FIGHTING THE
WAR
ON
TERROR

FIGHTING THE
WAR
ON
TERROR

A COUNTERINSURGENCY STRATEGY

JAMES S. CORUM
Professor, U.S. Army Command and General Staff College

Foreword by SIR MICHAEL HOWARD
President Emeritus of the International Institute for Strategic Studies

ZENITH PRESS

First published in 2007 by MBI Publishing Company LLC and Zenith Press, an imprint of MBI Publishing Company, Galtier Plaza, Suite 200, 380 Jackson Street, St. Paul, MN 55101-3885 USA

Zenith Press titles are also available at discounts in bulk quantity for industrial or sales-promotional use. For details write to Special Sales Manager at MBI Publishing Company, Galtier Plaza, Suite 200, 380 Jackson Street, St. Paul, MN 55101-3885 USA.

To find out more about our books, join us online at www.zenithpress.com.

ISBN-13: 978-0-7603-2868-2
ISBN-10: 0-7603-2868-4

Printed in the United States of America

Library of Congress Cataloging-in-Publication Data

Corum, James.
  Fighting the War on Terror : a counterinsurgency strategy / By James Corum.
    p. cm.
  Includes bibliographical references.
  ISBN-13: 978-0-7603-2868-2 (hardbound w/ jacket)
  ISBN-10: 0-7603-2868-4 (hardbound w/ jacket) 1. Counterinsurgency—United States. 2. War on Terrorism, 2001- 3. United States—Armed Forces—Stability operations. 4. United States—Military policy. I. Title.
U241.C685 2007
355.02'18—dc22
                                        2006029041

CONTENTS

FOREWORD

BY SIR MICHAEL HOWARD

Let us admit it fairly, as a business people should,
We have had no end of a lesson: it will do us no end of good.
—Rudyard Kipling, 1903

Thus wrote Rudyard Kipling a little over a century ago, in the aftermath of the Anglo-Boer War in South Africa. In that war, after spectacular initial triumphs, the British Army had been bogged down by two years of guerrilla fighting that absorbed almost its entire manpower, involved methods that deeply divided opinion at home, and earned it the hatred and contempt of all its European neighbors. Further, it was a war that had been planned and urged on by a small but powerful faction within the British government motivated as much by commercial as by ideological interests, and supported by a public opinion smarting from former humiliations and determined to assert the primacy of British Imperial power. We have, in short, been here before.

It's unlikely anyone in the U.S. government considered the precedent of the Boer War when the United States attacked Iraq in 2003, if indeed any of its members had ever heard of it. The military power of the United States was so overwhelming that the United States was assured of military victory. The U.S. military had been assured by its advisors—or those to whom it paid any attention—that once the tyranny of Saddam Hussein was removed, the

Iraqi people would welcome their liberators and automatically embrace "democracy." The boil that was poisoning Middle East politics would thus be lanced and American troops could return to ticker-tape triumphs—all at minimal expense to the American taxpayer.

The first part of this scenario certainly went according to plan. The invasion itself did indeed prove, in the happy words of one neocon commentator, "a cakewalk." But the invasion was only a preliminary, and the dismal events in Iraq since 2003, political as well as military, have ensured that those brilliant initial triumphs are now almost forgotten. The United States and her allies in the Coalition have certainly had "no end of a lesson." The important thing now is to ensure that it has done us no end of good.

What went wrong? In this brilliant book, James Corum draws on his own long experiences with the U.S. Army both to explain the basic causes of these disasters, and advise how to put them right.

The fundamental mistake, Corum shows, was that the Pentagon—and with it the White House—believed that the defeat of the Iraqi armed forces would in itself be enough to achieve the purposes of the war; that is, make the Iraqi people accept peace on our terms. Further, they assumed that such a defeat would in itself provide the basis for a more stable international order. They therefore planned a campaign that they expected would itself settle the issues of the war, and looked no further ahead. They had plenty of warning that it was likely to be only the beginning of a long and difficult involvement, but chose to ignore it. As Corum puts it, the generals thought tactically rather than strategically, but their political masters did not encourage them to do anything else. The alternative was too expensive, politically as well as financially, for them to contemplate.

But in the modern world such an approach is not enough. Preparation for war must involve seamless planning, not only for the military campaigns themselves, but for the establishment of order after them and the management, and ultimately the reconciliation, of the peoples in whose territory the fighting has taken place. In this second "post-hostilities" phase of operations, the military must still play the leading part. Order has to be established and maintained before more positive and creative measures of "nation-building" can take place. In fact, the United States was once rather good at this. The *Small Wars Manual* published by the U.S. Marines in 1940, based on experience in the Philippines and Central America, remains a model textbook on the subject. During World War I, President Woodrow Wilson assembled some of the best brains in the country to advise him on the settlement of postwar Europe. During World War II, General George C. Marshall was planning for the occupation of Germany within months of Pearl Harbor. Why wasn't this done with Iraq?

Some blame, Corum admits, must be allotted to "the American Way of Warfare" itself, as it has developed since the Civil War: that is, the mobilization of all resources to crush the enemy, with little concern as to what happens afterward. As President George W. Bush unwisely (and quite mistakenly) once put it, Americans "do not do nation-building." When put to it Americans "do nation-building" very effectively; but it is true that American soldiers are not encouraged to see it as an intrinsic part of their duties. This mind-set, as Corum emphasizes, has been greatly reinforced by the increasing *dehumanization* of warfare as high technology has increased its grip on the American Armed Forces—especially the so-called "Revolution in Warfare" that seeks to reduce war to combat between machines rather than men, and eliminates the need to understand the adversary as a human being if one is to engage with him effectively. But for that, as Corum comments ruefully, one needs an education in the humanities of a kind that is positively discouraged in the U.S. Army today.

But there is another, more secular trend that undermines the capacity of traditional American doctrine to deal with the complexities of warfare in the twenty-first century, and it is this: The defeat of the opponent's army will only result in the capitulation of his people if the strength of that people is effectively embodied in their armed forces, as it was in the case of the Confederacy and of the Germans in World Wars I and II, when the exhaustion of those armies left their peoples with no resources to fight. If it is not so embodied, the defeat of the army may be only the opening phase of a prolonged "people's war." To quote another historical analogy, it took the armies of Prussia and her German allies only four weeks to defeat the French

Imperial Army in 1870: it took them another four months to compel the French to make peace. The United States was to have much the same experience in the Philippines thirty years later. By the mid-twentieth century, such people's wars and insurgencies had become a global norm. Indeed, paradoxically, the more rapidly and decisively the professional armies of the adversary are defeated, the more resources are available for dissident elements in the population who probably never identified themselves with those armies in the first place; and who, whatever their political beliefs, can probably count on the sympathies of a population instinctively hostile to foreign occupying armies, whatever ideology they may profess. In dealing with such opponents high tech is of limited value, as the United States discovered in Vietnam. So if the United States seriously intends to fight further "preventive wars" to root out terrorists from whatever bases they use to threaten the American homeland, she needs a thorough reexamination and overhaul of the doctrine, if not indeed the structure, of her armed forces.

This book is a manual of what needs to be done, and the first lesson is that it cannot be done on the cheap. "Stabilization strategies," writes Corum, "involve large troop commitments." They also involve an understanding of the cultural environment of the peoples with which those troops have to deal: counterinsurgency, he reminds us, "is about humans interacting with humans." As the British General Rupert Smith has put it, war today is fought, not *against* peoples, but *among* peoples—peoples whose cultures are likely to be very different from one's own but which we must learn to understand. But whatever their culture, the first requirement of an occupied people will be *security*—not "freedom," as politicians so windily put it. Unless the occupying forces can provide that security, they can never win the war.

Security, the provision of basic law and order, both requires and makes possible further constructive activities. First there is intelligence, itself impossible without a good command of languages. Then public relations and propaganda, "winning the hearts and minds," and isolating the insurgents. There must be positive action to rebuild the infrastructure and provide such facilities as schools and clinics. Finally, there must be careful indoctrination and training of indigenous forces to reinforce and eventually replace the occupying troops. All this requires money; it requires preparation; and above all it demands *time*. The most successful counterinsurgency campaign on record, the British pacification of Malaysia, took fourteen years. There is no reason to believe that Iraq will need much less.

It might have been expected that the United States would have learned all these lessons a generation ago in Vietnam, but apparently it did not. Now that it is having to start all over again, this book is a very good place to begin.

CHAPTER ONE

CONTEMPORARY INSURGENCY AND TERRORISM

War cannot follow its own laws, but has to be treated as part of some other whole; the name of which is policy.
—General Carl von Clausewitz, 1832

The conduct of small wars is in fact in certain respects an art by itself, diverging widely from what is adapted to the conditions of regular warfare....
—Colonel C. E. Callwell, British Army, 1899

The first step for developing an effective strategy for a particular conflict is to understand the nature of the conflict. Insurgency has been around for a long, long time and so has counterinsurgency. While sometimes insurgents have adopted the organization, strategies, and tactics of conventional states and armies and fought a highly conventional war (the American War of Independence follows this pattern), in most cases the insurgents eschew conventional tactics and wage irregular or guerrilla war against the government.

Insurgents are rarely strong enough or have the arms to defeat an organized government with regular military or police forces—at least in the first stages of an insurgency. So insurgents follow the traditional strategy of the weak against the strong—they harass and demoralize the enemy through small raids and attacks. Insurgents often wear civilian clothing and are indistinguishable from the civilian population. Insurgents commonly use terrorism as a tactic to demoralize the government and to intimidate any in the civilian population who might oppose them.

One thing is very clear. Insurgencies are wars—but not the conventional wars our own forces are trained to fight. These are wars that have none of the strategic targets of conventional states such as capitol cities, defense industries, large conventional forces, or a visible state infrastructure—all of the things our military forces are trained to locate and attack.

Wars waged by nonstate forces are, by their very nature, quite different from state-on-state wars. However, because wars involving conventional states against nonstate forces are a very old phenomenon, certain conditions, patterns, and experiences are constantly repeated. In this chapter, I will outline the most common strategies of insurgency and counterinsurgency, the most common historical patterns, and the aspects of insurgency that are relatively new as a step in working toward a strategy to counter current insurgencies.

Insurgencies, conflicts in which factions attempt to take over state power by force, have been around almost as long as there have been organized states. Indeed, insurgency is one of the most common types of conflict. Most major empires have faced armed rebellions by national groups wishing to assert their own independence. For example, in Josephus' *History of the Jewish War* we have a detailed account of a well-organized insurgency by the Jews from AD 66 to 73, when they attempted to drive the Romans out of Judea and regain their independence. In the fifteenth century the Swiss cantons organized themselves and won independence from the Hapsburg Empire in a short and sharp war. Indeed, the United States was born out of a successful insurgency by the Americans against the British Empire.

Historically, most insurgencies have failed. This is usually due to the political and military weakness of the insurgents when they are pitted against the substantially larger military forces and economic resources of the ruling state. However, some insurgencies, and the American example comes to mind, have been spectacularly successful. The success of those insurgencies provides encouragement to national groups and factions that look to successful models in planning their own revolutions.

Until the late nineteenth century there were no general theories of counterinsurgency, nor was there anything resembling a "how to" manual for the soldier or strategist facing an insurgency—especially an insurgency where the enemy was composed primarily of unconventional forces. The spontaneous rising of thousands of Spaniards who organized irregular forces to fight the occupation of Spain by Napoleon's armies and who fought a guerrilla war (Spanish, meaning "little war") of ambush and harassment against French rear detachments, played an important part in the eventual defeat of the French Empire. While the Spanish guerrillas were too weak to fight major battles against the French, they nevertheless inflicted a large number of casualties in constant small raids and skirmishes. The guerrilla war diverted large numbers of French soldiers from the main armies as they tried in vain to suppress the Spanish rebellion. Eventually, the French were decisively defeated by the British and Allied armies on the battlefield, but not before being considerably weakened by guerrilla war. Clausewitz, in his grand theory of war, briefly touched on the subject of people's war and clearly had the example of Spain before him. Yet he quickly passed over the subject because he recognized that a war with irregular forces was, in fact, a very different kind of war from one fought between conventional states with conventional state forces.[1] Clausewitz recognized that war with a nonstate enemy would require its own theory.

The Western armed forces and governments had to wait until the end of the nineteenth century to see the development of a general theory of insurgency and counterinsurgency. The first theorist to write a major work concerning conflict with nonstate enemies was British Major General C. E. Callwell, who wrote *Small Wars: Their Principles and Practice* in 1896. Callwell's book went through several editions in the early twentieth century and was popular reading in the British Empire, where the military and political leaders had to deal with numerous rebellions in the colonies, and also in the United States, whose military forces were facing their own problems of dealing with insurgency in the Philippines and Caribbean nations.

Callwell defined small wars as "campaigns undertaken to suppress rebellions and guerrilla warfare in all parts of the world where organized armies are struggling against opponents who will not meet them in the open field."[2] The enemy consisted mainly of "irregular forces," which included everything from semiorganized armies to tribal forces and bandits. One essential point was that the enemy forces were not organized under control of a modern state but were, in essence, nonstate enemies. Callwell emphasized that warfare against irregular, nonstate enemies was fundamentally different from fighting an enemy state: "But the conditions of small wars are so diversified, the enemy's mode of fighting is often so peculiar, the theatres of operations present such singular features, that irregular warfare must generally be carried out on a method totally different from the stereotyped system [state-on-state warfare with regular forces]."[3] He took a characteristic British approach to small wars by stressing practicality rather than theory. However, his approach was also well rooted in Clausewitzian theory in that he insisted the colonial power first had to determine the nature of the war, assess the capabilities of the enemy, establish clear objectives, and devise tactical and operational solutions to realize the objectives.[4] Callwell, as indeed the British Empire before World War II, viewed insurgency mainly as a military problem to be dealt with by defeating the rebels in battle. Callwell's theory was a useful first step toward helping Western powers to understand counterinsurgency, but was deficient in that it reflected a lack of regard for the social, economic, and political aspirations of the native peoples under British dominion.

The Americans adopted a generally more sophisticated approach in dealing with the nationalist insurgency in the Philippines between 1902 and 1908. While waging a military and police campaign to defeat rebel forces in the field, the U.S. military also stressed the nonmilitary aspects of the campaign. U.S. regional commanders established local self-government, civic action programs such as schools and medical care that directly improved the lives of the people, and programs to co-opt rebel leaders by granting amnesty to any willing to lay down their arms and recognize American sovereignty over the Islands. Former guerrillas were even accepted into the ranks of the local and regional governments. Although not codified at the time as a theory of counterinsurgency, the U.S. approach—emphasizing a "hearts and minds" campaign that addressed the causes of discontent among the population—provided a good model for future counterinsurgency operations.

As counterinsurgency theories were developed by the major powers, the concepts of revolutionary war, or people's war, also became more sophisticated. The first insurgency that can be called a people's war in the modern sense was the rebellion of the Irish nationalists against British rule from 1916 to 1922. After attempting an open, conventional battle against the British during the Easter rising of 1916, the Irish nationalists realized the impossibility of trying to fight the British armed forces head-on and began waging a ruthless guerrilla war that lasted from 1919 to 1922. As in so many insurgencies, it was a war of small raids and skirmishes. The war pitted small groups of rebels—who assassinated British officers and agents, raided police stations, and ambushed British army patrols—against large and clumsy operations by conventional forces that tried to clear areas of rebels. The rebels easily evaded the British sweep operations and chose battle only on their terms. Though the small attacks by the Irish inflicted little damage to the British military in any grand strategic sense, they still created enough casualties to cause dissatisfaction in Britain over the cost of holding Ireland in the Empire.

Equally important was the success of the Irish nationalists in setting up an underground government complete with finances, law courts, and an underground press. As British governmental authority retreated into highly protected enclaves, the day-to-day running of the country, especially in the rural areas, was effectively taken over by the highly organized nationalist civil authorities. The Irish nationalists were eventually accepted by the majority of the Irish as the legitimate government, and the British as foreign interlopers with no true legitimacy outside of their military force. Although the Irish nationalists never won any major military victories, and their military forces were basically broken by the overwhelming force of the British military and police by 1922, the Irish won independence simply by staying in the field and convincing the British public and politicians that holding Ireland was simply not worth the trouble.

Faced with considerable disorder in the Empire and a series of nationalist revolts in Palestine, India, Iraq, and elsewhere in the 1920s and 1930s, the British army slowly moved away from the heavy-handed Victorian approach to suppressing insurgencies and adopted a more subtle approach for using force to suppress dissidents. Formerly the British had taken the approach of collective punishment, holding entire tribes or villages accountable for the outrages or rebellion by some members. But techniques that emphasized brute force were considered too blunt for a modern colonial administration. In the 1920s and 1930s senior British officials in India, including the

Viceroy, disapproved of punitive actions and collective punishment by British airpower on the sensible grounds that such actions were not only morally doubtful but politically risky as they were likely to increase the hatred that some tribes felt for the British.[5] After some ugly incidents in dealing with violent nationalists the British learned that excessive force often inflamed the population even further.[6] Thus, the new official doctrine was to employ the minimum possible force necessary to restore a basic degree of order and allow the civil government to function again. The importance of addressing social and economic grievances was understood, but as an issue for civilian authorities to deal with after the military and police had quieted the situation.

American counterinsurgency doctrine generally followed the lines laid down in the Philippines early in the century. In the 1920s and 1930s the U.S. Marine Corps, then called "the State Department's army," served as the primary American intervention force in the Caribbean and Central America. In those years the Marines developed the doctrines for counterinsurgency and military occupation to a high art. In the administration of Haiti as a virtual American colony from 1914 to 1934, during the interventions in Nicaragua in the 1920s and 1930s, and in other interventions in the Caribbean region, the U.S. Marine Corps gained considerable experience. These operations included fighting insurgents, supporting pro-American indigenous governments, training local constabularies, building local infrastructures, and even administering small countries. This experience was collected and edited by a group of Marine officers with long experience in these operations and was officially codified as the *USMC Small Wars Manual*, published in 1940.

The four-hundred-page *Small Wars Manual* has long been considered one of the classics of counterinsurgency and low-intensity operations. While some sections dealing with the specific tactics of infantry operations are dated, most of the *Small Wars Manual* deals with fundamental issues of military operations and strategy that have remained unchanged. There are sections dealing with the coordination of the civilian and military arms of the U.S. government, and the requirement for U.S. political leaders to set clear political objectives and to link military operations to the political objectives. The *Small Wars Manual* also discusses the conduct of intelligence operations in counterinsurgency, training local forces, and even organizing the military occupation of a country. Throughout the *Small Wars Manual* there is an emphasis on conducting U.S. operations within the framework of international, American, and local law. Developing and maintaining good relations with the local population is held to be an essential art. The *Small Wars Manual* also reminds the reader of the importance of establishing the political legitimacy of U.S.-supported local government and institutions. Although the Americans at the time were fighting a variety of insurgents, rebels, and bandits, throughout the *Small Wars Manual* a heavy-handed approach toward counterinsurgency is ruled out.[7] The minimum practical amount of force is recommended, with the understanding that maintaining good long-term political relations with the local inhabitants is always the paramount goal.

Inspired by the successful communist revolution in Russia and fueled by a wave of nationalism, insurgency theory took a quantum leap forward in the first half of the twentieth century with the theories of Mao Tse-tung. Mao developed the most comprehensive and influential theory of insurgency during the 1930s and 1940s as he fought the Nationalist government of Chiang Kai-shek and mounted a resistance movement against the Japanese. In a series of essays and lectures written over more than a decade, Mao's approach to revolutionary warfare was proposed as a strategy for insurgents to defeat superior government forces—a standard people's war. It was, indeed, a highly successful model that drew from classical military and Marxist theory (Mao knew his Clausewitz as well as his Marx), military history, and an analysis of the particular conditions of China. Mao's theory of people's war, which proved quite successful in China, has influenced many insurgent groups throughout the world for the last six decades.[8]

Mao's concept of a people's war begins with an assumption that for such wars to be successful, they are most likely to be protracted wars. At first, even where there is widespread dissatisfaction with the government, the revolutionaries are never strong enough in terms of military force or economic resources to mount an effective campaign against the superior strength and organization of the government. Mao believed that the revolutionaries' best hope for victory was to develop a superior political organization, to win the mass of people to their side, to build up "liberated areas" as bases for continued operations, to continually attrit and weaken government forces by guerrilla war and, finally, to take the government down by force once the measures of relative strength favored the insurgents.

Mao's model follows Clausewitz's dictum in that it starts with a political ideology and political goals. The revolution will be centrally led and directed and depends on a well-trained cadre of carefully selected leaders who can recruit and organize civilian and military forces and keep them focused on the political goal of the revolution. Having organized the revolutionary cadre, military action is undertaken in a process to wear down the government forces. At first, the military side of the war is guerrilla war. The small and usually poorly armed guerrilla forces fight with surprise and stealth, attacking isolated government garrisons or ambushing government supply trains. When confronted by large regular forces, they retreat and survive. The military results of such operations, however, are not the main aim. Often, the military action is a means of simply showing the population, which is likely to be indifferent at first, that the government forces are not invincible. Guerrilla war also forces the government forces to withdraw from large areas of the countryside—leaving such rural areas and populations open to being taken over by the rebels.

In the first stages of the revolution, the emphasis is on recruiting and winning over the population. Mao enjoined his military forces to treat the peasants in a considerate manner, and not to confiscate food and goods (in the tradition of Chinese soldiers) but to pay for food and carry out civic action programs. Once the good will of the revolutionaries toward the peasants is established, the revolutionary army then recruits and organizes the population with an emphasis on educating the people in the revolutionary ideology. In time, whole regions of the country become "liberated zones" where the revolutionary insurgents hold sway and can form an alternative government complete with a judicial system, schools, and a local government. The requirement to continually build and expand the base of popular support through a broad public education and propaganda campaign is considered more important than winning military victories. As the insurgency progresses, the goal is to win legitimacy for the revolutionary movement in the eyes of the people while undermining the legitimacy of the ruling government.

In practice, Mao's model of revolutionary warfare accepts terrorism as one of the standard tactics used in the military side of the campaign.

Government officials and collaborators were commonly assassinated as a means of undermining the authority of the government and deterring others from supporting the government. If the government forces could be provoked into employing terrorist tactics of their own, such as destroying villages friendly to the rebels or executing large numbers of suspected rebel sympathizers, then such actions also served the long-term interests of the revolutionaries, for they increased the mistrust of the population toward the government and pushed the survivors of government brutality into the hands of the revolution. In short, strong-arm tactics by the government can work as a recruiting tool for the insurgents as long as the insurgents are not squeamish about the suffering of the civilian population. Most revolutionaries, including Mao, usually aren't. After passing through stages of organization, buildup, guerrilla war, and the strategic defensive, the revolutionary forces will be strong enough to take on the now-weakened conventional forces of the government and defeat them in outright battle.

In general, Mao's approach to revolutionary war provides a fairly effective model. It worked well under Chinese conditions, in which the revolutionaries had a large landmass to work and hide in and a large rural population at their disposal that could be organized and trained in relative safely from government attacks. Mao also benefited greatly from large-scale Soviet assistance after 1945 that included military trainers and large stocks of captured Japanese weapons. Finally, Mao had an advantage in fighting a corrupt, incompetent and badly organized Chinese government that failed to establish a program to win the hearts and minds of the rural population.

In the post–World War II era many insurgencies sometimes consciously, sometimes unconsciously, followed a variation of Mao's people's war model. Mao's model was most effective for conducting insurgency in countries whose populations consisted mostly of poor peasants. Adding fuel to the postwar disorder was the rise of strong nationalist movements in Europe's African and Asian colonies. Even some European nations such as Greece, which had a large and impoverished rural population, were susceptible to revolutions led by communist parties. Many nationalist and communist revolutionaries studied Mao's model, adding their own variations to the theme. The Vietnamese insurgency against French rule (1946 to 1954) provides a good example of adapting the Chinese model to local conditions. Truong

Chinh, a leading Vietnamese communist theoretician, understood the necessity for a protracted war to defeat the French but disagreed with Mao's concept of guerrilla forces, in which such forces would be turned into regular troops as the revolution progressed to the stage of mobile warfare. Truong Chinh developed a particularly Vietnamese strategy of a "war of interlocking," in which both guerrilla and regular insurgent forces would conduct simultaneous operations against the French government forces.[9]

In the revolt of the Algerians against French rule, some aspects of Mao's model were employed, while others were dropped or adapted to local conditions. Particularly, the Algerian revolutionary ideology eschewed Mao's atheistic communism and, instead, emphasized nationalism and Islam. The careful development of the Algerian party organization under a central leadership was similar to the Chinese model as was the understanding that the war would be protracted—one fought with guerrilla tactics and terrorism. Indeed, the Algerians, faced with enormous French military power, never seriously considered changing their campaign from a guerrilla war to a conventional war as Mao had done in China. In the end, it wasn't necessary. The French government, exhausted by the cost of maintaining its presence in a largely hostile Algeria, essentially abandoned the country to the insurgents who had been beaten on the battlefield but whose underground political organization had survived.

The notable successes of Mao's revolutionary insurgency theory and its variants quickly pushed the non-Communist powers to find an effective doctrine to defeat insurgency. Britain and America found that the new model of people's war, based largely on nationalist fervor and peasant dissatisfaction, could also be defeated by Western powers when they took a comprehensive approach to counterinsurgency strategy. The first major counterinsurgency test for the Western powers came in Greece, which faced a major communist insurgency between 1944 and 1949.

SUCCESSFUL COUNTERINSURGENCY CAMPAIGNS

The Greek communists had used the period of German occupation from 1941 to 1944 to organize and arm themselves, first as a national resistance force but increasingly with the intention of seizing power when the Germans withdrew. In 1943 the main procommunist and non-communist

Greek resistance groups forgot about the German enemy, who were clearly losing the war, as they went to war with each other to better position themselves for postwar control of the country. In early 1944, the Greek government in exile cobbled together an uneasy truce between the factions and later admitted several Greek communists to the cabinet of the interim provisional government that would assume power when the Germans evacuated Greece. When the British army landed in Greece with a small force in October 1944, the shaky power-sharing agreement between the communist and non-communist factions was barely holding. Skirmishing erupted between the factions as the Germans left and both sides tried to seize government buildings and strategic centers. The uneasy coalition of the interim Greek government quickly fell apart when the six communist cabinet members resigned on 1 December. Within days a full-scale civil war erupted between the communists and their allies, who controlled most of the countryside, and the Greek government, supported by the British and non-communist resistance units.[10] After a sharp fight for control of Athens, which was won by the British and Greek government forces, war continued with renewed violence in the countryside. The civil war escalated as the British poured in arms and advisors to assist the Greek government and the USSR sent aid to the communists through their allies in Yugoslavia, Bulgaria, and Albania. By 1947, the war was at a virtual stalemate and the British government, bankrupt from the cost of World War II, told the American government that Britain could no longer afford to support the embattled Greek government. In March 1947, the Truman administration took up the challenge and announced the "Truman Doctrine"—a pledge to provide economic and military support to nations threatened by communist insurgency. The U.S. provided the Greek government with a large amount of economic and military aid, sending hundreds of military advisors to help train and organize the Greek army. It was the start of a comprehensive American strategy to contain the Soviet Union and its attempt to increase its power and influence by supporting communist revolutionary movements in countries ravaged by the recent World War.

Greece was a desperately poor and war-wracked nation and the high level of poverty ensured a large recruiting pool for the insurgents. Much of the U.S. support to Greece therefore went to build up the Greek economy and ensure that jobs could be found for Greek workers. Greek civilians fleeing the areas of heavy fighting were resettled and cared for by government agencies. On the military side, General James Van Fleet, the chief of the U.S. military mission, pushed Washington for additional money to finance an increase in the Greek army. Using U.S. aid as a lever, he pushed the Greek government to retire ineffective officers and place a new crop of officers, identified by the Americans as the most capable men, into the top military positions.[11] In 1948, under better leadership, the Greek army started to make headway.

One advantage of the Greek government was a poor insurgent strategy. Having handled the army roughly in earlier campaigns, the communists tried to fight a conventional war under cover of heavily fortified positions in the mountains of northern and western Greece. This played to the advantages of a revitalized and better-led army that had recently been equipped with plenty of heavy firepower. In a series of battles through 1949, the army broke the rebel defenses and forced the communist survivors across the border into exile in communist lands. By the end of the year the insurgency was broken.

For fighting the insurgents, the Greek army was organized into several types of units. Specially trained and equipped elite units under top leaders bore the brunt of direct operations against the insurgents, supported by regular Greek army units. Several dozen additional battalions, with less equipment and training and not capable of offensive operations, secured areas recently cleared of rebels by the army and protected the population from harassment and terrorism by communist guerrilla forces.

In the Philippines, a major communist rebellion challenged the newly independent Philippine government from 1946 to the mid-1950s. As in Greece, the insurgency had its roots in longstanding social problems, especially the high level of rural poverty among the landless peasant laborers of Luzon and other islands. The Philippine Communist Party and its military arm, called the Huks, developed and grew out of the wartime resistance movements. By the time the American forces reoccupied the Philippines, the Huks were a large and well-organized force, especially on Luzon. Having helped America and the Philippine government in exile to liberate their nation from the Japanese, they were not content to disarm and return to the state of poverty, petty corruption, and oppression by the great landowners that had characterized rural life in the Philippines for centuries. The new government had few troops or resources to deal with these problems. Within three years, the Huks had recruited thousands of fighters and held large areas of Luzon under their sway.

At the height of the Huk insurgency, the United States was so involved in the Korean War that it could only spare a few advisors along with some military and economic aid for the Philippines. In fact, this was fortunate because it pushed the Filipinos to seek their own solutions to their own conflict— backed up by the American assistance program. At first, the Philippine government, trying to fight the insurgency as a military campaign, made little headway. But in 1950, a brilliant and reform-minded politician, Ramon Magsaysay, was appointed defense minister. Magsaysay turned the war around, closely advised by American Air Force Lieutenant Colonel Edward Lansdale, an officer who had long service in the Philippines and knew the country intimately. Together, Magsaysay and Lansdale developed a comprehensive counterinsurgency strategy that emphasized civic action by the military and fundamental social and economic reforms by the government to improve the lives of the Filipino peasants. While some of the military forces tracked rebels in the jungle, other forces built roads, water systems, medical clinics, and schools that dramatically improved the standard of living for the rural people. Magsaysay worked tirelessly to visit the rural people, listen to complaints, and address the most pressing issues. Land reform was introduced, and thousands of formerly landless peasants were granted title to plots of public land. There was a crackdown on government corruption. Added to the military and civic action programs was an amnesty program that not only encouraged the guerrillas to surrender, but also provided them with land and financial help to get started as independent farmers.[12]

Over time, the comprehensive civil/military strategy paid off. The Huk force quickly declined as its recruiting base, the rural peasants, saw their lives improve under the military and government programs. Offered incentives to surrender, guerrillas began streaming in from the hills to take up a peaceful life. Although a hard-line cadre remained, by the mid-1950s they were more of a minor irritant than a serious threat to the Philippine government.

In the British colony of Malaya, postwar disorder and the rise of the Malayan Communist Party during World War II set the stage for a major communist insurgency that broke out in 1948. The communist insurgents were recruited primarily from the large Chinese population of the colony (more than 40 percent of the population). Of these, the rebel fighters and supporters mostly came from the hundreds of thousands of landless peasant laborers. At first, the British tried to deal with the insurgency in military terms. Forty thousand British army troops were committed to Malaya, the ten-thousand-man police force was increased to forty thousand, and tens of thousands of Malayan home guards were recruited to guard the mines and rubber plantations that produced most of Malaya's wealth. The massive application of military power against a relatively small insurgent army, approximately ten thousand men backed up by many thousands of active sympathizers, was enough to stabilize the situation and prevent insurgent victory, but by 1951 the British commanders admitted that they were making no progress in defeating the insurgents.

In 1952 the military and civilian authorities received new leadership in the person of General Gerard Templer, a British army officer who took over as head of the civilian administration as well as the military command. Unifying command of both the civilian government and the military under an especially capable commander was an important step. Whereas before, cooperation between the military and civilians had been sporadic and ineffective, Templer pushed the police and military to work together. The intelligence system was reformed, with the police and military now sharing information and cooperating at every level. Direction of the war was coordinated through small committees of key military and civilian leaders from the national down to the district level, and the effectiveness of the military and police forces was dramatically improved.

Templer and other senior commanders understood that counterinsurgency is not just a military operation. Hundreds of thousands of Chinese rural villagers, who generally supported the insurgents, were moved from areas of high rebel activity to areas under government control and settled in new villages. These new villages were provided with clean water, schools, and free government medical clinics. The Chinese peasants, heretofore landless, were given title to plots of land allocated to them. A political campaign was waged to give the Chinese a greater voice in Malayan affairs and to recruit them into the previously all-Malayan civil service and police. While the rebels hiding in the jungles were relentlessly hunted by small army and police units specially trained in jungle warfare, the government also mounted a large media and psychological warfare campaign publicizing the benefits of surrendering and accepting the government authority. And the benefits were considerable. Although the insurgency continued until 1960, the insurgent power steadily declined through attrition and rebel surrenders until the tiny remnants of the rebellion were no longer a threat to the government.

COUNTERINSURGENCY THEORIES

In the aftermath of insurgencies in Greece, Malaya, and the Philippines; and with a major conflict heating up in Vietnam that featured both an internal insurgency and an outside conventional attack by North Vietnam, several highly experienced British and American practitioners of counterinsurgency wrote books outlining some of the basic principles learned from recent campaigns.[13] Taken together, the works of the British and American practitioners amount to a comprehensive theory and operational model for counterinsurgency that was firmly based on the practical experience of fighting and defeating enemies who employed variations of Mao's strategy of prolonged war. The American and British counterinsurgency experts outlined the following basic principles of counterinsurgency warfare:

1. The civilian population is understood as the center of gravity in an insurgency. One cannot fight insurgents effectively without winning the support of the population. Ideally, the counterinsurgency strategy should be geared to driving a wedge between the population and the rebels.

2. Successful counterinsurgency requires a comprehensive strategy that combines military and police operations with social, political, and economic action. Since insurgencies grow out of

large-scale dissatisfaction with the government, the means must be found to address the social, political, and economic problems that provide the fuel for insurgency.

3. There needs to be a unity of effort by the government forces, that is, close coordination between the military and civilian agencies at every level.

4. Effectively fighting the insurgents, who usually live among and draw support from the civilian population, requires good intelligence. Military and police action without good intelligence is largely a wasted effort. To fight the insurgent one has to find him.

5. Military and civic action campaigns need to proceed simultaneously and be coordinated with each other.

6. The government needs to wage an effective media campaign to reassure the population and undermine support for the insurgents.

7. Military and police power needs to be applied carefully and with discrimination. A heavy-handed approach is wasteful and can cause discontent among the populace.

In addition to the British/American theory of counterinsurgency, some officers in the French army developed their own theory. France had the experience of fighting an unsuccessful campaign against insurgents in Indochina from 1946 to 1954 and was embroiled in a counterinsurgency campaign in Algeria from 1954 to 1962. The French view, expressed by French Army Colonel Roger Trinquier and published as *Modern Warfare* in

1961, was widely read in both French and English editions. The French model differed considerably from the British/American model. Trinquier, who had long experience in counterinsurgency, outlined some very useful tactics in dealing with urban rebellion, including discussions of how to seal off a city district, collect comprehensive data on the population and register the whole population as a means to identify insurgents from outside the area, and limit the ability of insurgents to move within the country. Trinquier's theory differed enormously from the Anglo-Saxon model on several key points. First of all, he saw counterinsurgency primarily in military terms. For Trinquier, establishing a military presence and crushing the insurgents by force was the first priority. In contrast to the British and American view that military action had to be carried out simultaneously with civic action programs, Trinquier argued first for military action to crush the insurgents. While civic action programs were important, they would be carried out only after the insurgency had been crushed by force. Whereas British and American theorists of the 1950s and 1960s believed that building up a legitimate civilian government and supporting indigenous institutions were key elements of counterinsurgency strategy, there is little of this in Trinquier's work. Essentially, Trinquier believed in strongarming the population into compliance with French rule.[14]

Trinquier's approach could bring short-term success. The most notable example was Algeria, where the French army essentially broke the back of the insurgent movement by 1960. However, in the long run, by ignoring the need to build public support for the government, the French approach led to strategic failure. One illustration of the French approach's lack of political considerations was in the policy of torturing and abusing insurgent prisoners in Algeria. Trinquier advocated torture as a means of obtaining intelligence information, although he did not advocate the widespread use of such means. He failed to understand the breakdown in army discipline that occurs when moral and legal boundaries are crossed. Once the French army had adopted a torture policy, it immediately got out of control and torture became the primary intelligence-collecting technique. While torture sometimes produced intelligence information of value, in the long run this kind of ruthlessness undermined support for France among the Algerians and eventually undermined support for the war among the French civilians at home as stories from Algeria slowly leaked out.

The French approach can be contrasted with the approach to counterinsurgency promulgated by British counterinsurgency leaders, Sir Robert Thompson and General Frank Kitson. Both served in counterinsurgency campaigns and in the 1950s and 1960s wrote works based on their experience that are still considered useful references on the subject. Using Malaya as a guideline, Thompson insisted that counterinsurgency operations be conducted within the rule of law. Under the rule of law, a government could still set and enforce strict controls on the population and upon movement and commerce. A government could also set drastic penalties, including the death penalty, for acts of terrorism or providing support to the insurgents. Under the British policy, the punishment of individuals had to be conducted within proper rules of arrest and detention, and legal representation was mandated for suspected Malayan insurgents going on trial. Proclaiming clear rules of behavior that could be understood by the whole population, as well as insisting that the ultimate political aim of all military and police activity be understood by the government and its forces, was vitally important.[15]

Failure to Learn in Vietnam

One of the notable events of the post–World War II counterinsurgency era was the failure of the U.S. government and military to use recent models and hard-won experience in developing an effective strategy to fight the war in Vietnam. In the early 1960s, Lansdale, by then an Air Force general, and Sir Robert Thompson, acting as an advisor to the U.S. government, urged the U.S. military to undertake a concerted counterinsurgency campaign in Vietnam. They argued for a comprehensive civil/military strategy to be based on the example of the successful campaigns in Malaya and the Philippines. Unfortunately, the U.S. military leaders at the time could only think in terms of large-scale conventional war and, starting in 1965 with the introduction of American combat divisions to Vietnam, they largely ignored the counterinsurgency aspect of the conflict and concentrated on the big battles against the North Vietnamese army. While the United States was usually successful in the field, this did not support the legitimacy of the South Vietnamese state or provide effective security to the peasant villagers of South Vietnam.

At the time, the top counterinsurgency experts strongly advocated expanding the programs to help the Vietnamese defend themselves.[16] Sir Robert Thompson, who had served in Malaya and understood Southeast Asian conditions, was brought in as a special advisor to the U.S. high command in Vietnam. He told the U.S. military commanders in 1969 that the U.S. conventional war strategy was "a failure" and argued that the United States should have concentrated on building up the South Vietnamese Army and supporting political and economic reforms from the start.[17] Along with American experts, Thompson noted that the highly successful U.S. Marine Corps program of training local defense forces in the thinly settled northern sector of the country would also work well in bringing security to the majority of the population that lived in the south.[18] Thompson advised that the successful Malayan strategy of clearing and pacifying one district at a time would also have been appropriate for South Vietnam.[19] Unfortunately, General Westmoreland, the senior U.S. military commander in Vietnam from 1965 to 1969, and the American Joint Chiefs of Staff, focused their efforts on fighting a conventional war against North Vietnam and generally ignored the counterinsurgency aspects of the war. The final result was the collapse of South Vietnam in 1975.

The U.S. military leaders—the same people who refused to employ a counterinsurgency strategy in Vietnam—took away the false lesson from that war that counterinsurgency strategies did not work. In contrast, several scholars have argued that Vietnam was by no means an "unwinnable war" and that the Americans, in partnership with the South Vietnamese, might have won if a comprehensive counterinsurgency strategy had been practiced in much of the country and the American combat role been limited to protecting South Vietnam against the North Vietnamese main forces.

Through the 1950s and 1960s, the Viet Cong made steady progress in gaining effective control of much of the South Vietnamese countryside, especially the Mekong Delta region. However, in early 1968 these gains were largely wiped out when the formidable Viet Cong force engaged in large-scale conventional attacks against the South Vietnamese and American forces during the nationwide Tet Offensive. The Viet Cong, generally superior to government forces in small-scale guerrilla operations, were thoroughly decimated while directly challenging the enormous firepower advantage of the American and South Vietnamese forces. After the Tet Offensive, the Viet Cong insurgents were a broken force, and a window of opportunity existed for embracing a broad counterinsurgency program in rural South Vietnam. But American leaders missed the opportunity to ensure the security and support of the rural population.[20] Ironically, the Tet Offensive, while a striking military defeat for the insurgents, ended up as a political and strategic victory in that it helped turn much of the American public opinion against the Vietnam War. The ability of the Viet Cong to mount a major offensive provided the media with the very false perception that the American and South Vietnamese could make no progress in the war. Faced with the perception of an unending war, American patience and will began to fade and, with them, the confidence that America could win the war.

REFINING COUNTERINSURGENCY DOCTRINE AFTER VIETNAM

By the 1970s, the most influential American military officers accepted as dogma the view that the U.S. military was unsuited to fighting wars like Vietnam. General William E. Dupuy, who had enormous influence upon U.S. Army doctrine in the 1970s as the first chief of the Training and Doctrine Command, believed the path for renewing the low morale of the post-Vietnam army was to return to the conventional war tradition and prepare the army for a war against the Soviets on the Northern European plains. Dupuy and a corps of smart and visionary senior officers effectively restored the morale and confidence of the U.S. Army during the decade following the Vietnam War, ushering in what many consider a renaissance of military thought and doctrine. Dupuy did a superb job of rebuilding and retraining the army for a major conventional war. Nevertheless, a great deal of valuable experience won in Vietnam was rejected as irrelevant—so sure were the senior officers that the United States would never again fight a major counterinsurgency campaign.[21] The most negative consequence of the post-Vietnam reforms is that the U.S. Army became a one-trick pony capable of fighting just one type of war. The U.S. Air Force, frustrated by the Vietnam War experience, also turned its collective back on counterinsurgency and returned to conventional war roots with a renewed emphasis on the science of strategic bombing.[22]

A general rejection of the counterinsurgency experience within the U.S. military did not, however, mean that the United States would no longer engage in counterinsurgency operations. In 1980 a major Marxist insurgency began in the poor and troubled nation of El Salvador. As President Ronald Reagan took office in 1981, he decided to help the government of El Salvador fight an insurgency that, if left unchecked, could undermine other nations in the region. While the United States could not realistically consider sending troops to fight in Central America only a few years after Vietnam, America could still provide aid, military equipment, training, and advisors to the Salvadoran government. Since U.S. advisors were kept to a strict limit by Congress (there were never more than 120 U.S. military personnel at any time in El Salvador), the Americans could not consider the option of taking the war over from the locals. American military and State Department personnel assigned to support the Salvadorans were forced by the circumstances to concentrate on counterinsurgency basics. The American advisors determined that the Salvadorans had to initiate broad reforms in the military and civilian spheres; that the economic problems of the nation had to be addressed; that Salvadoran security forces had to be retrained and reformed, and an emphasis placed upon civic action and human rights throughout all levels of government—something quite alien to the tradition of military dictatorship that had prevailed in El Salvador for decades. It all had to be done with U.S. advice and training, using U.S. aid as a lever to push the Salvadoran government to accept the changes that were needed to defeat the insurgents.[23]

The war in El Salvador would be considered prolonged by any standard. It was finally concluded in 1992 when the insurgent groups signed a peace treaty with the government, essentially on the government's terms. El Salvador, in the course of the war, had been painfully transformed into a democratic nation. Most of the fundamental issues that had motivated the insurgents had been addressed by a series of reformist governments. The small group of American military and State Department personnel who served in El Salvador ignored the prevailing conventional war doctrine and culture of the U.S. military, developing a strategy that followed the classic British/American doctrines of counterinsurgency—all of which were validated by the course and outcome of the war. Americans who served in El

Salvador drew some soundly based conclusions from their experience, and this led to a renewed interest in counterinsurgency among a small group of American military officers. For them, counterinsurgency was not a dirty word, for El Salvador had proven that a major insurgency could be defeated with the help of the West and the proper strategy.

Ambassador Edwin Corr and Courtney Prisk, who had served in the Central American region, outlined the importance of comprehensive political, social, and economic reform to winning in El Salvador.[24] Max Manwaring, who served for several years in El Salvador helping to craft a comprehensive strategy for the Salvadorans and Americans, argued for a "new people-oriented model. Every policy, program, and action—military, political, economic, opinion making—must contribute directly to the maintenance or enhancement of political legitimacy. As much must be focused on preconflict and postconflict periods as on the conflict itself."[25] Manwaring was not arguing for a new doctrine but was mainly restating some principles that had been forgotten after Vietnam. For example, Manwaring argued that the war was not just about military action but equally about social, political, and economic reform: "The ultimate outcome of any effort to deal with a given conflict is not primarily determined by the skilful manipulation of violence in one of the many military/police battles that might take place."[26] El Salvador was compared with other insurgencies and a useful matrix was drawn up, outlining the many tasks that a nation needed to address in order to successfully defeat the insurgents.[27]

An important aspect of the war in El Salvador also relates to Malaya and other campaigns. In El Salvador, one of the obstacles to establishing a comprehensive civil/military strategy to support the government and defeat the insurgents was the difficulty of getting the various American government agencies (including the Department of Defense and State Department) to work effectively together.[28] A measure of cooperation was achieved in the end, but bureaucratic friction delayed the implementation of what proved to be a successful strategy that incorporated expansion and training of the Salvadoran armed forces along with government and economic reforms. One of the paramount lessons taken from El Salvador was the importance of creating a management structure that ensured cooperation and coordination as a first step in establishing a general strategy. Ambassadors Edwin Corr and David Miller recommended that the U.S. approach counterinsurgency organization with an established doctrine rather than the ad hoc approach that had been used in El Salvador. The two ambassadors noted that, "on the job training is a high risk, inefficient way to prepare personnel to understand and cope with LIC (Low Intensity Conflict)."[29] However, this lesson from El Salvador never "took" in the bureaucratic culture of Washington and the problem of coordinating government agencies would remain a problem for future operations.

In summarizing the lessons from the El Salvador experience, Max Manwaring, one of America's leading counterinsurgency theorists, outlines the primary issues that have to be addressed by a nation in order to defeat an insurgency: "Control of the situation is determined by

1. the degree of legitimacy of the government;
2. the organization for unity of effort;
3. the type and consistency of external support for the targeted government;
4. the ability to reduce outside support to an illegal opposition;
5. the effectiveness of intelligence; and
6. the level of competence and discipline of a government's security forces."[30]

Manwaring argues, quite convincingly, that concentrating on these six issues (known as "Manwaring's Paradigm") is the first step on the path to establishing a coherent counterinsurgency doctrine. The small group of U.S. military personnel who studied counterinsurgency in the 1980s and 1990s have come to appreciate these insights, and the central importance of legitimacy has been underscored in American thinking.

INSURGENCY AND TERRORISM IN THE 1970S AND 1980S

Variations of revolutionary theory developed throughout the 1970s after the successful models of insurgency in China, Vietnam, and Cuba. One variation of revolutionary insurgency, known as the "Foco theory," argued that the strategy of initiating insurgent military action only after a long period of political organization and preparation was unnecessary. Che Guevara, the famous colleague of Fidel Castro, argued that an insurgency could start with guerrilla warfare by the people's army as the first step. Organizing the political base of the people could come later as the people would be drawn to the insurgent cause by the initiation of military action. Guevara tried his theory in Bolivia in the 1960s and failed miserably, losing his life and the lives of his cadre in the process while demonstrating the flaws in the Foco theory.[31] In insurgency, as with other forms of warfare, good planning and careful preparation are essential for success.

Another form of insurgency that enjoyed some popularity in Latin America between the 1960s and the 1980s was urban guerrilla war. In Venezuela, Colombia, and several other countries, Marxist revolutionaries initiated programs of terrorism carried out by small cadres. The terrorist strategy at first targeted government institutions and the police. The revolutionary strategists hoped that their actions would provoke the government into overreacting, initiating ruthless measures of repression that would, in turn, delegitimize the government in the eyes of the people and foster dissatisfaction with the regime. The revolutionaries relied upon keeping close contacts with churches, embassies, international jurists, and the international media to ensure that any government use of violence and repression in response to terrorist acts would receive maximum media play and bring international condemnation upon the government. This strategy failed every time it was employed. The strategy of targeting the police for terrorist attacks backfired on the rebels. Instead of winning support for the revolutionaries it quickly turned the mass of the population against the authors of terror. Most of the police in South America who were the primary targets of bombing and murder campaigns were working-class men with large families. Average urban residents identified more with the police victims than with the mostly upper-class revolutionaries who killed them. The resulting backlash to terrorism increased public support for the government and served to delegitimize the revolutionaries.[32]

The 1970s and 1980s saw the rise of terrorism on several fronts. In Europe, small radical groups, usually of an anarchist inclination, sought to destabilize and demoralize Western nations through acts of public and calculated terrorism. These groups, like the Red Brigades of Italy or the Red Army Fraktion in Germany, cannot be classified as insurgents because they had little popular support and had little interest in winning a mass base. For such groups, acts of indiscriminate violence became an end in themselves. In the Middle East, groups that used terrorism extensively as a tactic arose or came to public prominence, such as the Palestine Liberation Organization (PLO) and Hezbollah in Lebanon. They can be fairly classified as insurgents since they sought and won a mass following and had the political objective of destroying Israel (the PLO) or forcing Israeli forces out of Lebanon (Hezbollah).[33]

Terrorism was employed by the PLO against Israeli interests in many nations as part of a long-term strategy to undermine the Israeli state and to reduce international support for Israel. Terrorist acts also became the focus of the military campaigns by Hezbollah. It was a strategy of the weak against the strong and it worked with some effect. Constant political agitation, demonstrations, and terrorism pushed the Israelis to directly negotiate with the PLO in the early 1990s. Hezbollah was even more successful. After an eighteen-year war with Hezbollah terrorists in southern Lebanon, Israel finally withdrew its occupation forces.

Seen from a political/strategic context, terrorism is not an irrational act but part of a rational general strategy. Christopher Harmon outlined the five major effects that groups hope to achieve by employing terrorism as part of a general strategy. Terrorism is used to:

1. create social dislocation and/or anarchy;
2. undermine an enemy government;
3. inflict military damage;
4. cause economic dislocation; and
5. affect international policy and relations.[34]

Terrorism alone cannot win a military victory but it can still have enormous effects. The terrorist attacks on New York City and Washington on September 9, 2001, inflicted military damage (the Pentagon attack), caused America billions of dollars in economic damage, and won a kind of worldwide respect for al Qaeda. In the Muslim world, where the attack on America was often celebrated, al Qaeda won popularity among the masses and a following that continues today. The dramatic actions of 9/11 gave al Qaeda a worldwide credibility that makes this organization and its many offshoots exceptionally difficult to suppress. Having created such notable strategic effects, terrorism is now a favored tactic of insurgent groups that oppose the United States and U.S. allies and interests.

CHANGES IN THE MOTIVATION FOR INSURGENCY

While terrorism has become a primary tactic of insurgent warfare, other aspects of insurgency have also changed in the last two decades. Generally, one or more of the following factors motivate people who join an insurgent organization:

1. Ideology, a desire for a new system of government to meet the social and economic needs of the people. Marxist insurgencies, such as in El Salvador, usually fall into this category.
2. Nationalism, the desire of one nation or people to win independence from another nation. The colonial insurgencies, such as Indochina from 1946 to 1954 and Algeria from 1954 to 1962, were primarily motivated by nationalism.
3. Ethnic nationalism, the desire for independence or autonomy for one's tribe or ethnic group. An example of this is the insurgency in Guatemala from 1963 to 1996. It was motivated primarily by the desire of the Indian population to be autonomous from the Spanish-Guatemalan culture.
4. Religion, the desire to make one's religion supreme and to suppress other religions. Religion is a primary motivator of the Hezbollah guerrillas who have fought the Israelis from 1982 to the present and was also a major motivation for the Taliban in Afghanistan.

In the era from World War II to the end of the Cold War, most insurgencies were motivated by ideology or nationalism or a combination of the two, as in the examples of Malaya and the Viet Cong in South Vietnam. However, the end of the Cold War was accompanied by the revival of long-suppressed ethnic rivalries in countries such as Yugoslavia and the former Soviet Union.

With the general rise of disorder in the world and the collapse of the bipolar political alliance system, the primary motivations for most insurgencies changed. From 1990 to the present, most of the major insurgencies have been motivated by ethnic nationalism or religion. Often, as in the case of the rebellion of the Chechens against Russia, there is a combination of the two. The civil war in Afghanistan, which had been raging for years before the American attack against the Taliban government in 2001, was waged mostly along tribal and ethnic lines. The current insurgency in Afghanistan against the pro-Western government of Afghanistan continues along the old tribal/ethnic lines, with elements of religious fervor thrown in as non-Afghani al Qaeda supporters travel to Afghanistan to conduct a crusade against the U.S. and Western forces and the freely elected Afghani government allied with them. In Iraq, the insurgency began primarily along ethnic lines with the Sunni Muslim minority, which formally ruled Iraq, fearing the loss of power to the Shiite majority. Adding to the ethnic motivation for insurgency is the religious element, radical Sunni and some Shiite clerics calling on the faithful to wage war against the non-Muslim forces in the country and to create a pure religious state in Iraq. Thousands of al Qaeda members and sympathizers, motivated by religion, have come to Iraq from many nations to wage war against the infidels.[35] Many have proven their dedication to the cause by becoming suicide bombers and therefore holy martyrs to Islam. As of this writing, it is notable that the majority of those fighting the Coalition forces in Iraq have been Iraqis, but the majority of suicide bombers have been non-Iraqis.

This trend of combined ethnic and religious motivations for insurgents makes counterinsurgency more difficult. Often a compromise or broadly acceptable political solution can be found to convince people motivated by nationalism or ideology to lay down their arms and turn away from an insurgency. Historically, it has been possible to negotiate with nationalists. The British defused some of the nationalistic elements of the Malayan insurgency by granting Malaya independence in 1958. The French might have defused the Algerian nationalist movement if they had granted some form of meaningful home rule to the Algerians before 1954. In El Salvador and the Philippines the government reduced peasant support for Marxist ideology by enacting fundamental economic and political reforms that provided a better life. People very commonly change their political and ideological positions—just note how many ex-communists have turned to capitalism and democracy since 1990. In contrast, people are born with their ethnicity and rarely change their religion. Though it is still possible to defuse such issues and protect the rights of ethnic and religious minorities in order to convince them to stop support for an insurgency, it is a task of much greater magnitude.

The development of the religious/political ideology of the Muslim Brotherhood in Egypt in the 1950s provided much of the motivation for the current war waged against America and the West by Islamic radical groups. This religion-based ideology has a broad and growing appeal throughout the whole of the Islamic world. While the founders of the radical approach to purify Islam have been dead for a generation, Osama bin Laden is one of many who picked up the teachings and have carried them to their inevitable conclusion of open conflict with the West and with the "impure" Muslim states as well. Essentially, the current conflict with radical Islam is not about economics, or the social needs of the people, but a conflict rooted in a view of religion that amounts to a huge, international insurgency of radical Islam against the West and its allies. In the strategic view of the Islamic radicals, America, as the leading nation of the West, is the political/ideological/economic pillar. If America is crippled, then the whole West is crippled.

Osama bin Laden's religious decree of 1998 amounted to a straightforward declaration of war against the United States. His *fatwa* (religious decree) cites specifically Islamic reasons for declaring war, including the need to "purify" the holy Arabian Peninsula from the presence of "Crusaders" (unbelievers, of whom America is the leading nation), and because America supports the Jews. The Koran is quoted as justification to "kill Americans and plunder their money wherever and whenever they find it." Osama's *fatwa* allows that his forces may kill civilians as well as military personnel and also authorizes war against any Arab nation that allies itself with the United States.[36] Notable Islamic scholars and their interpretation of the Koran are quoted to prove that war on America is in compliance with "Allah's order." War to destroy America is seen as an act of self-defense for Islam: "As for the fighting to repulse an enemy, it is aimed at defending sanctity and religion, and it is a duty as agreed (by *ulema*—Holy Law)."[37]

An insurgency that is motivated primarily by religious fervor, and in which those who carry out suicide bombings against civilian unbelievers are praised and honored as holy martyrs, is exceptionally difficult to combat. Traditionally successful counterinsurgency strategies that deal with the political and economic grievances of the population have less relevance in undermining support for an insurgency motivated by religion. Any successful counterinsurgency strategy must first understand the motivation for the insurgency and then deal with it. In this case, a broad push to support a more moderate approach to Islam and the more moderate Islamic states would be in order as a central element in counterinsurgency strategy.

INSURGENT ORGANIZATION

From World War II to the collapse of Communism, most insurgencies followed some variation of the Maoist model. The insurgents, usually possessing a Marxist worldview and political ideology, normally started an insurgency already possessing a central leadership and highly developed political organization, a clear political program, and a long-term military/political strategy to achieve their ends. The end of the Cold War brought not a peace dividend but a period of nonstop disorder through much of the developing world. Since 1990, many of the national, religious, and ethnic tensions that had been present during the Cold War (but often ignored by the great powers) have risen to the surface, triggering a series of implosions of small nations as well as civil war in many others. The insurgencies based on ethnic or religious motivations developed a different organizational form from the highly centralized Maoist type of insurgency seen during the Cold War. The *intifada*, the uprising of the Palestinians in the territories occupied by Israel that began in 1987, and which has been carried on in its current incarnation since 2000, developed a new and very loose form of organization in contrast to the formally centralized leadership of the PLO. The *intifada* became a popular rebellion organized through a network of small local groups. Within a month of the *intifada*'s spreading through the occupied territories, the following three levels of insurgent leadership had evolved: neighborhood leaders of popular committees that came to the fore; the United National Command of the Uprising (a network of local leaders who cooperated and coordinated their efforts); and a loose network of Palestinian academics, journalists, and official representatives who worked with the local and national groups to publicize the Palestinian cause to the world. For the latter group, their connections with the international media were especially important.[38]

The loose network of the Palestinian insurgents defeated Israel's attempt to squelch the rebellion by finding and arresting the leadership. The local committees and the leaders of the United National Command, unlike guerrilla leaders in the past who emphasized personal charisma and leadership, chose to remain anonymous. Handbills produced by the local committees were simply signed "UNC" (United National Command). Israeli roundups of local committee and national Palestinian leaders failed to cripple the organization. New leaders arose and simply produced new editions of the handbills that were circulated through the Palestinian territories. In short, the *intifada* leadership effectively reconstructed itself and continued the resistance after every Israeli strike or roundup.[39]

In the Israeli-occupied region of southern Lebanon, where the Israelis faced a growing insurgency by the Lebanese Shiite community after the 1982 invasion of Lebanon, the Israelis faced a similar problem in trying to identify and decapitate the leadership of the Hezbollah insurgents, who were making life increasingly unpleasant for the Israeli forces. The Lebanese Shiites had for generations maintained close connections with Iraq, where the Lebanese Shiite mullahs went for their theology education. Hezbollah was organized around a council of mullahs in Lebanon who, thanks to their close connections with the mullahs of the Iranian Revolutionary government, could count on money, arms, training, and support from Iran. The Hezbollah leadership, which remained largely anonymous through the eighteen years of Israeli occupation of southern Lebanon, decided upon a strategy of constant harassment by small raids and terrorist attacks, featuring suicide bombers as a standard tactic. A relatively small force of a few highly trained men, highly motivated by their faith, carried out the military raids and terrorist operations. The relentless campaign of bombing known Hezbollah camps and bases had little effect since Hezbollah always had plenty of volunteers to replace the few men lost to each raid. Even strategies of decapitating the Hezbollah leadership failed. In 1987, a brilliant Israeli commando raid captured Hezbollah leader Sheik Abdul Karim Obeid. In

February 1992, the Israelis conducted an air attack that killed the secretary general of Hezbollah with a helicopter-mounted missile. Yet Hezbollah was scarcely affected by such raids and attacks on the leadership. After every successful Israeli operation, the small attacks and suicide bombings against the Israelis continued as before.

Although Israel took a heavy toll on the Lebanese Shiites, killing them at a ratio of ten Lebanese for every Israeli, the Hezbollah fighters were not deterred. They were willing to take heavy losses to achieve the political aim, while the Israelis were not willing to take constant casualties to maintain their position in southern Lebanon. After eighteen years of struggle, Hezbollah won and Israel simply pulled out of southern Lebanon. The Hezbollah type of insurgency had defeated a nation of great military prowess, armed with the latest American high-tech and precision weaponry. They had done it with some of the tried and true insurgent tactics: inflicting constant harassment with constant small losses for the enemy, and having the will to take punishment and endure over the long term.[40]

Among the most effective tactics of the Palestinians and Hezbollah has been their use and manipulation of the media to support their cause. The Palestinians developed good contacts with the international media and made sure that their version of events dominated the world press. Heavy-handed Israeli reaction to Palestinian violence was usually portrayed on the television news with images of unarmed Palestinian civilians being bullied by heavily armed Israelis with armored vehicles and helicopters.[41] During the battles with the PLO in Lebanon in 1982, the Palestinians emplaced military equipment such as antiaircraft guns in civilian neighborhoods and on hospital grounds in Beirut and parked armored vehicles next to foreign embassies in the hope that the Israelis would bomb these clearly military targets—actions fully allowed by the laws of war—and cause civilian casualties that could then be shown to the world's media as proof of the "genocidal" and "immoral" Israeli approach to warfare.[42] The Palestinians, Hezbollah, and many other insurgents have been quite prepared to sacrifice innocent civilians in order to create effective propaganda for their cause in the international media.

The fairly loose organization of the Hezbollah organization and of the Palestinians' does not lend itself to major military or conventional operations.

Attacks and suicide bombings are not controlled or commanded centrally but are often carried out under the initiative of local groups and commanders, with only a general strategic coordination by the insurgent council. This form of insurgent organization finds it difficult if not impossible to agree on a broad political program. Usually the long-term political goal is very simple—drive out the foreign forces and their allies. After that, all is unclear. During the conflict in southern Lebanon, Hezbollah cooperated with other insurgent groups for the short term but failed to form a long-term political program. While any large-scale coordinated strategy and campaign is ruled out by this very loose network of insurgent and terrorist groups, the advantage for the insurgents is that it is difficult if not impossible for the government forces to cripple the insurgents by bombing their headquarters or killing their leaders. One can imagine that if Chiang Kai-shek had managed to kill Mao in the mid-1930s, the Chinese revolution would likely not have succeeded. If the French had killed Ho Chi Minh or General Vo Nguyen Giap in 1946, the outcome of the French colonial war in Indochina would very likely have turned out better for the French. But the newer forms of loosely organized and networked insurgent groups are not reliant on charismatic leaders or central command like the classical Maoist forms of insurgency.

In Afghanistan, the insurgency against the Soviet-backed government in the 1980s and the current insurgency against the U.S.-backed Afghan government are organized primarily around tribal groups, although considerable support from radical Islamic groups is also present. Traditionally, Afghani tribes have found it impossible to cooperate for any length of time, and tribal conflict is a normal part of Afghani culture. From the Western perspective, Afghani politics is bewildering. Afghanistan contains more than a dozen major tribal groups with a long history of fighting each other and maintaining short-term alliances to prevent any tribe or alliance of tribes from dominating the country. During the long conflict with the Soviets, some Afghani tribes would ally themselves with the Soviet-backed Afghan government for a while and wage war against a neighboring tribe. In the next fighting season, some tribes would switch allegiance and end up in an alliance fighting the Soviets. The Afghan resistance against the Soviets was led by a very loose organization of tribal elders who met occasionally to bicker over dividing up aid from outside Afghanistan. Aside from that, there was no general strategic coordination of the Afghani resistance in the 1980s. While the Afghanis could not coordinate a general strategy, the Soviets were unable to make any decisive strike against the Afghani leaders. The tribes were so constituted that when the Soviets killed a leader, it was easy through the tribal law to select a new one.[43]

INSURGENT ORGANIZATION AND IRAQ

The current insurgency against the U.S.-supported Iraqi government is a further example of an insurgency organized into loose groups and networks. When the regime of Saddam Hussein was overthrown, the Coalition forces should have expected trouble from the strongest supporters of the old regime: mainly the Sunni Arab minority of Iraq. However, a great deal of trouble with Saddam's supporters might not have occurred if the United States had not officially disbanded the Iraqi army in late May of 2003—an act that precipitated open insurgency by the former Baathist regime supporters. Disbanding the army not only put hundreds of thousands of Iraqis out of a job, it was a signal that there would be no place in the new Iraq for former Saddam supporters. Four days after the Iraqi army was officially disbanded, the bombs started going off in Fallujah, a Sunni and Baathist stronghold. Essentially, the Iraqi insurgency was originally motivated by nationalist and ethnic considerations. Although the overwhelming majority of the Iraqis welcomed the Coalition forces as liberators from the vicious dictatorship of Saddam, the Sunnis proclaimed the insurgency as a resistance to a foreign occupier. Using the political networks of the old regime, and with considerable weaponry and Baathist Party funds readily available, the Sunnis began a program of harassment and terrorism against the Coalition forces and, even more disturbing, a program of assassination against Iraqis cooperating with the Coalition forces in forming a new and democratic government and working with the administrative or security forces of the new Iraqi government.

With Saddam captured and in prison by December 2003, there was no central figure to organize an insurgency around. The Iraqi insurgency now took the form of numerous small groups and factions, mostly ex-Baathists, who stepped up the campaign of violence to destabilize Iraq. As of mid-

2005, the numerous insurgent groups in Iraq have not managed to create either a coherent political organization or a political program. The only program that all the insurgent groups have is a desire to have all foreign forces leave Iraq and to undermine and destabilize the Iraqi government. In short, they want Iraq to turn into another Lebanon of the 1980s—a land wracked by perpetual ethnic warfare and division, a place where armed groups might come to the fore and seize their share of power.

Added to the loose mix of Sunni Arab resistance groups, several thousand foreign fighters, motivated by their vision of radical Islam, have found their way through the unguarded borders and joined with the Sunni Arab insurgents in attacking the American and Coalition forces and the Iraqi government. As for the Sunni Arab insurgents, there is no single commander or organization for the radical Islamist groups operating in Iraq. The most notable tactic of the foreign insurgents in Iraq has been the suicide bomber. A disproportionate number of the suicide bombers in Iraq have been non-Iraqis. Also notable about the foreign fighters and tactics has been the indiscriminate nature of the suicide bombings, with Iraqi civilians, mostly Shiites, being targeted as frequently as soldiers and government officials. This shows the largely negative goal of Iraqi insurgents: simply to make Iraq ungovernable. If Iraq can't be governed, and the American and Coalition forces leave, the world will perceive the Iraq War as an enormous U.S. failure and a victory for radical Islam. Many of the Sunni Iraqi insurgents, of course, have a very different vision for a future Iraq—power for themselves—and would probably not get along with the radical Islamic terrorists if the Coalition forces did pull out. In the meantime, however, the two factions have formed an unofficial alliance and are cooperating together. As of 2005, there are an estimated ten to fifteen thousand active insurgents in Iraq, with as much as 20 percent of that number being foreign terrorists.

The Ansar al-Islam (Partisans of Islam) group provides an example of how the foreign/indigenous terrorist groups network in Iraq. These are guerrillas closely linked to al Qaeda and based in Kurdistan. The group formed in the mid-1990s as a group of Islamicist factions that split from the Islamic Movement of Kurdistan. Some members of the group are Kurds, but the group consists mostly of Arab leaders and cadres. Ansar al-Islam reportedly started with $300,000 to $600,000 in seed money from al

Qaeda, and the foreign presence soon grew to between 80 and 120 al Qaeda regulars. Members have included Iraqi, Jordanian, Moroccan, Syrian, Palestinian, and Afghan fighters. In their stronghold in a mountainous region of Kurdistan they have tried to establish a Taliban-like regime. The group already existed under the regime of Saddam but laid low. After the Coalition invasion of 2003, they bounced back. Soon, there were clashes between Ansar al-Islam and the Kurdish security forces. It is also suspected that the group receives aid and support from Iran, yet another aspect of the frighteningly complicated world of Middle East politics.[44] Ansar al-Islam is believed to be behind the suicide bombing of the offices of the Kurdish Democratic Party and Patriotic Union of Kurdistan on February 3, 2004, which killed over one hundred people including many leaders in Kurdish politics.[45]

While many of the factions fighting in Iraq are operating as classical insurgents (that is, local people trying to seize power by violence), we are also seeing new, networked organizations of insurgent and terrorist groups flourish, some of them motivated by religious fervor rather than by nationalism or ethnic nationalism. The network organization of insurgents and foreign terrorists operates more locally and regionally, hindering the development of any clear strategy or political program. On the one hand, networked insurgents are unable to coordinate military efforts on a national level. On the other hand, the network organization of the insurgency means that it cannot be destroyed by any simple strike at the organizational leadership. For the Iraqi government and the Coalition forces, each faction must be hunted down, rooted out, and destroyed, one by one, a long and complicated process.

THE U.S. DOCTRINAL RESPONSE TO THE IRAQI AND AFGHANI INSURGENCIES
Despite the extensive experience of operations in Colombia and El Salvador from the 1980s to the present, the U.S. Army has been so reluctant to deal officially with the problem of ongoing insurgency that it took the campaigns in Iraq and Afghanistan to finally push them into publishing a new counterinsurgency doctrine. In October 2004, the U.S. Army published the first official doctrine manual on counterinsurgency since 1965, Army Field Manual FM 3-07.22 *Counterinsurgency* (October 2004). The new manual

includes a good deal on the tactical lessons of counterinsurgency operations recently learned in Afghanistan and Iraq: how to clear urban areas, how to move in convoys, and how to provide local security. At the operational and strategic level, the basic teachings of the Manwaring Paradigm, essentially the classic counterinsurgency strategy of putting the legitimacy of the supported government at the heart of all operations, is clearly emphasized. The basic rules of a civil/military program—long known to counterinsurgency specialists and validated by many successful campaigns—are repeated. Although new technologies are available to support the tactics and operations, the strategies for success in counterinsurgency have not changed, and the new manual delivers this message with clarity.

In most respects, the new U.S. doctrine (mostly an old doctrine) is a huge step forward in American military thinking on counterinsurgency. However, there are some serious flaws in the doctrine that demonstrate U.S. military thinking is still behind in understanding the fundamentals of some newer aspects of insurgency. The major problem in the new U.S. Army doctrine is that it still expects insurgency to follow a Maoist model of organization, a centrally led insurgent force operating under a unified insurgent command. This is the type of organization the U.S.-supported Colombian government faces, but is clearly NOT the type of insurgent organization that the U.S. military faces either in Iraq or Afghanistan now or is very likely to face in the future.

The new type of loosely networked insurgent organizations in no way invalidates the basic strategic guidelines for counterinsurgency outlined in Army Manual FM 3-07.22 proven over many years. However, a poor understanding of insurgent organizations can hamper U.S. tactics by encouraging the targeting and destruction of a central insurgent organization that simply does not exist. In short, the American doctrine is likely to push the U.S. Army to think in terms of decisive strikes against the leadership as a primary operational method in the hopes of a rapid, decisive victory. With the networked form of insurgent organization, the hope for a rapid, decisive victory in counterinsurgency is likely to be an unachievable goal.

The new army manual on counterinsurgency was developed as a rush product to provide some general guidance to the U.S. unit leaders fighting

insurgencies in Afghanistan and Iraq and is in use today as an interim doctrine as the army conducts further study and analysis. Current debates
within the U.S. Army and Department of Defense (DOD), especially
among the senior leaders, will shape the content of the next edition of
army counterinsurgency doctrine. The key issues at dispute are not about
tactics and techniques but about the place of insurgency and counterinsurgency in general military theory. After so many years of exclusive focus
on fighting conventional wars against conventional states, most of the
senior military officers have been conditioned to view insurgency as simply a subset of conventional war—with enemy forces just a bit less organized and less well equipped than those of a major state enemy. Viewed in
this manner, the traditional terminology of "rapid, decisive operations"
and the old principles of war (mass, offensive, maneuver, firepower, and so
on) can still be conveniently applied with only minor modifications. On
the other hand, those who have carefully studied insurgency and counterinsurgency almost universally regard war with nonstate enemies as a
completely different kind of war, a war in which the principles of conventional state-on-state war do not apply. Counterinsurgency warfare
requires an entirely different set of principles and theoretical models,
many of which are very much at odds with the U.S. military's traditional
constructs of warfare. Fighting nonstate enemies requires military and
civilian leaders to get out of their intellectual comfort zones and adopt a
different way of looking at America's security problems. The success or
failure of the U.S. efforts to fight insurgencies motivated by radical Islam
will depend largely on how well our military leaders can adapt their thinking. The interim doctrine on counterinsurgency offers at least a hope that
the U.S. military might adapt to new conditions by returning to its own
historical traditions for answers.

CHAPTER TWO

AMERICA'S "NEW WAY OF WAR": UNFULFILLED PROMISES

For all but the resolutely sightless, it is now obvious that air combat determines the outcome in modern war.
—General Merrill McPeak, USAF, 2003

Thousands of human lives are sacrificed to military buzz-words—assuredly not from evil intention, but simply from lack of independent thought.
—Colonel General Hans von Seeckt, 1935

The collapse of Communism as a state system between 1989 and 1990, combined with the Gulf War (1990–1991), was a major turning point for American military theory, doctrine, and organization. In the aftermath of the incredibly successful U.S.-led military campaign against Saddam Hussein's Iraq and the successful end of the Cold War that left America as the world's only military superpower, a broad consensus was established among America's military leaders, political leaders, and defense experts. This consensus was that the nature and conduct of war had fundamentally changed. The old principles of war, codified since the Clausewitz era in the nineteenth century and which had dominated our military doctrine and theory during the Cold War, were no longer relevant—these leaders said. The common belief among the service staffs in the Pentagon and at the military staff colleges, where the majors and lieutenant colonels are trained for higher command, was that the Gulf War had demonstrated a "Revolution in Military Affairs"—and these became favored buzzwords in U.S. military circles. The common American view that technology had become the single

51

most decisive aspect of warfare gave rise to a whole family of new jargon terms such as "hyperwar," "full-spectrum conflict," and "third-generation warfare." By any reckoning, it was the most buzzword-rich era in the history of American military thought, with new terms to go with the new perception of reality.

The events in the Persian Gulf were indeed dramatic. The United States fought a major war in 1991 in which a six-week air campaign and four-day ground campaign decisively and dramatically wrecked one of the world's largest and best-armed military machines—all at the cost of fewer than 150 combat fatalities. For most of the U.S. military, and most of the American public, the Gulf War seemed to prove that American technology presented such an overwhelming advantage that the United States could apply the same formula to defeat almost any potential enemy quickly, efficiently, and decisively—and at minimal cost. Space-based surveillance gave the United States a detailed, real-time view of enemy forces. U.S. aircraft armed with the latest sophisticated avionics, employing stealth technology and precision bombs, could quickly paralyze a highly modern air defense system and leave a major enemy open to devastating attacks on command centers, military industries, and fielded forces. Highly trained American ground forces, equipped with the world's most advanced armored vehicles and most precise artillery systems, networked together by the world's most sophisticated communications systems, could attack, maneuver, and cover ground with a rapidity never before seen in modern warfare. All this was backed up with enormous and precise aerial firepower. Against American air and ground operations, Saddam's huge army first was paralyzed and then quickly collapsed. To those who experienced it and those who watched from the sidelines, it seemed the U.S. military had at last discovered the right combination of precision, intelligence, weapons, and tactics to guarantee decisive victory—at little cost to our own forces and with minimal collateral damage to the enemy's civilian population.

After the great success of U.S. arms in the Gulf in 1991, there appeared a kind of euphoria among the U.S. military leadership. After Vietnam, there had been a twenty-year process of rebuilding the army and reorienting the training and doctrine system for the armed forces to fight large-scale conventional war. Now, it had worked better than anyone in the military had imagined. The U.S. victory against Iraq made conventional war look almost easy, and there was a rush to apply the new lessons. The Gulf War victory was so dramatic, with its televised scenes of precision-guided bombs plunging through Iraqi headquarters' air vents, followed by almost comical images of Iraqi soldiers trying to surrender to unpiloted reconnaissance drone aircraft, it's no wonder that so many in the American military and civilian leadership concluded that they had developed a revolutionary answer to modern warfare and that old wisdoms about war should simply be discarded.

Richard Cheney, secretary of defense during the Gulf War, was one of the leaders most impressed with this vision of high-tech warfare. Shortly after the conflict, he commented, "This war demonstrated dramatically the new possibilities of what has been called the 'military technological revolution in warfare.' "[1] During the 1990s, many U.S. military leaders went further than Cheney in expressing their belief in a "new U.S. way of war." General Eric Shinseki (Army Chief of Staff 1999–2003), as a three-star general and chief of army operations in the early 1990s, reportedly announced to a conference of army officers that Clausewitz was no longer relevant to American military doctrine. Carl von Clausewitz, the brilliant nineteenth-century philosopher of war, argued in his theory of conflict that all military operations are carried out under conditions of "fog" (confusion, uncertainty, lack of information) and "friction" (even simple tasks become very difficult under war conditions). But General Shinseki argued that both these elements had been eliminated. Modern high-tech assets, such as space-based surveillance and networked computer communications, had eliminated the "fog" from warfare, and U.S. commanders in the future would fight with a complete intelligence picture of the battlefield. "Friction" was being eliminated by the instantaneous and accurate information flowing through every level of the military command, providing commanders with the ability to seamlessly coordinate the actions of forces across huge expanses.[2]

Enthusiasm permeated the U.S. military leadership, and the military literature abounded with articles explaining how the nature of war had dramatically changed.[3] Nowhere in the U.S. military was the enthusiasm for the "Revolution in Military Affairs" more pronounced than in the U.S. Air

Force, where the long doctrinal tradition of winning wars through strategic bombing was combined with a corporate desire to seize the title of dominant U.S. military service.

The U.S. Air Force mind-set produced an advocacy literature to support an "airpower alone" solution to modern warfare that bordered on fanaticism. The U.S. Air Force's most influential theorist in the 1990s, Colonel John Warden, proclaimed after the Gulf War, "The world has just witnessed a new kind of war—hyperwar!"[4] After the Gulf War, several USAF colonels involved in developing service doctrine privately told me of their belief that armies and navies were largely obsolete and that to win future wars, all one really needed was a large and very high-tech U.S. Air Force. The vision of the radical airpower theorists of the 1920s such as General Giulio Douhet and General Billy Mitchell that argued that bombing strategic targets could paralyze and defeat whole nations in weeks had finally come to pass. In the wake of the Gulf War, some U.S. Air Force officers made even more strident claims in the professional military journals. One lieutenant colonel wrote, "Douhet's basic tenet that warfare had fundamentally changed can now be understood. The airplane is the supreme offensive weapon. It is not an inherently supportive creature—it can win wars all by itself."[5] Another U.S. Air Force officer argued that, thanks to American precision weapons, U.S. airpower alone could prevent insurgents from defeating an indigenous government.[6]

Although the official U.S. Air Force doctrine refrained from expressing the extreme views common among air force officers—because they would have caused an open rift with the other services—it still abounded with inflated claims for airpower. In an outline of U.S. Air Force doctrine written in the mid-1990s, U.S. Air Force Chief of Staff General Ron Fogleman proclaimed that "The Air Force also recognizes the emerging reality that in the 21st century it will be possible to find, fix, or track and target anything that moves on the surface of the earth."[7] The U.S. Air Force officers were the most explicit in arguing that the high-tech new way of war had eliminated the need for ground armies, but some senior soldiers jumped on the bandwagon as well. The chairman of the Joint Chiefs of Staff, Army General John Shalikashvili, expressed his own vision of modern high-tech war in a series of new doctrinal buzz phrases such as "full-spectrum dominance," "precision engagement," and "information superiority." The old form of planned and sequenced operations was gone, he claimed. "Instead of relying on massed forces and sequential operations, we will achieve massed effects in other ways. Information superiority and advances in technology will enable us to achieve the desired effects through the tailored application of joint combat power."[8]

Such statements were common in the 1990s. The lessons of the Gulf War were quickly codified and published by all the services in a rush to claim their share of the defense budget in the post–Cold War cutbacks and realignments that were the top priority for the administration after the successful war. Each service argued that it had mastered the art of synergistic joint operations, effective communications, precision engagement, and decisive operations (all popular military jargon). Each argued that it was well prepared to engage America's enemies in the context of the Revolution in Military Affairs (known simply as "RMA"). In the postwar budget debates, the air force was the best positioned of the services: It was the most rapidly deployable, could penetrate the best air defense systems with little loss, and could employ devastating firepower with a precision undreamed of a generation before. In World War II, for example, it took hundreds of B-17s carrying hundreds of tons of bombs to destroy one point target—usually with significant losses for the air force. In the Gulf War, one or two planes could achieve the same effect with no losses and minimal collateral damage to nearby civilians. Moreover, the air force was backed by an incredible array of space-based surveillance and communications systems to assist in intelligence, targeting, and navigation.

In the postwar competition for funding, the army had a mediocre, low-tech showing in comparison with the U.S. Air Force. The air force could deploy its fighter and bomber units to the far side of the world by air and be ready for large-scale conventional combat in a matter of days. On the other hand, the army's heavy divisions required weeks to load and transport all their heavy weapons (tanks, armored personnel carriers, and artillery) from the United States to the front lines by sea. Even under the best conditions, the army's primary forces—its heavy armored and mechanized divisions—are slow to get into the fight.

The army seemed to have additional drawbacks in this new age. Ground warfare was manpower intensive, and although the commitment of troops might make a victory certain, it also held the prospect of significant casualties. One of the fundamental assumptions of U.S. military and civilian leaders after Vietnam was that the American public would never support a long casualty list. This belief that the American public is adverse to military casualties was widely held as a matter of faith and drove the formulation of our military strategy and doctrine from the Vietnam War until 2001. (Interestingly, this point was disproved by several studies during the Gulf War that showed that the American public could accept heavy losses if a military operation were clearly in the national interest.[9]) Further, a large professional military carries with it some heavy long-term personnel costs, such as training infrastructure, U.S. and foreign bases, logistics requirements, family support, medical care, and generous retirement packages for those who have served twenty to twenty-five years. These issues all added up. The Pentagon sponsored several studies in the early 1990s in which it considered cutting the eighteen-division active army to a total of between four and a half and twelve divisions (a total army, including support troops, of between 145,000 and 180,000 soldiers). During the elder Bush and then Clinton administrations—which were eager to cut the defense budget and realize a post–Cold War peace dividend—the personnel-intensive army became the primary target for force reduction.

Cutbacks were also proposed for other branches of the military. The defense planners considered the navy to be too personnel-intensive and cost-inefficient; carriers and planes proved less capable than the air force's land-based aircraft and several times more expensive to operate. Defense analysts called for cutting the navy carrier force from fifteen task forces to seven. The size of the air force was also to be reduced. However, its high-tech glamour was left intact. The air force would receive full funding to build and deploy expensive new planes and precision weapons that were even better than those used in the Gulf War. Moreover, the most expensive and high-tech of all the U.S military assets—the air force's space systems—would receive *increased* funding and support under every proposed budget scenario.[10]

In the cutbacks of the 1990s, the Pentagon compromised on a twelve-wing air force (wing = one hundred to one hundred thirty aircraft), a ten-division army, and an eleven-carrier group navy. Many of the top defense analysts argued that the army and navy were still too large, since in future wars America could surely rely on an air campaign, rather than ground forces, as the primary means of applying force.[11]

A few of the most competent and experienced defense analysts cautioned against building a set of strategic dogmas on the thin evidence of the Gulf War. Immediately after the Gulf War, U.S. Air Force Secretary Donald Rice commissioned some outside scholars to put together a thorough, objective, and critical study of the air war with a view to outlining the deficiencies of the aviation forces as well as their strengths. The *Gulf War Air Power Survey* employed dozens of air force officers as well as outside scholars and ran to eight volumes. As expected, the *Survey* praised the many remarkable successes of the American and Coalition Air Forces in the campaign. It also pointed out deficiencies, such as the failure to find and destroy any of Saddam's Scud missiles, problems with accurately assessing the damage done to military targets, and difficulties with disseminating intelligence collected by air force satellites to the ground commanders in a timely fashion. While the *Survey* generally praised the performance of airpower, the primary authors, academics Eliot Cohen and Thomas Keaney, pointed out that many of the postwar analysts had made extreme claims about the role of airpower—claims the authors argued "went too far." They pointed out that many of the elements of airpower touted as "new" and "revolutionary," such as a master attack plan and air tasking order (specific daily missions for all air units in a combat theater), had long been in use in NATO.

The authors of the report also pointed out that the campaign to suppress enemy air defenses, the employment of precision munitions, and the attempt to paralyze the enemy through bombing were by no means new developments.[12] Cohen and Keaney argued that Iraq was essentially a minor power that confronted the world's only superpower and fought with every disadvantage. As for drawing radical conclusions about a revolution in warfare from this relatively minor conflict, they cautioned, "True revolutions in war may take decades and require not merely new technologies but new forms of organization and behavior to mature."[13]

A few other critical voices pointed out the obvious: during 1990 and 1991, the U.S. had enjoyed the advantage of a remarkably stupid enemy in Saddam, and it was unlikely America could expect future enemies to be as incompetent. For example, immediately after seizing Kuwait, Saddam had an open road to seize Saudi Arabia's major Gulf ports, which lay within easy striking distance of his armored forces. For a few weeks, the only ground forces deployed to stop his armored divisions were some lightly armed units of the 82nd U.S. Airborne Division. If Saddam had seized the ports vital to landing and supplying the U.S. and Coalition forces, the Coalition forces would have had to land their heavy armored forces at the Red Sea port of Jeddah and then fight the Iraqis at the end of a several-hundred-mile-long supply line. It could have been done, but it would have complicated Coalition operations enormously. Luckily for the United States, Saddam failed to act.

It was also clear that the quality of Saddam's soldiers didn't even come close to matching the quality of their Soviet-supplied equipment. Aside from the Republican Guards units, the mass of the Iraqi army was poorly trained; each soldier or tank gunner was allotted only a few rounds of ammunition a year for practice. Iraqi officers were poorly trained and chosen more for their loyalty to the regime than for their competence. The Iraqi army had been a remarkably mediocre force since its creation in the 1920s. Although equipped with large quantities of modern weapons, in every campaign it had fought against Israel (1948, 1967, and 1973), it had been handily beaten. Despite the fact that the Iraqis possessed great numerical superiority in planes, tanks, and artillery pieces during the Iraq-Iran War (1980–1988), the Iranians beat the Iraqi forces back to the border and forced the war into a draw.

With this tradition of consistent defeat, morale in the Iraqi forces was low even before the Coalition began its sustained air attacks. While doing nothing to improve his army's notable weaknesses in command and training, Saddam gave the Coalition nations a gift of six months to mobilize and deploy large forces, establish a huge logistics infrastructure, and conduct intensive training and preparation. And the U.S. and Coalition forces used that six months well to carefully plan and prepare for a huge ground campaign. Finally, Saddam was diplomatically isolated from the rest of the world, with only Jordan as a supportive neutral.

Under these conditions, one can fairly question whether the Gulf War really demonstrated any revolutionary principles of war. One side had superbly trained forces, competent military leadership, cutting-edge equipment, and massive air superiority. It handily beat a power with poorly trained soldiers, incompetent officers, inferior equipment, and no airpower. What's revolutionary about that?

After dozens of books had extolled the performance of the U.S. forces and technology in the Gulf War, one of Washington's most respected defense analysts, Jeff Record (who served in Vietnam as a regional advisor and spent years as a top congressional defense staffer), in 1993 wrote a prescient book called *Hollow Victory*. In it, Record pointed out that, for all the touted military success, the war had still not achieved the political aim of eliminating Saddam Hussein as a long-term threat to the region. He predicted that the United States would probably have to go back again at a later date and finish the job. Record took on the official service histories and the Pentagon argument that the Gulf War would serve as a model for future warfare. He argued this attitude might even be good for America's third world enemies because it encouraged an attitude of overconfidence among U.S. military and civilian policymakers. By thinking that war had become cheap and easy, he wrote, we just might get ourselves into trouble.[14]

But these were only a few dissenting voices. In the meantime, word had spread among the military that if you wanted to get ahead in your career, you had better get on the high-tech bandwagon and show how your service, branch, or unit was relevant to the revolutionary changes in warfare. Dissent from the prevailing Pentagon mind-set was not only ignored—it was quietly suppressed in the Pentagon's bureaucratic tradition. Some first-rate officers, assigned to the above-mentioned *Gulf War Air Power Survey* project, one of the best critical analyses of a U.S. military campaign ever produced, found their careers cut short and were quickly retired as lieutenant colonels.

Although the *Gulf War Air Power Survey* had documented the success of American airpower in the Gulf, it had avoided hyperbole and had also documented some deficiencies. What the air force leadership preferred was an uncritical public relations document, which they found in the semiofficial history of the war, *Storm over Iraq: Air Power and the Gulf War*, written in 1992 by the air force's chief of history, Richard Hallion. *Storm over Iraq* was filled with factual errors and panned by many reviewers who saw it not as official history but as an official advocacy piece. Still, the book's argument that airpower was now the dominant and decisive element of warfare was just what the senior officers wanted to hear—especially as the budget discussions got under way.

CONFLICTS OF THE 1990S AND THE PENTAGON'S "NEW WAY OF WAR"

The failure of the U.S. military intervention in Somalia in 1992 to 1994 ought to have served as a wake-up call to the U.S. military as some glaring holes in its strategy and doctrine were exposed. In 1992, President George H. W. Bush deployed U.S. forces to Somalia with the vague objective of supporting the United Nations (UN) humanitarian effort and improving conditions in that unstable, war-torn nation. There was, however, no coherent, long-term planning or strategy. The Clinton administration took over Bush's nonstrategy, and the U.S. and UN peacekeeping forces drifted into a war with one of the leading tribal chiefs, Mohammed Aideed, in mid-1993. With no clear guidance from Washington as to U.S. policy in Somalia, U.S./UN forces carried on a desultory war with Aideed's faction until the bloody battle of October 1993 in Mogadishu, in which eighteen Americans were killed, more than eighty were wounded, and two helicopters were lost—all described in the book (and movie) *Black Hawk Down*. As battles go, it was a fairly minor operation that included a failed raid on Aideed's leadership and a daylong street battle in Mogadishu in which the U.S. forces killed hundreds—perhaps as many as a thousand—Somali warriors.

Seemingly paralyzed by the loss of a few troops, the United States failed to follow up and punish Aideed for inflicting those U.S. losses. In fact, U.S. forces handed the warlord a strategic victory when, after avoiding further combat, they withdrew a few months later. Quite a few strategic and tactical lessons might have been learned from the Somalia episode by the U.S. civilian and military leadership—but they weren't. One lesson was the need for coherent policy guidance for intervening in and rebuilding failed states. Another lesson concerned the limitations of high-tech intelligence and the urgent requirement for old-fashioned human intelligence—people who spoke the language and knew the culture of the people the United States was fighting. Finally, the vulnerability of American helicopters, light vehicles, and light infantry in third world urban combat was made obvious.

The U.S. military might have ignored these lessons from Somalia, but others did not. Osama bin Laden and other radical Islamic leaders studied the U.S. operations and learned several important pieces of information:

1. The Americans have no tolerance for casualties.
2. If you stand up to the Americans, they will back down.
3. You can inflict casualties on the Americans and demoralize their government if you are willing to take heavy casualties yourself.
4. By fighting in urban areas, you can nullify many of the American advantages in high-tech equipment and firepower.
5. Light and readily available weapons (machine guns, light rocket launchers) can take out U.S. helicopters and vehicles in close battle.

America's next major military operation came in 1995, when the United States deployed its military power as part of a UN and European coalition that was trying to push a settlement for the exceptionally brutal Serb-versus-Croatian/Muslim civil war that had been raging in Bosnia for three years. The Bosnian Serbs, who had carried out a program of genocide against the Croats and Muslims and refused to compromise on any power-sharing agreement for Bosnia, were seen as the main obstacle to peace. After years of fruitless negotiations, the U.S. government—with European and UN approval—decided to apply limited American force in the form of a six-week bombing campaign, designed to take out some carefully selected Bosnian Serb military targets and send a message that the Serbs could expect more serious damage if they didn't pursue a peace agreement. The U.S./UN/European pressure worked, and in late 1995 the Bosnian Serbs signed the Dayton Accord, which granted the Croat/Muslim Federation 51 percent of Bosnia and left the Serbs with 49 percent.

In the official U.S. Air Force study of the conflict, the U.S. air campaign was cited as evidence that strategic bombing alone could decide the outcome of wars and that the United States could use its high-tech airpower to ensure victory without the politically messy decision to use ground troops and risk more casualties. Indeed, the only role for ground troops in the Balkans was to come in after the conflict was won and act as peacekeepers.

The USAF study of the Bosnia campaign is a good example of how public relations and advocacy pieces have replaced objective analysis in the Pentagon culture. The report runs to more than five hundred pages and includes a series of monographs by ten USAF officers and one USAF civilian employee, and a USAF colonel edited it. Praising all the USAF generals involved in the campaign, it features a type of purple prose that recalls the "glories of the Imperial Army heroes" style of the Victorian age. One author took the extreme micromanagement of the tactical operations exhibited by USAF Lieutenant General Michael Ryan (which came under intense private criticism from many USAF officers involved in the operation) as evidence of his "strong and comprehensive leadership" and swooned that Ryan had "exhibited a style of leadership more reminiscent of Napoleon Bonaparte's personalized 'great captainship.' "[15] And this was not the only instance in the report of comparing Ryan to Napoleon.[16]

In arguing that airpower and strategic bombing had been decisive in settling the war, the USAF authors barely noted that the air campaign took place at the same time as an exceptionally successful Croat/Muslim ground offensive that forced the Serbs into retreat (the ground action was mentioned on only three of the five-hundred-plus pages). The offensive was threatening to overrun some of the largest Serb population centers when the Serbs quickly decided to accept a cease-fire. Yet the USAF official study adamantly maintained that it had been the U.S. air campaign and not the international sanctions or ground war that had really done the trick. Dr. Norman Cigar, a highly experienced defense analyst who—unlike the USAF authors—is fluent in Serbo-Croatian and a recognized expert on Yugoslavia, argued that it was the successful ground offensive that pushed the Serbians to concede. He contended that a huge influx of destitute Serb refugees from the threatened city of Banja Luka into Serbia proper would have quickly destabilized the already shaky regime of Slobodan Milosevic. Such an argument, based as it is on an intimate knowledge of Serbian and Balkan politics, makes a great deal of sense. However, Cigar's analysis was published in a fairly obscure journal and was scarcely noticed by the Pentagon strategists, in their euphoria that U.S. high-tech warfare had apparently been successful again.[17]

Unexpected Outcomes

In 1999 the U.S. carried out another bombing campaign in the Balkans, this time to force the Milosevic regime to pull the Serbian army and security forces out of the province of Kosovo. The goal was to allow self-rule and eventual independence for the majority Albanian population, then engaged in a low-level civil war against the Serbs. The 1999 campaign was characterized as the first conflict fought, and won, with airpower alone. Yet again, it seemed that the high-tech approach to warfare had been vindicated.

In fact, the air campaign had not been as successful as advertised. At the strategic level, the whole conflict was characterized by confusion. NATO and American negotiators expected that the Serbs would cave in to their demands for Albanian sovereignty in Kosovo under the mere threat of air attack, and that it wouldn't be necessary to use military force at all. When the Serbs failed to give in to NATO, the NATO and U.S. military staffs had to go ahead with an air campaign, but they had only a three-day plan. NATO and the United States were forced to cobble together a strategy and plan virtually from scratch after the conflict started in March 1999. The strategy had to be approved by the whole NATO Council, and there was broad disagreement between the Americans and British, who both favored a large-scale campaign, and the French, who favored a restricted application of force. Strategic policy became mired in friction. For fear of losing aircraft, NATO and U.S. warplanes were ordered to fly above fifteen thousand feet, where they would be above Serb air defenses. Yet attacking at high altitude also meant that it was harder for NATO and the U.S. Air Force to find and destroy the Serb forces then carrying out a massive ethnic cleansing campaign against the Albanian population.

For seventy-eight days, NATO air strikes were unable to interfere with Serb army operations against the Albanians of Kosovo. Airpower did not seem to be infallible here. It was one thing to hit tanks in the open desert of Iraq. It was quite another to track down and find an enemy that carefully dispersed heavy weapons in the mountains and forests; understood the art of camouflage; and set out large numbers of decoy tanks, guns, and even bridges to attract the attention of the NATO fighter bombers.

Several weeks into the campaign, NATO, in essence, stumbled across a fairly effective strategy of coercing the Milosevic government by attacking the assets of the regime and its supporters. The campaign finally ended with a combination of successful coercion and NATO compromise. The Serbs agreed to end the ethnic cleansing and pull their army out of Kosovo, but NATO caved in on the originally nonnegotiable demand that elections be held in Kosovo and independence be allowed if the majority voted for it (as would certainly have happened, considering that more than 80 percent of the population was ethnically Albanian). The Serb forces would leave to be replaced by a NATO peacekeeping force. However, the Serbs would retain legal sovereignty over the province and the demand for an independence vote would be dropped.

Although the conflict was portrayed as a NATO victory and Serb capitulation, in the end it was the Serbs who won their primary negotiating point. Kosovo might be occupied for a time, but it was still going to be internationally recognized as a legitimate part of Serbia. As it stands now, Kosovo's Albanians can gain independent status—the essence of what they were fighting for—only if NATO violates its solemn treaty. Was this a tactical victory for airpower? Perhaps. A glorious victory for U.S. or NATO foreign policy? Hardly.

Beyond the political outcomes were questions about the results of the fighting. Within the military, intensive debate took place regarding the effectiveness of the NATO air campaign. During the war, the USAF claimed the destruction of hundreds of Serb tanks, armored vehicles, and artillery pieces. Then, when the cease-fire came, the Serb Third Army came out of its lairs in the forests and villages of Kosovo with plenty of tanks, guns, and armored vehicles. That the Serb army was in such good shape and could withdraw with most of its equipment intact came as a shock to the U.S. and NATO staffs. How was this possible?

First of all, U.S. and NATO intelligence estimates of Serb forces had been way off the mark. The Serbs committed thousands more troops to Kosovo than NATO had ever discerned, even with its array of high-tech intelligence equipment. Second, the DOD had grossly overestimated the effect of its bombing campaign against the Serb military. Toward the end of the bombing campaign, the DOD claimed that it had destroyed 120 tanks, 220 armored personnel carriers, and 450 artillery pieces in 744 air strikes. Secretary of Defense William Cohen said that these attacks had "severely crippled Serbian military forces in Kosovo."[18] In fact, what the NATO military assessment team that moved into Kosovo immediately after the Serb withdrawal and examined the reported bombing sites saw close up bore little relation to what pilots and surveillance devices had seen from thousands of feet above. The military assessment team actually found the wreckage of only 14 tanks, 18 armored personnel carriers, and 20 artillery pieces. They also documented that the NATO planes had taken out a large number of cleverly constructed wood and scrap-metal decoys.[19]

The enormous discrepancy between the destruction claimed by the DOD and the evidence found on the ground meant either that there was something terribly wrong with the U.S. intelligence and battle damage assessment system, or that the Serbs had managed to create the most efficient wrecked-equipment cleanup and removal system ever seen in military history. Not surprising to anyone who knows the Pentagon culture, it was the latter hypothesis that predominated in some of the postwar air force briefings that this author attended.

The official DOD view presented to Congress declared that U.S. intelligence had performed quite well. Of course, numerous studies within the DOD told another story.[20] But by 1999, the new, high-tech, airpower-oriented way of war had become such Pentagon dogma that even the unsettling hard data provided by the department's own experts appeared to make no impression on the minds of the senior defense leadership.

What the "new way of war" had actually proved was that, in the case of Bosnia in 1995 and Kosovo in 1999, airpower could be effectively used, along with an array of other mechanisms, including ground forces and sanctions, to coerce small and weak nations to make limited political concessions. Not quite a case of forcing an enemy to surrender unconditionally or of inflicting paralysis upon a weak enemy.

In fact, the limits of coercing or damaging terrorists with high tech and standoff weapons that avoided risking American soldiers' lives had been demonstrated in June 1998. Near-simultaneous bombings of the U.S. embassies in Tanzania and Kenya by the al Qaeda terrorist network killed 257, including 12 Americans. In this case, the United States was confronted by a straightforward act of war carried out by an identifiable enemy. Although most of the al Qaeda network operated underground, with its personnel and assets hidden in many countries, it had some identifiable targets in the form of training camps in Afghanistan. The Clinton administration's response to this act of war was neither to send manned aircraft capable of leveling the camps with heavy bombs, nor to annihilate known al Qaeda centers with paratroops and commandos. Such actions would have been more effective but would have likely resulted in U.S. casualties. Rather, it was to rain seventy-five ship-launched, unmanned cruise missiles on a Sudanese pharmaceutical plant and on some camps in Afghanistan. The damage to al Qaeda was negligible—a few buildings destroyed and a reported twenty-one minor operatives killed.[21]

The al Qaeda commander in the Khost area that was attacked, Mullah Jala Ludin Hakkani, ridiculed the American missile attack. He pointed out that it was minor compared to what the Russians had done—and he had defeated the Russians. Important targets such as large ammunition dumps remained mostly untouched.[22] Considering the high cost of cruise missiles (approximately $569,000 each)[23], the expense of killing these low-level terrorists came to more than $2 million per terrorist.

Al Qaeda had to be pleased with the results. They proved that al Qaeda could strike a serious blow to U.S. interests in well-planned, simultaneous attacks, and such operations won the organization enormous prestige among the radical elements in the Muslim world. What is more, al Qaeda handily survived heavy, high-tech U.S. attacks with damage so minimal that it could jeer at U.S. efforts. By carefully crafting an airpower-alone attack that refrained from putting any air personnel or soldiers in harm's way, the United States sent al Qaeda a clear message that the Americans were so fearful of casualties that they would be easy targets for future attacks. Rather than being impressed by America's vast technological capabilities and deterred by its ability to precisely deliver munitions by aerial means, al Qaeda and other terrorists perceived America as the proverbial helpless giant. Clinton's weak policy toward terrorism soon convinced radical Islamic factions that attacking the United States directly was a low-risk strategy. In the wake of the September 11, 2001, attacks the senior leader of the Taliban regime ridiculed the American demand that he turn over the al Qaeda leaders who had planned and ordered the massive terror attack on New York and Washington. Mullah Mohammed Omar said on a radio broadcast to the Afghani people that "Americans don't have the courage to come here." He believed that he could deter the Americans by announcing, "If you attack us, there will be no difference between you and the Russians."[24] Apparently, the new high-tech way of war favored by the United States was interpreted differently in different cultures.

By 1999 to 2000, the Clinton administration's policy of favoring airpower and a high-tech approach to national defense had resulted in a serious drop in the army's effectiveness and capabilities. In an attempt to transform itself into a lighter, more high-tech force, the army had for years cut back on training, personnel, and operations funds to build up the cash to buy expensive new helicopters, communications gear, and light armored vehicles. Repeated peacekeeping missions were wearing down the army and soaking up what remained of the budget. In the mid-1990s, the army troop levels fell to the lowest point in fifty years, with only 475,000 troops to carry out a set of broad, worldwide missions. By 1999, the Army Secretary and staff were lobbying the DOD for 20,000 to 50,000 more troops—but the DOD turned down the request.[25] So, to keep the deployable units at full strength, the army mortgaged its future and gutted the Training and Doctrine Command—leaving some training centers at only 66 percent of their authorized strength. Failing to fully staff and fund the training infrastructure meant reducing the number and scale of the large-unit exercises that had worked so well to prepare the army for the Gulf War. The range of specialist training courses had to be cut back and small-unit exercises and courses reduced in length.[26] The payback came in the Iraq War when many of the quickly mobilized Army National Guard and Reserve support units complained that they were sent into action unprepared for the full range of missions required in a war with no clear front.[27]

The New Bush Administration: More of the Same
The administrations of George H. W. Bush and Bill Clinton had firmly committed the U.S. military establishment to a policy favoring a technology-intensive approach to warfare. When President George W. Bush came to office, his defense team, led by Secretary of Defense Donald Rumsfeld, not only favored this policy—they accelerated it. Defense was to receive additional funding, but the increases were to go to the high-tech end of

the U.S. arsenal. "Transformation" became the slogan of the DOD, and this meant that the supporters of the "old" means of war, such as heavy armored and mechanized divisions, were leaned on to adapt and "get with the program."

So intense was the pressure to support the high-tech approach to war that disturbing reports about Pentagon activities began to circulate in the military. Some of America's top soldiers charged that the Pentagon had rigged the outcome of tests and war games to "prove" the validity of the new concepts. One of them was retired Marine Lieutenant General Paul Van Riper, the highly respected former chief of the Marine Combat Development command. In 2002, he walked out in protest after playing the role of enemy commander in an elaborate three-week war game designed to test the validity of the Pentagon's approach to a major theater war. Van Riper led the "red force" opposing the U.S. "blue force," and he came up with a variety of clever tactics that would nullify some of the Americans' high-tech advantages. According to Van Riper, after the red force had inflicted heavy losses on the blue force, superiors disallowed some of Van Riper's tactics. The game was then restarted in midcourse to ensure an American victory. When Van Riper walked out, he complained to colleagues that the major exercise "was in actuality an exercise that was almost entirely scripted to ensure a blue win."[28]

For the last two decades, the Pentagon has tended to view the supporters of a more traditional military structure as irrelevant or simply reactionary. In a time of budget cuts, that perspective is made concrete. Even in a very pro-defense administration, defense spending is not unlimited. The conflicts in Bosnia and Kosovo indicated to the new defense leaders where cuts could and should be made: in the increasingly irrelevant army. The first Pentagon spending plan drawn up by the new secretary of defense and his core staff in April 2001 called for an additional $25 billion a year for fighter jets, including an additional $11.2 billion for the F-22 air-to-air fighter; an $8 billion increase in missile defense technologies; and $2.7 billion for the air force's space-based laser system. While the Pentagon pushed for an impressive 42 percent increase in the weapons budget, no significant budget increases were planned for pay or personnel.[29] In every case, the army was the big loser in the long-term Pentagon budget strategy.[30]

Even after the shock of 9/11, the Bush administration remained firmly committed to a policy of high-tech force at the expense of manpower. The Pentagon leadership and the army rank and file drew diametrically opposed lessons from the 2001 to 2002 campaign in Afghanistan. Many army officers believed that, if more U.S. ground forces had been committed to the Afghanistan campaign, the Taliban and al Qaeda forces that took refuge in the mountains of eastern Afghanistan might have been completely annihilated instead of simply being badly damaged. Now, as army chief of staff, responsible for training and equipping the whole army, General Shinseki had modified his enthusiasm for the new, high-tech way of war in light of the army's broad new missions, which went well beyond small conventional wars or peacekeeping operations of the 1990s. He quietly argued for a larger and more robust army to meet the long-term commitments of fighting a worldwide terrorist threat that might require U.S. forces to be committed simultaneously in several regions. A larger army, and a larger military in general, would be needed simply to take some of the stress off the active and reserve forces who would otherwise face back-to-back deployments as trouble spots arose. After 9/11, common sense would also have argued for a significant increase in the National Guard, the force with the primary responsibility for homeland defense and security.

Yet the Pentagon drew an entirely different conclusion from the events of 9/11 and subsequent campaign in Afghanistan. It remained firmly on course with a strategy that favored high-tech operations. In 2001 and 2002, defense leaders floated proposals to actually cut the army from the current ten to eight divisions. Army officers privately complained about Stephen Cambone, the undersecretary of defense for intelligence and a key Pentagon insider, who reportedly favored increasing space funding and support for the national missile defense at the expense of ground forces.[31] The attempt to *cut* the army in wartime was beaten back; the Pentagon nonetheless refused to increase the army strength. Max Boot, a journalist whose writings on U.S. intervention have found great favor with the neoconservatives, coined the term "The New American Way of War" in an article of that name that described the early operations in Afghanistan in 2001 as a model for the new, high-tech war doctrine. The "New American Way of War" features the perceived lessons from Afghanistan and the 2003 invasion of Iraq coupled with the American experience in Kosovo. In this new approach, America would leverage its overwhelming technological superiority, especially its information superiority, and swiftly defeat its enemies using minimal manpower. It is a notion of "hit and run, not fight and stay."[32] The rapid success of American arms in the conventional stages of the Afghanistan and Iraq campaigns lent some credence to the view that America had, indeed, found a "new way of war." In the military, friction grew between those who supported the new concepts of the "New American Way of War"—mostly Air Force officers and academic political scientists—and its preference for rapid, low-manpower operations, and those who were skeptical—mostly U.S. Army and Marine Corps officers—who still saw some utility in maintaining armed forces capable of fighting and staying in long conflicts.

Partly because of these issues, by 2003 the relationship between the army and the secretary of defense was worse than at any time since the 1960s era of Robert McNamara. Within the army there was a near-universal perception that Secretary Rumsfeld and his senior civilian assistants were staunchly "anti-army" and would tolerate no dissent from their views. General Shinseki was summarily and rudely retired. Senior DOD civilians failed to come to his retirement ceremony, a snub that had occurred in the past only when members of the civilian and uniformed leadership were at loggerheads. The army was now in the unusual position of being without a formally appointed chief of staff (the army had to make do with an acting chief). The prevailing story was that none of the army four-star generals wanted to work with Rumsfeld. For most of 2002 to 2003, this conflict between the Pentagon's civilian leaders and the army's top generals was the lead story in the *Army Times*, the weekly newspaper that most closely reports on army issues. Finally, after several months, a retired four-star, General Peter J. Schoomaker, was recalled from retirement to take the post. Going to the retired list to find a chief of staff is unprecedented in U.S. Army history.

This is how things have stood between the army and the Pentagon in the post-9/11 world, with widespread hostility over funding cuts and status and disagreement over the "new way of war" promoted by the administration. Such "culture wars" often occur between branches of the military. They also are not unusual between senior defense civilians—who are commonly drawn from the business and management world—and career soldiers. In many cases, this culture clash leads to healthy tension and debate. However, when it degenerates into semipublic hostility and palpable mistrust, it becomes decidedly unhealthy. And this was the atmosphere from the start of the Bush administration. While Rumsfeld and his strategy for high-tech warfare and transformation have met with great approval from the mainstream of the air force officer corps, the majority of the army has remained highly skeptical. Throughout the army, Secretary Rumsfeld has often been referred to as "another McNamara." In some respects, the comparison is a fair one. Both McNamara and Rumsfeld are men of limited military experience: McNamara was an Air Corps staff officer in World War II; Rumsfeld served for three years as a navy aviator in the 1950s. Both were highly successful business executives. Both talked of using business and management techniques to achieve greater efficiencies within the DOD, and both came to the office with a clear agenda to carry out major changes. Both have had a reputation for impatience and for intolerance of career officers who oppose their views.

Immediately after 9/11, Rumsfeld and his crew of senior civilian policymakers in the DOD saw the chance, even the duty, to put their ideas into practice. Now was their opportunity to show that the U.S. could not only win wars—but could do so quickly, at low cost, and with minimal deployment of troops. It was a lot to hope for.

AFGHANISTAN AND THE NEW WAY OF WAR
Only weeks after the September 11 attacks, the United States responded with a campaign that destroyed the Taliban regime in Afghanistan. Some defense analysts claimed that the U.S. air campaign in support of the Afghan Northern Alliance forces in late 2001 through early 2002 signified a revolutionary model of war.[33] From October to December 2001 in Afghanistan, a few elite U.S. Special Operations Forces (SOF) personnel, acting as liaisons with Afghan allies, directed the full weight of U.S. precision airpower to bear on the Taliban and their Arab (mostly al Qaeda) allies. With only a handful of specialist U.S. forces on the ground, U.S. airpower and the Northern Alliance defeated the Taliban forces in a matter of

six weeks, and Kabul and all of Afghanistan's major cities easily fell to the Northern Alliance forces.

For the United States, providing air support to local partisan/irregular forces locked in battle with enemy regimes was not a new form of warfare. The country has a long history of providing such air support as part of a conventional war campaign. During World War II, the U.S. Army provided liaison and advisor teams that enabled lightly armed guerrilla units to successfully take on better-equipped and better-trained conventional forces. This was a successful feature of the campaigns to retake Burma and the Philippines. However, in every case where this tactic had been applied in the past, the partisan/guerrilla forces served only as auxiliary support for large conventional forces that carried the main burden of battle. It was an efficient way to fight the war and maximize the use of personnel. The partisans with air support took some of the load off the regular forces, enabling them to fight more efficiently.

However, indigenous irregular forces had never before been used as the primary ground force in a U.S.-led campaign. Afghanistan was the first major operation in which this was the case, and the scope and scale of the air support provided to the anti-Taliban alliance was unprecedented. A relatively small force of SOF and Central Intelligence Agency (CIA) personnel provided effective coordination to a powerful aerial strike force deployed by the U.S. Air Force and Navy. Against the predictions of numerous pundits and military analysts who had cautioned against fighting in Afghanistan in the winter, the Northern Alliance forces, supported by U.S. airpower, broke the Taliban regime's main forces in a matter of weeks, killing many and sending the remainder of the Taliban and al Qaeda forces into headlong retreat.

Not surprisingly, many in the U.S. military leadership and the Bush administration touted the early victories as another successful demonstration of the Pentagon's new focus. The United States, they said, could fight and win with a combination of local forces and a few light U.S. forces supported by overwhelming airpower.[34] For a time, it appeared that the old political problem of committing U.S. troops to battle had been sidestepped. If the Afghanistan model were applicable to other conflicts, it would indeed be a revolutionary development. One campaign fought under unique circumstances, however, does not provide an adequate basis for a new doctrine of war. Moreover, the war in Afghanistan did not end with the fall of Kabul and Kandahar. The Taliban forces and their al Qaeda allies simply retreated into the mountainous country near the Pakistani border to reorganize and regroup. As the United States was to find out, they might have been beaten up—but they were not beaten. They were soon ready and willing to take on the Northern Alliance and its American allies with other tactics on other ground. The next rounds would prove far tougher than the first round of the war.

The follow-on campaigns against al Qaeda and Taliban forces at Tora Bora in December 2001 and Operation Anaconda in March 2002 highlight-ed the limitations of an airpower-based strategy against an enemy that was now fighting in the role of the insurgent. The U.S. Central Command (CENTCOM) realized the United States would have to commit ground troops to Afghanistan, both to help secure the authority of the new Afghan government in the main cities and to help track down and destroy the remaining Taliban and al Qaeda forces. This led to a debate between CENT-COM and the Pentagon on the size and scale of the U.S. commitment to Afghanistan.

Hundreds of SOF troops had been in the country since October 2001 and were serving with the Afghans. In late 2001, a few thousand more U.S. support personnel arrived to operate allied air and logistics bases at Bagram and the larger cities of Kabul and Kandahar. As to fighting forces, the Pentagon insisted on going in as lightly as possible with only a few battal-ions from the army's 101st Airborne Division and 10th Mountain Divisions—essentially light infantry forces organized to fight without armored vehicles and with much less artillery than the army's "heavy" mech-anized and armored divisions. The American troop commitment was pared down even further when the army commanders were told to leave their inte-gral artillery units and even light fire support units, such as mortars, at home. Airpower would substitute for army heavy weapons, they were told. Army planners were left in a state of confusion in setting up the complex operation of moving troops and equipment to Afghanistan.

The Pentagon repeatedly insisted that there was no "force cap" for U.S. troops committed to Afghanistan, that the army commanders on the ground would receive all the forces they requested. However, that was not how the army commanders perceived it. Requests for units to deploy to Afghanistan were met with resistance from the Pentagon along the lines of, "Do you really think you need your mortars, your liaison teams, a 105mm artillery battery?" Soon, the consensus was that there were indeed strict caps set on the commitment of forces to Afghanistan, although no one knew just what the force caps were. For the various headquarters and planning staffs, it was an active guessing game as to how many U.S. troops could be deployed. In order not to offend senior Pentagon leadership, troop planning for the campaign was pared again and again, and ad hoc organizations were quickly created. Many vital units and parts of units that would normally be deployed in a combat campaign were left behind to help "lighten up" the force. This was not the way that the army, in particular, had been trained or organized, and this would have a major impact upon its subsequent operations.

In addition to apparently setting this mystery cap on ground forces, the Pentagon failed to provide for an adequate command setup or fully staffed headquarters in Afghanistan to carry out the (ideally) final campaign against the Taliban and al Qaeda forces. Ad hoc task forces were set up in Afghanistan, all with their own complex reporting mechanisms for CENT-COM or the Pentagon. In the first three months of operations in Afghanistan, General Tommy Franks, the CENTCOM commander, created three joint special operations task forces and numerous other commands, resulting in overlapping responsibilities and conflicting command relationships. A few days before the March 2002 Anaconda operation was launched, General Franks named Army Major General Franklin Hagenbeck as the joint task force commander for the operation, but Hagenbeck did not have operational control of all the forces necessary to carry out the mission. Under reported pressure from the DOD to keep the forces as small as possible, CENTCOM did not set up Afghanistan as a separate theater of war with a single commander, headquarters, and staff. That would have required moving hundreds of soldiers, along with planeloads of communications gear, into Afghanistan. Instead, General Franks would command the Afghan campaign from CENTCOM headquarters in Tampa, Florida—seven thousand miles and ten time zones away from the battlefront.[35] It was an arrangement reminiscent of the U.S. command setup in Vietnam, complete with overlapping and competing commands, and with basic issues of tactics and combat deployments not being decided by the commanders on the ground but rather micromanaged by Pentagon civilians and senior officers half a world away. The new way of war on which the Pentagon had pinned so many of its hopes turned out to be a highly flawed model when confronted with the realities of Afghanistan.

The situation in Afghanistan, in fact, had changed greatly in a few months. After the fall of Kabul and Kandahar, the Afghan campaign moved into a new stage in which the primary enemy was not the poorly trained Taliban militia force, but the well-trained and much more effective al Qaeda bands in Afghanistan. These insurgents, in contrast to most of their Taliban allies, learned quickly and adapted to the new American doctrines. The surviving enemy forces in Afghanistan, in the battles of Tora Bora in December 2001 and Operation Anaconda in March 2002, were able to limit the effectiveness of U.S. high-tech surveillance and intelligence collection by successfully concealing many of their fighting positions from American airpower. During Operation Anaconda, the United States focused all of its considerable reconnaissance assets, including space surveillance platforms and the latest-model unmanned aerial vehicles, on a 10-kilometer-square battlefield. Nonetheless, fewer than 50 percent of all the al Qaeda positions ultimately identified in the course of the fighting on this battlefield were discovered before the ground contact.[36] Just like Arab rebels that fought the British in the 1920s, the al Qaeda and Taliban forces had learned to adapt to Western airpower.[37] At the Tora Bora battle, air-delivered precision munitions were far less lethal to al Qaeda fighters than the U.S. military had anticipated. Al Qaeda's fighters were in well-sited and well-prepared defensive positions. Even though their losses to airpower were heavy, enough of the enemy survived the air strikes to mandate a tough and costly ground battle.

During Operation Anaconda three months later, the Pentagon's unofficial force caps got the U.S. forces into a lot of trouble. For example, air support for ground forces in a close battle requires a specially trained team of air force ground controllers to coordinate the targeting and talk the aircraft "onto" the target. Without such a team, the possibility of friendly-fire casualties increases. And without the air-to-ground communications systems of

75

the air force team, targeting can be delayed for minutes—or even hours. The 18th Air Support Operations Group, normally assigned to coordinate support for the army's 10th Mountain Division, was left off the 10th Division's deployment orders to Afghanistan despite General Hagenbeck's request to assign them to the campaign. According to the 10th Division staff, a higher headquarters denied their request to deploy the air force unit.[38] The result was that only one small, overworked air control team with limited communications gear was available to handle the air coordination for a large operation. According to one of General Hagenbeck's key staff officers, the fire support coordinator for the operation, it sometimes took hours for the air force to deliver requested air support to the ground forces engaged in desperate, close combat.[39] Ordinarily, air support would not be critical for the army in this kind of battle—but the 10th Mountain Division had left its primary fire support (105mm howitzers) back in the states and, aside from a few mortars, lacked the basic firepower that it relied upon in going to war. The forces had no choice but to rely completely on air support.

Were these weapons restrictions necessary? There were no operational reasons why the army could not have brought a few artillery pieces and heavy mortars to the fight in Afghanistan. Mortars and 105mm guns and their ammunition are light. C-130 transports can easily carry them and can fly into short and primitive airstrips. Plenty of air transport was available to get more troops and weapons to Afghanistan. Army planners are traditionally careful, and, when possible, they like to "bring a gun to a knife fight."

Indeed, most soldiers who are below the rank of general, who have to deal with the daily realities of training troops and planning for war, are still devout believers in Carl von Clausewitz and his theory of conflict, with its "fog" and its "friction." Despite Pentagon assurances to the contrary, fog and friction are out there—and army planners like to have plenty of soldiers, supplies, and weapons available just in case things go wrong. Even today, weather and communications glitches can inhibit the use of airpower. In such cases, the army likes to have a backup means of providing heavy firepower for its infantry. Yes, this approach is based on the old-fashioned, inefficient, pretransformation concepts of war that have been so out of favor in recent administrations. However, such an approach would have worked a lot better in Afghanistan than the high-tech, minimal-troops plan favored by the Pentagon.

Result of Committing Too Few Troops, Indigenous Troops

A study by Dr. Stephen Biddle of the Army War College casts doubt on the utility of the Afghan War as a model for other conflicts and points out some operational problems encountered in the Afghan campaign. Biddle argued that if one's indigenous allies are as well trained as one's opponents, then precision airpower support can have a decisive effect in defeating the enemy. In Afghanistan, some of the Northern Alliance forces were fairly competent—equal or superior in their training to most of the Taliban forces, who tended to be untrained tribal militiamen. In cases where the Northern Alliance forces, supported by American airpower, went up against Taliban militia, the Taliban force was quickly defeated. However, as many as fifteen thousand of the Taliban forces were well trained, and the several thousand highly committed al Qaeda Arab fighters were much less likely to collapse in the face of a strong enemy. Although Northern Alliance troops supported by U.S. airpower performed well in the early stages of the war against the poorly trained Taliban militia, even airpower could not tip the balance in their favor when they faced the well-trained al Qaeda forces at Tora Bora and the Shah-i-Kot Valley (Operation Anaconda). In short, for the Afghan model of airpower to work elsewhere, the United States' indigenous allies need to be equal or superior in training and leadership to their enemy.[40]

Another problem with the U.S. concept of employing airpower and high-tech assets against terrorists is the problem of unreliability among third world forces—who might be well-trained troops or, more likely, poorly trained and indifferently led tribal militias. Using indigenous forces to fight the ground battle makes the issue of militia reliability central to the success of the operation. The reality is that local forces have their own agendas, which may not be anything close to the strategic goals of the U.S. government. In 2001, once the primary objectives of the cities of Kabul and Kandahar had fallen to the Northern Alliance forces, the motivation of those troops to finish the destruction of the Taliban and al Qaeda forces dropped considerably. Although Tora Bora and Operation Anaconda were tactical successes, the Northern Alliance forces allowed many of the Taliban and al Qaeda forces to retreat through the alliance's lines rather than close and fight a battle of annihilation that might have proven costly to themselves.[41] In short, although Anaconda and Tora Bora were tactical victories in that many enemy troops were killed, they were by no means decisive. Because the United States relied mainly on local forces to conduct the ground war and committed only a very limited U.S. ground force to those battles, many of the more experienced al Qaeda and Taliban soldiers survived and escaped to Pakistan—there to retrain, reorganize, and reequip to fight another day. Indeed, the guerrilla war in Afghanistan continues as of this writing (2005).

IRAQ AND THE NEW WAY OF WAR

The U.S./Coalition campaign to take down the regime of Saddam Hussein in 2003 was one of the most successful conventional war operations in history. In a high-intensity campaign between March 19 and April 9, three fast-moving American divisions and one British division, supported by accurate and overwhelming U.S. and UK airpower, wrecked the 400,000-man Iraqi military, overran all of Iraq's major cities, and toppled the Saddam regime while suffering only a few hundred casualties. What made the campaign more impressive is that it used fewer troops than the army had planned for. Moreover, an offensive from the north by the Fourth Infantry Division never came off because Turkey reneged on a deal to allow the U.S. forces to use its territory.

The incredible efficiency of the Allied forces, documented live by "embedded" journalists, again seemed to justify the Pentagon's preference for quick, decisive, high-tech, low-cost wars fought with a minimum of troops on the ground. However, sober postwar scrutiny by some of the army's best analysts points out that the effectiveness of U.S./Coalition forces and tactics only partially explains the remarkable victory. A great part of the Coalition's success can be attributed to the amazing incompetence of Saddam as a commander and strategist.[42]

In fighting the American and Coalition forces, Saddam made every mistake in the book and even invented some new ones. The greatest U.S. fear was that Saddam would prepare Iraqi cities for defense and force U.S. troops to fight through densely populated city blocks, resulting in heavy civilian and American/Coalition casualties. Urban warfare would have nullified, or at least severely limited, many of the U.S. advantages in airpower and long-range standoff weapons. Urban warfare is a slow process that mandates large numbers of attacking forces. Battling each Iraqi city in turn might have taken months of hard fighting and required a commitment of many more troops to Iraq with the consequent political problems for the U.S. administration.

Fortunately for the Coalition forces, Saddam had failed to train either his regular forces (Republican Guards and regular army) or his paramilitary Fedayeen in city fighting. In the race through Iraqi cities, U.S. forces encountered no obstacles, mines, or barriers. The Fedayeen had not prepared the interiors of buildings as fighting positions, as any minimally trained city fighter would have done. Instead, the Fedayeen prepared fighting positions in open areas where they were fully exposed to aerial observation and direct fire. Saddam's poorly armed and trained irregular forces were killed in large numbers simply as they stood up and fired rockets and machine guns at U.S. armored vehicles.

Saddam deployed his regular forces in large units to fight the Coalition in open terrain—which provided the Coalition air forces an ideal opportunity to locate and decimate his heavy forces long before the Coalition ground troops reached them. As had been the case in the Gulf War, Iraqi military morale was already weak before the Coalition offensive. Now the regular forces, deployed as inviting targets, began to melt away.

However, some Iraqi units did avoid U.S. surveillance and were positioned to ambush advancing U.S. armor. On April 4, at Objective Montgomery, a Republican Guards tank battalion lying in wait for the U.S. forces ambushed a U.S. armor column from the flanks at a range of eight hundred to one thousand meters with its tank guns. The Iraqis got off the first shots at the surprised Americans, firing sixteen rounds from their highly lethal 125mm main guns. For tank warfare, this was almost point-blank range. Unhappily for the Iraqis, every shell missed. Although Saddam had one of the world's largest ammunition stockpiles—estimated at more than five hundred thousand tons, though no one knows for certain—he had limited his tank gunners to only eight practice rounds per year, and Iraqi tankers were not provided with enough ammunition to properly sight their guns. U.S. tankers, who fire a few hundred practice rounds per year, returned fire and wiped out the Iraqi tank battalion in five minutes with no U.S. losses.

This kind of story was repeated throughout the campaign. Given the Iraqis' good equipment, a force with halfway decent leadership and more than minimal training might still not have won the war—but could easily have inflicted serious casualties and won some tactical battles. The information superiority of the United States had been overhyped. The story that was promoted was one of U.S./Coalition forces using technology to gain a complete picture of the battlefield while the enemy fought blind. Throughout the campaign, however, Iraqi scouts in civilian clothes continuously reconnoitered U.S. positions and reported to their headquarters with cell phones, land telephones, and couriers. In some cases, the Iraqis had more accurate intelligence on U.S. positions and movements than the United States had on theirs. However, the highly compartmented Iraqi command system did not allow for the sharing of information across unit boundaries, and Iraqi division commanders did not have any situational awareness beyond their immediate area. Hence the Iraqi inability to exploit Coalition gaps and weaknesses. Another stroke of luck for the Coalition was the Iraqis' failure to draw the Coalition into an urban fight and then concentrate their irregular Fedayeen forces against the highly vulnerable Coalition supply lines that reached far back into Kuwait.

Finally, the U.S. air plan to win immediately and decisively by decapitating the regime (that is, putting a bomb on Saddam) failed on several occasions. It was a good idea and might have worked, but simple survival was the one military tactic in which Saddam was a master. That should teach an important lesson. As good as U.S. bombers are, they still could not decapitate a regime or paralyze the enemy command system.

In conclusion, the much-vaunted "new way of war" that the Pentagon and successive U.S. administrations had been proclaiming for more than a decade has failed to live up to its promise. Fog and friction and all the other aspects of conventional wars still remain. The successful U.S. and Coalition operation that used relatively few troops and turned high-tech advantages into a quick, decisive, and low-cost victory still makes a poor guide for planning future operations: Coalition success was heavily dependent upon the stupendous level of incompetence demonstrated by Saddam. Those who were on the ground know how much worse it could have been. A moderately competent enemy with a moderate level of training could have inflicted significant casualties on the Coalition forces and turned a campaign of a few weeks into a campaign that lasted for months.

If the lessons of the Iraq War are taken as normative guidance for the future, and if we plan our doctrine and force structure on this foundation, we're liable to get into terrible trouble. Military history is replete with armies taking dramatic success in battle and using it as the foundation for future doctrine. The most explicit example is the Allied powers of World War I, which assumed that the firepower-intensive, methodical battle of 1918 would be the norm for future warfare. Instead, in 1940 they learned that warfare had evolved quite differently from their expectations. A military doctrine and strategy built on the assumption that future enemies will be as incompetent as Saddam might be the most negative thing to come out of the Iraq War.

CHAPTER THREE

CONTROLLING POPULATIONS: A TRICKY BUT NOT IMPOSSIBLE ART

If you think ten thousand men sufficient, send twenty; if one million pounds is thought enough, give two; you will save both blood and treasure in the end. A large force will terrify, and engage many to join you, a middling one will encourage resistance, and gain no friends.

—Lieutenant General Thomas Gage, 1774

For the profession of arms, it's no longer sufficient just to be militarily proficient. You really need to understand dimensions beyond the military dimensions. You need to understand politics and economics. And you need to understand cultures. These aren't pure military operations anymore...

—General Anthony Zinni, USMC, 2003

Victory or defeat in a counterinsurgency campaign depends on how effectively the government or occupation forces can control the population. Controlling a population is much more than just a police operation to keep order—although that is first on the task list of any government facing an insurgency or occupying a hostile country. Population control also includes a large political element as well as social and economic elements. The ultimate goal of controlling populations is to establish some semblance of peace, order, and rule of law. All actions should be geared toward separating the rebellious elements from the main base of the population and convincing a usually skeptical population that supporting the government or occupation power is in their best interests. Control policies require building up the base of popular support by making progress in the local economic life (creating jobs and promoting economic growth), and by enhancing the social infrastructure (establishing better schools, fair courts, and political systems that allow for peaceful resolution of local issues).

Some countries have controlled populations and suppressed insurgencies through sheer terror. The German occupation forces in Greece had little trouble from the Greek resistance because they took hostages and threatened to kill one hundred Greek civilians for every *Wehrmacht* soldier killed by guerrillas. The Soviet Union suppressed rebellions in the 1920s by shipping to the gulag anyone who might be seen as a class enemy or otherwise inclined to oppose Soviet control, a category that included whole ethnic groups. That most of the population was not inclined to actively oppose the new Soviet rulers mattered not. By sending vast numbers of people to the gulag, innocent and guilty were swept up alike and fear became the universal motivator. In Guatemala in the early 1980s General Rios Montt, who had taken power in a coup, effectively broke a rural insurgency by relocating whole villages and placing them under a ruthless military government. Poor Indians were compelled to join the civil defense militia and go on patrol against the rebels, with whom many sympathized. Any reluctance to fight or kill rebels meant summary execution at the hands of government troops. Montt was only in power for less than two years, but that was long enough to completely demoralize the rebels—who eventually made peace on the government's terms.

Although there are some black spots on the American record of fighting insurgencies—notably some incidents during the Indian Wars and suppressing the Filipino rebellion in 1899 to 1902—U.S. policy has historically eschewed extreme measures such as those applied by the Germans or Soviets or Guatemalans. For one thing, the American military has a strong moral tradition, and even though we have had the occasional commander go berserk and slaughter civilians or suspected insurgents as did Lieutenant William Calley at My Lai in Vietnam, such actions have not been part of our national policy. The overwhelming majority of our officer corps has been, and remains, a group of decent people raised in a Christian and Western tradition. Few would allow ruthless counterinsurgency policies for long. And although the public might occasionally get into a lynch-mob mentality and want to see the enemy punished ruthlessly—for instance, many Americans, including some policymakers, wanted to see Germany kept ruined and impoverished after World War II—the Western and democratic traditions of the American people always prevail. Indeed, no democratic country will long tolerate a program that allows their armed forces to carry out merciless occupation or counterinsurgency policies. And the military of any democratic nation are also well aware that they are answerable to the national legislature for their actions. Thus, as the arm of a democratic nation, the U.S. military must operate within strict moral and legal limits. While some might see that as a disadvantage, historically it has been one of our strengths as a nation and one of the reasons why the U.S. military has usually been successful in controlling populations and conducting counterinsurgency operations.

The U.S. military exists to defend the nation and win the nation's wars. Professional soldiers tend to see all the other things—such as nation-building in obscure countries, peacekeeping, training foreign forces in occupying countries, or countering insurgencies—to be side issues that detract from their primary duties. Indeed they are. However, the military also exists to serve the national policy and it may be, and often is, national policy to fight insurgents, occupy nations, conduct nation-building in impoverished countries, or keep the peace among fractious Balkan peoples. These are all legitimate military missions and they play a large part in the history of the U.S. armed forces. In the unsettled world of the twenty-first century, these side missions are going to take up a huge part of our military forces and effort—whether the military likes it or not. The mission of controlling populations is not going to go away.

Controlling populations is an art, an art in which the U.S. military has considerable experience. For most of the nineteenth century, the main job of the U.S. regular army was to deal with hostile American Indian tribes. Despite the images from the popular press or the legacy of Hollywood westerns, real battles between Indians and the army were rare events. Most army campaigns were essentially constabulary operations in which small army units would round up small bands of hostiles with as little fighting as possible.

More often it was the job of the army to carry out negotiations with the many tribes and even to dispense government aid to Indians who accepted the reservation life, as all were eventually compelled to do. As in all successful counterinsurgency operations, the army relied heavily upon the indigenous population to fight the insurgents. A key element in the army's successful campaign against hostile Indians was the use of Indian Scout Units, figuring sensibly that the most qualified people to fight Indians were other Indians. By the 1870s and 1880s, the army had four thousand Indian Scouts on the army payroll; the army could never have tracked down Geronimo and other hostile leaders were it not for the efforts of the Indian Scouts serving alongside the army soldiers. Indeed, there were more Apaches serving with the army to fight the famous Geronimo in the 1880s than were in Geronimo's hostile band.

In the imperial era, the U.S. Army drew on its frontier experience to occupy Cuba and the Philippines after the Spanish-American War. Cuba was an easy matter, for the Cubans were able to establish their own government; the U.S. military presence was there mostly to ensure that the island remained orderly, and that a pro-U.S. government was elected and put into power. The Philippines (the new colony in Asia) were another matter entirely. Unprepared for a major insurgency, in 1899 the U.S. Army had to recruit a large number of troops and rush them to the Philippines to counter a large and well-organized independence movement. After the Americans easily defeated the main rebel forces in conventional battles, the rebels hunkered down for a guerrilla campaign that lasted three years. The United States had to root out the insurgency province by province, pacifying the population; establish U.S.-supervised local governments; recruit Filipinos to serve in the U.S. administration; and make enough progress on the economic, social, and political side that the majority of the population came to support the U.S. colonial administration. It is one of America's least-known major wars, though an important one for the development of the modern army. In the end, the U.S. Army learned the subtle art of civil affairs, population control, and the judicious use of force. In 1902, with most of the country pacified, the army was able to declare the insurgency over and turn the Philippines over to civilian control.[1]

After World War I, the U.S. Army occupied a sector of the German Rhineland until 1920. In the traditionally unstable Caribbean, U.S. forces, usually the marines but supported by the army and navy, intervened in several nations to suppress disorder, establish some kind of stable government, and make the region secure for U.S. interests (read business). From 1914 to 1934, the U.S. Marine Corps ran Haiti for what would be the only period of good government in the history of that unhappy country. In Haiti, the marines dispersed rural bandits, trained a native constabulary, built roads and numerous public works projects, supervised a relatively competent local government, and set the foundations for a sound economy. The Dominican Republic also came under U.S. occupation, but for a much briefer time. In Nicaragua from 1925 to 1934, U.S. Marines and soldiers supported a pro-U.S. government and built up a capable indigenous army. Officers who served in these various interventions and occupations collected and published their insights in the 1940 U.S. Marine Corps' *Small Wars Manual*, one of the best works on counterinsurgency, military occupation, and nation-building ever written. Much of the *Small Wars Manual* is about winning the support of the population and establishing an effective local government. Force is to be used, but mostly in subtle ways, and the *Small Wars Manual* warns against the kind of heavy-handed approach that would turn the population away from the government. The *Small Wars Manual* contains numerous nuggets of good advice about how U.S. troops can deal with the local culture, collect intelligence, and build a civil administration. *The Small Wars Manual* is much like Clausewitz's *On War* for the counterinsurgency practitioner. While much of the manual is dated to the technology and culture of the early twentieth century, the greater part is timeless—essentially sound guidelines for dealing with civilian populations and various local political factions and establishing some kind of order amid chaos.

If anyone believes that the U.S. military is a poor tool to occupy nations or effectively control populations, then one only need look at the U.S. Army occupation of Germany and Japan after World War II. Indeed, the U.S. Army did a brilliant job in West Germany from 1945 to 1954, and in Japan from 1945 to 1950. With complete authority to manage large civilian populations and economies, the army set sound policies; got the two devastated nations functioning again; and effectively transformed both nations from totalitarian and militaristic states into models of democracy, prosperity, and stable government. Although the U.S. military recruited a corps of civilian experts—including economists, educators, health officials, and administrators—to help manage the occupation of Germany and Japan, the people in charge at every level were U.S. line officers, few of whom had any specialized training or background to serve as governors of a subject populace.

One of the reasons why the occupations of Germany and Japan were so successful lies in the character of the U.S. Army officer corps. Military officers are, by nature, practical problem solvers. In today's jargon they are "mission oriented"—give them a task and they will try to do the best they can with whatever resources are available. Military officers are used to dealing with complex organizations and carrying out a wide variety of administrative tasks. Moreover, they are good at management, especially when there are straightforward jobs to do, such as repairing the infrastructure or moving food supplies. This kind of talent is especially important in meeting the basic needs of a civilian population. One simply can't imagine a carefully selected team of Ivy League academics doing half as well in running Germany or Japan after World War II. For one thing, academics aren't very good at following orders or carrying out someone else's policy. A star academic team would have dithered so long about the nature of the occupation policy and the theoretical foundation for dealing with the occupied populations that one can easily imagine an academic-led effort collapsing in chaos.

Another reason U.S. officers have been very competent at occupying foreign nations is the social nature of the officer corps. American officers are overwhelmingly from the middle class and bring many of the strengths of the middle class to their own profession. Since World War II, American officers have been, in the main, a highly educated group (with a preference for business and management degrees) and representative of mainstream America and mainstream American values. As "military" as professional officers might become over the course of a career, they also bring a great deal of positive cultural baggage with them from their civilian upbringing.

In postwar Germany and Japan, American officers were generally able to apply the best skills from their military experience and civilian education and life and apply them in a practical manner. Moreover, there are plenty of talented and well-educated people in the present U.S. military who enlisted via ROTC or officer training school who intended to serve for just a few years, but found they liked the military life and stayed on. The ability of the U.S. officers to deal effectively with politically complex issues and exotic foreign populations has been proven more recently in Bosnia, Kosovo, and Iraq. Through the interventions of the 1990s to the present operations in Iraq and Afghanistan, many captains, majors, and colonels responsible for districts with large civilian populations have shown an impressive ability to solve problems, manage the rebuilding of war-torn regions, and deal with local leaders and factions. When faced with a dearth of policy guidance from on high, midlevel commanders have forged ahead and created their own programs to meet the needs of the populace and get the local economy and infrastructure going again. In fact, the midlevel management of the occupation of Iraq has been a success story. The confusion over policy and the lack of coherent planning for the occupation of Iraq was not the fault of the lower or middle levels of leadership—those problems originated at the senior command levels.

SMALL WARS DOCTRINE PRIOR TO THE IRAQ WAR

During the Reagan era, when the army was large, military budgets generous, and the Cold War conventional doctrine reigned supreme, the army almost eliminated its civil affairs units—the specialist units responsible for dealing with foreign civilian populations in wartime, humanitarian emergencies, or counterinsurgency. The Army Reserve maintained a small cadre of a few thousand soldiers in civil affairs units, but in the context of the Cold War they didn't have much of a mission. In one of the periodic economy campaigns, the Pentagon looked for extraneous units and missions to cut in order to maintain spending momentum for the conventional combat forces. Civil affairs units didn't cost much, and cutting them would have saved the army a minuscule sum. But Pentagon leaders love to go to Congress and show that they are cutting "fat" out of the military forces and saving the taxpayers money. And, having made some largely symbolic cuts, could they please have some more funding for a new high-tech program? In addition, with the army leadership infected with the Vietnam Syndrome ("We don't do insurgencies."), few could imagine that the United States might ever need civil affairs units for counterinsurgency operations. With the army then concentrating its forces and doctrine to defend Europe against the massive Warsaw Pact forces, the idea that the United States might ever again occupy an enemy country—and need specialists to do it—seemed ludicrous. So civil affairs was put up for the axe.

Luckily, the Civil Affairs Association, an organization composed of reserve civil affairs personnel, mounted an effective lobbying campaign in Congress and the units were retained. While the Civil Affairs Branch of the regular army was reduced to a tiny cadre, ten thousand affairs specialists were kept in Army Reserve units, almost as an afterthought. The reserve civil affairs forces were no one's model of combat troops. Lightly armed and equipped with only a few jeeps, trucks, and radios, civil affairs units were composed mostly of officer and NCO specialists who were organized into detachments that dealt with local administration, education, security, public works, and finance. Since these were reserve units, they attracted officers from related civilian professions. It was not uncommon in the reserve civil affairs units to have officers who were city managers in civilian life, slotted as city managers in a civil affairs detachment. Officers and NCOs who were police officers in civilian life were detailed to the public security detachments of civil affairs units, and reservists who worked for the power company were assigned to supervise public works. Although these people would not have lasted long against a Soviet tank battalion on the European Front, any of the Army Reserve civil affairs companies could have taken over the administration of a mid-sized city and made a good go of it.

With the collapse of Communism and the end of the Cold War, the army was fortunate not to have eliminated the civil affairs units a few years before. Within three to four years, the army's civil affairs units went from being the lowest-priority units in the reserves to the units most deployed to third world hot spots. Unfortunately, by the early 1990s the army had cut its active duty civil affairs force down to only one small battalion (96th Civil Affairs Battalion) with four hundred men, even though civil affairs specialists were suddenly in big demand. In Somalia, the army needed civil affairs personnel to coordinate humanitarian relief planning with the UN and civilian aid agencies. This type of planning is not in the toolbox of the regular infantry officer, but it is part of the training of civil affairs soldiers. First with the deployment of U.S. forces to Somalia (1992–1994), Haiti (1995–1996), Bosnia (1995–forever), and then Kosovo (1999–forever), plus several other humanitarian operations, the civil affairs specialists of the regular army were quickly overextended. In a three-year tour with the army's civil affairs force, headquartered at Fort Bragg, North Carolina, a typical NCO or officer could not expect to see a single Christmas at home.

Rather than expand the overworked regular army civil affairs units, the army decided to mobilize reserve units to handle civil affairs operations in Haiti, Bosnia, Kosovo, and elsewhere. By the year 2000, civil affairs reserve soldiers could expect to spend two years on active duty out of every five. Such constant deployments have taken a toll on the reserve civil affairs units and morale. No matter what protections Congress might pass for the mobilized reservist, being called to active duty hurts civilian careers (I know this from hard, personal experience as a U.S. Army Reserve officer). If you're a small businessman, then you might be able to weather a one-year deployment, but a second deployment will ruin a business. Constant deployments also mean that nondeployed units are ransacked for personnel to beef up the deployed units suffering from personnel shortages. For the last fourteen years, U.S. Army Reserve civil affairs personnel have made enormous personal sacrifices to faithfully carry out U.S. policy. But reservists' accomplishments and sacrifices have been generally ignored by an army and Pentagon establishment that has historically held little regard for reservists.

The post–Cold War interventions and humanitarian operations have not produced much of a record of success. In Somalia, U.S. and UN forces ended the famine, but got caught in the crossfire of tribal/clan conflict, and were forced to withdraw in a humiliating manner after suffering losses to one faction. In Haiti, the United States intervened and threw out a criminal gang running the country and tried to aid the poorest people in the Western Hemisphere by organizing and directing various public works and infrastructure projects. U.S. forces brought a modicum of security and trained a new police force for Haiti. Of course, as soon as the U.S. forces withdrew, Haiti reverted to its old political habits and is now run by a government just as corrupt, violent, and undemocratic as the ones that went before it. That's another country that will require U.S. intervention in the future. In Bosnia, the Serb/Croatian/Muslim war was tamped down and the country put under international control—essentially a military occupation. While that sector of the Balkans has quieted down, both sides would go to war again if international forces were withdrawn. So the U.S. deployments go on and on and on, and I suspect that my grandchildren will probably spend time as peacekeepers in the Balkans. In Kosovo in 1999, NATO and U.S. troops ended the Serb program of ethnic cleansing and brought down the level of violence—but ethnic violence still occurs and would break out in full force if NATO and U.S. forces were withdrawn. Another occupation with no end in sight.

In all these places, the civil affairs specialists played a central role. On the ground, at the local level, the civil affairs units could point to an impressive record of success—of infrastructure restored, schools opened, functioning civil governments created, fair elections supervised, a respectable level of public security established, and so on. With few people and very limited funds and resources they accomplished a lot. If these interventions and operations have not been very successful at the strategic level, it is because the U.S. and Western governments have failed to develop long-term plans to solve the fundamental problems of these countries and have never seriously considered allocating aid sufficient to ensure economic growth or sustain effective civil governments. The "CNN effect," in which governments are driven to intervention by images on the evening news, was in full play from Somalia to Kosovo, and it plays in Europe just as much as in the United States. Western powers intervened in the 1990s to get the images of starving faces of refugees off the television screens and prove that the government was "doing something" about the problem. As soon as something was done and the images were dropped from the nightly news, the U.S. and European governments quickly lost interest. Yet the troops remained and more than a few are still cynical about their duty tours in these countries. They don't complain that they were sent to miserable places to do tough jobs. It's that we deployed them for cynical and local political reasons, and did not allow them to succeed when success was possible.

In Haiti, for example, the army civil affairs teams surveyed the nation's economy, infrastructure, and resources and developed an aid plan that, if carried out, might have given Haiti a good chance of becoming a stable nation with a standard of living above the extreme poverty line. Civil affairs officers who served in Haiti were enthusiastic about their plan because they sincerely wanted to see that country salvaged. As one officer who served there told me, "Ninety percent of the Haitians are very gentle, decent, and hard-working people who are ruthlessly oppressed by the ten percent who are thugs." Many U.S. Army personnel wanted to stay longer in Haiti just to help out people who were mired in seemingly inescapable poverty. However, it was all cut short in the rush to get the U.S. forces out of Haiti. The problem was that the civil affairs plan that would have given most Haitians the opportunity to progress would have cost an estimated $6 billion over ten years. With the Clinton administration under pressure to cut foreign aid in favor of new domestic spending programs, Haiti was never given the chance to rebuild. That's the problem with reacting to foreign crises in the "CNN mode." Haiti will collapse again and we'll be back—but the next time conditions will be even worse, and the problems more intractable.

As frustrating as these indecisive humanitarian interventions and peace operations have been for the army over the last fifteen years, some benefits have accrued. An army that had been almost completely focused on conventional war now found itself with a large cadre of soldiers who have some direct experience in civil affairs, population control, nation-building, and peacekeeping. Although the civil affairs soldiers have been the most involved forces in this kind of work, many infantry, armor, and engineer officers spent time in Bosnia or Kosovo and gained experience in an occupation force. American lieutenants, captains, and majors have had to learn to deal with violent demonstrations, unfriendly populations, terrorist threats, obstreperous local leaders, and assorted ethnic factions who would gladly slaughter their next-door neighbors if the U.S. troops weren't inconveniently in the way. It was a thankless task that went unappreciated by the army's senior leaders who saw all of this as a distraction from their "real mission" of conventional war.

For more than a decade, the officers who carried out the nation-building and peacekeeping operations in assorted third world hellholes received no recognition or appreciation. Indeed, international peacekeeping tours could even hurt your professional advancement. One officer who served a tour with a UN peacekeeping mission told me that one peacekeeping tour would neither help nor hurt his career. However, a second tour doing such operations was career suicide in the eyes of the Pentagon personnel specialists. This competent and experienced American peacekeeper pointed out that, even if an officer showed a real knack for the work and was successful at it, he should avoid making such operations a specialty. Even when the United States was embroiled in numerous peacekeeping operations, the senior military leadership had little use for officers who dealt with things outside mainstream conventional war operations, and successful peacekeepers would likely end their careers as lieutenant colonels. Rather than create a small cadre of colonels and generals who were very good at peacekeeping and nation-building, the U.S. military culture tended to punish officers who stepped out of the mainstream. This ensured that, as we entered the twenty-first century, any in-depth understanding of such esoteric operations would be rare indeed among the senior ranks of the armed forces.[2]

Despite the U.S. military's disapproval of peacekeeping and nation-building operations, a great many midranking officers picked up a lot of valuable lessons and, luckily, wrote them down. A fairly extensive literature dealing with peacekeeping, nation-building, and small wars issues began appearing in obscure places, websites, and journals. Detailed after-action reports from operations in Haiti and Somalia were circulated throughout the army. The Army Center for Lessons Learned at Fort Leavenworth published (and still publishes) a series of short but useful booklets on all aspects of population control, nation-building, peacekeeping, and counterinsurgency. Little of this is grand theory or anything that would appeal to academics, as most of the literature consists of tactical bulletins or outlines for tactical training exercises (how to set up a checkpoint, how to deal with angry demonstrators, how to legally apply deadly force, and so on). Still, for the commander who has to deploy on a peacekeeping or occupation mission, these reports and booklets are a good starting point for planning and training.

For a more academic and strategic discussion of these issues there is the Army War College's Strategic Studies Institute, which has published a series of well-written, well-researched, and critical monographs covering the strategic aspects of nation-building, counterinsurgency, and military occupation. The Army War College also contains a group of small wars experts who have produced some of the best work on the subject. At the operational level the *Civil Affairs Newsletter* is widely circulated in the army and contains articles and discussion across the whole range of military doctrine—from small-unit operations to large-scale programs. That so much of this is online is a tremendous advantage. The U.S. Army and Marine Corps civil affairs chat rooms are some of the most informative and interesting military correspondence centers around. In short, by the time it came to plan for the invasion and occupation of Iraq there was a wealth of knowledge and experience available within several branches of the army, and much of the knowledge was very recent (Bosnia and Kosovo) and learned under tough circumstances (Somalia and Haiti).

POPULATION CONTROL AND COUNTERINSURGENCY

The first need for any people is a basic level of security. All of the economic development opportunities, infrastructure programs, education programs, and opportunities to participate in a democratic process mean little to the average person if he is afraid to leave his house for fear of being robbed or killed by criminals, forced to pay extortion to rebels, or simply made the victim of a random bomb. High crime and insurgent activity usually target the transportation system—which means that shipping goods from one town to another becomes an expensive and difficult operation. Criminal and insurgent activity inhibits foreign and local investment and job creation, which, in turn, creates high unemployment and lowers the standard of living and creates dissatisfaction among the population. An impoverished, dissatisfied, and jobless population, especially a population with a large number of unemployed young men, is an excellent recruiting source for insurgents and criminal gangs. Poor security ensures that there is little deterrent to taking up a life of crime and violence. It's a vicious circle and one that must be broken in order to make any progress on the economic and social fronts.

When General Gerard Templar took over as high commissioner and military commander at the height of the insurgency in Malaya, he insisted that the first and overriding mission of the British and Malayan government was to improve security for the population. His policy of security first and foremost was heartily criticized at home, and his policies were described—fairly accurately—as creating a police state in Malaya. Templar imposed strict measures of control under expanded security regulations and moved whole villages of the Chinese squatters, who provided support to the rebels, and established them in brand-new villages where they were carefully guarded and kept under protection of a police detachment and their travel and economic activity supervised. Templar's approach was effective. As the security of the population improved, so did the economy and the social conditions for building a democratic nation.[3]

When regimes are overthrown in conflict, violent disorder is bound to result. This rule not only applies to third world countries with few traditions of democratic self-government—but also to highly advanced nations. When the German Imperial government collapsed in 1918, the state authority officially transitioned to the leaders of the parliament. But, as the police and military apparatus had also collapsed along with the old government, numerous groups quickly organized, armed themselves, and initiated a violent revolution. It took a weak, but legitimate, national government more than a year to suppress the German revolution at the price of several thousand dead. After World War II, parts of Europe were again plagued by violence and revolution caused by the power vacuum left by the collapse of authority. For example, the end of the German occupation in Greece in 1944 led to an immediate civil war between competing wartime resistance factions, a bloody war that continued to late 1949.

The end of World War II in Asia left a power vacuum in Europe's colonial possessions that local groups exploited. The Vietnamese nationalists had been a minor political force under the French and Japanese occupation, but when the Japanese surrendered in August 1945 the Vietnamese saw their chance to take power, ruthlessly seizing control of the local governments before the French could return. The French, discredited by their wartime defeat, then fought a nine-year war to regain their former position and failed miserably. The Malayan Communist

Party had been no threat to the British rule of Malaya before the war but, with the collapse of the British administration in 1942 and occupation by the Japanese, they organized to emerge at the end of the war as a large, cohesive, and well-armed force. The Malayan communists were well positioned to exploit the disorganization of the postwar police (the police having collaborated or been imprisoned during the war) and to begin an armed revolution. The U.S. defeat in the Philippines in 1942 led to the creation of a large and well-armed resistance movement, much of it communist dominated (the Huks on Luzon). When the United States granted the Philippines their independence in 1946, the first problem facing the poor, weak, and thoroughly disorganized Philippine government was how to deal with the former Huk resistance fighters who had grown into a formidable army and controlled a large part of Luzon. A guerrilla war lasting into the 1950s began.

More recently, the breakup of the authoritarian and Serb-dominated Yugoslav Federation in the early 1990s led to a power vacuum, with several ethnic factions arming and competing for territory and power in a series of bloody campaigns that took several years and foreign intervention to quell. The collapse of the Soviet regime led to rebellion in hinterlands such as Chechnya, and there was even a violent coup attempt by some military forces in Moscow as Russia made a disorderly transition to democracy. A nation that can transition from an authoritarian to a democratic form of government without considerable violence and disorder is rare indeed.

When an authoritarian government collapses, people used to constant police repression and tight control by the government can be expected to exhibit a high degree of psychological disorientation. Also, in the aftermath of a war or conflict there are a lot of weapons about, along with large numbers of recently demobilized soldiers who know how to use them. Nature and politics abhor a vacuum, and when a power vacuum is created by a regime collapse every group and faction that can get itself organized and find a few guns will make a bid for power. In many cases, the ideology or party program of the group will be unclear. Many groups simply want to seize power first and worry about the program later.

However, there are several ways to avoid violence, revolution, and disorder in the aftermath of a conflict or state collapse. One is to have a broad agreement among all the major ethnic and political factions to ensure an orderly transition of power at the start of the process. This happened in 1989 to 1990 in Poland, Hungary, and Czechoslovakia when the communist regimes saw that their days were finished. One of the decisive factors in this case was the immediate commitment of economic aid and political support from the Western powers. But, historically speaking, such cases of a peaceful and orderly transition of power in the aftermath of a war or collapse of an authoritarian or colonial state are very rare.

One of the most common tasks of the U.S. military since World War II has been to intervene to settle civil wars or to reconstruct imploded nations as in the Dominican Republic in 1965, Somalia in 1993, Bosnia in 1996, and Kosovo in 1999. A consistent lesson from these operations is that a large ground force is initially required when conditions are chaotic and violent. The first requirement is to establish a basic level of security, without which other vital operations such as humanitarian assistance, reconstruction, and establishment of a peaceful civil society are impossible. A 1995 article by Rand Corporation analyst James Quinlivan in the Army War College's journal, *Parameters*, addressed the Clinton administration's policy for peace enforcement operations. He argued that intervention in the types of violent situations such as the British had faced in Malaya and Northern Ireland required a force ratio of more than twenty soldiers, police, and other security personnel per every thousand civilians. Other cases, such as the U.S. intervention in the Dominican Republic in 1965, had required more than ten troops per every thousand civilians.[4] Quinlivan also noted that the population growth in the third world has resulted in large and difficult-to-control urban populations and that a failure to establish control and security during an intervention would quickly drain away the perceived political legitimacy of the intervention. He concluded, "Therefore, establishing control over the large populations of such cities (capitols, major trade centers) must be a major objective at the start of any operation, from which the conclusion is that any intervention force must have large numbers at the outset of operations."[5]

Moreover, per Quinlivan's model, nations conducting intervention planning have to consider not just the size of the initial force to stabilize a chaotic security situation, but also had to consider the requirement of maintaining a stability force over a long period and relieving and rotating troops. Realistically, this means that the United States or any Western intervention force would need at least three to four battalions for every battalion deployed on peacekeeping or stability operations to allow for rest and retraining of units as well as preventing "burnout" of soldiers being constantly deployed. The obvious implication was that the army, at that time, was not large enough to handle a policy of foreign intervention and stability operations. In particular, the army and its reserve forces were already drastically short the logistics and support units—such as military police—necessary to adequately support intervention operations without causing significant morale and readiness problems within the army. It was an argument that the DOD and Clinton administration did not want to hear, for the devotees of high-tech warfare were in the saddle and viewed any argument for a larger army as a threat to their plans to pour money into new and expensive weapons systems.

For the U.S./UN intervention in Bosnia a few months after the article appeared, and the NATO intervention in Kosovo in 1999, Quinlavin's formula for troop levels proved an exceptionally accurate planning guide. In order to tamp down the civil war and disorder in Bosnia in 1995, the intervening Western nations sent in a force that amounted to 22.6 troops per 1,000 Bosnians. The situation was quickly stabilized, but conditions still required a large force to prevent the civil war from flaring up again. Only in 2001 did the successor Bosnia Stabilization Force fall below a ratio of less than 10 soldiers and police per 1,000 people. In the 1999 Kosovo intervention, NATO initially committed more than 50,000 troops to control a population of 2 million: a ratio of 23.7 soldiers per 1,000 people. Even then, Kosovo was plagued for months by riots, revenge killings, and terrorist acts. Six years later a smaller, but still sizable, force remains in Kosovo. In the wake of the U.S. intervention in Iraq in 2003, Quinlivan updated his data and returned to the theme of force ratios. He emphatically concluded that "no one has discovered successful stabilization strategies that avoid large troop commitments while trying to bring order to large populations."[6]

Anticipating Iraq

Without belaboring the point, things in postwar Iraq have not gone as the

Bush administration and senior DOD leadership expected. The military campaign went brilliantly; the Iraqis who fought were quickly annihilated, and the Iraqi forces that didn't fight (most of them) slipped away and went home in the middle of the campaign. Coalition casualties were under two hundred dead, and 3 1/2 weeks after the start of the war the world witnessed jubilant Iraqis cheering as the huge statue of Saddam was toppled in Baghdad's central square. From that moment on, however, the whole thing went sour. The economic state of Iraq and the state of its vital oil infrastructure was much worse than the Bush administration had expected. Reconstructing Iraq would cost far more than expected—partly due to the wave of looting that spread across the liberated cities and caused billions of dollars' worth of damage to Iraq's economic and government infrastructure. Decent Iraqis lived in a state of fear as criminal gangs (Saddam released the criminals from prison as his regime collapsed) unleashed a wave of banditry, murder, and kidnapping that neither the few remaining Iraqi police nor the occupying Coalition forces could control. Worst of all, within weeks of the end of the conventional war an organized insurgency sprang up and Coalition forces and Iraqis working to rebuild some semblance of civil society found themselves under constant attack.

Called to testify before Congress, DOD civilian and military leaders put forward a variety of explanations that illustrate the strategic process in the Bush administration and senior Pentagon ranks. In testimony to the House Armed Services Committee in July 2004, Army General John Keane, who served as acting chief of staff of the army in the summer and fall of 2003, admitted that many in the DOD leadership had been "seduced by the Iraqi exiles in terms of what the outcome would be after the war." He also admitted, "There were very few people who actually envisioned, honestly, before the war what we were dealing with now after the regime went down... We did not see (the insurgency) coming, and we were not properly prepared to deal with it." In a press conference in August 2003, Defense Secretary Rumsfeld defended all the aspects of the postwar planning but acknowledged that the problems in establishing security in the wake of Saddam's fall and the following insurgency had arisen due to "unforeseen circumstances."[7] Deputy Secretary of Defense Paul Wolfowitz told reporters, "There was a plan, but as any military officer can tell you, no plan survives first contact with reality.

Some conditions were worse than we anticipated, particularly in the security area."[8] Concerning the rise of disorder and insurgency in postwar Iraq, one top Bush administration advisor remembered that, "Every briefing on postwar Iraq I attended never mentioned any of this."[9]

In fact, a great many people in the DOD and State Department, including the small group of highly experienced officers and experts on the Middle East tasked with planning for the postwar stabilization and reconstruction of Iraq, predicted quite accurately what the United States needed to do in Iraq to meet the Bush administration's strategic goal of creating a stable, prosperous, and democratic nation in place of Saddam's totalitarian state. That the DOD pointedly ignored its own experts and staff officers and proceeded with postwar planning based on incredibly rosy and unfounded assumptions will provide an example of a faulty policy and strategy process that will be the fodder of academic and military studies for generations. Assuming that Keane and others are telling the truth, that they had no reason to question the optimistic assumptions about postwar Iraq put forward by the DOD leadership (and I believe that General Keane and other senior leaders have testified honestly), then we have to study the conditions and process that shut down serious debate or discussion within the military on a matter as vital as determining the appropriate means to achieve the administration's fundamental strategic goals.

One reason for the lack of detailed planning for postwar Afghanistan and Iraq can be found in President Bush's dislike of the concept of using the U.S. military for nation-building. In a campaign speech at the Citadel in 1999 Bush declared that the purpose of the armed forces was to deter, fight, and win wars. He promised to end U.S. peacekeeping missions to Bosnia and Kosovo, arguing "we will not be permanent peacekeepers... that is not our strength or our calling." According to Bob Woodward's book *Bush at War*, Bush told his war cabinet in a meeting in late 2001, "I oppose using the military for nation-building. Once the job is done, our forces are not peacekeepers. We ought to put in place a UN protection and leave."[10] Such sentiments were warmly welcomed by the U.S. military leadership who, since the end of the Vietnam War, had focused almost exclusively on fighting the big conventional wars and were in the process of transforming the U.S. military into a smaller, high-tech force. Any long-term occupation or nation-building project would likely threaten the funding and force structure for the wars that the military leadership is strongly committed to.

However, sometimes nation-building is an unavoidable task if national objectives are to be met. Secretary of State Colin Powell, a man with more combat experience than most of America's senior military leaders and considerably more military experience than the inner circle of DOD civilian secretaries, argued before the Iraq War for more planning to deal with the postwar conditions as he cited the famous Pottery Barn rule: "If you break it—you own it." If the United States brought down Saddam's regime, then the United States would be initially responsible for creating a legitimately and internationally recognized order in Iraq. This implied a full military occupation of the country. In fact, the Geneva Convention requires this. But Powell and the State Department were sidelined early in the planning as the DOD took over complete responsibility for directing all aspects of the Iraq War—including the postwar occupation.[11] With Powell largely out of the picture in the war planning, none of the senior military officers were inclined to challenge the views of either President Bush or the DOD's senior civilian leadership on the issue of nation-building. Indeed, the disdain for this kind of operation has long been fairly universal in the top military ranks.

The administration's prewar policy guidance on postwar Iraq was governed by several incredibly optimistic assumptions that also proved incredibly wrong. First of all, because Iraq is an oil-rich country, it was assumed that Iraq could quickly pay for its own reconstruction out of oil revenues. It was going to be a cheap war: fought rapidly with a minimum of troops and finished in record time. Postwar occupation costs would be small, for Iraq would rapidly recover from decades of tyranny, oppression, and corruption. However, little interest was shown in carefully determining the actual state of the oil infrastructure that would pay for rebuilding Iraq. If anyone had checked, they would have quickly learned that Iraq's oil infrastructure was in a shambles and would require years of extensive repair and rebuilding before the oil could flow in large enough quantities to guarantee an adequate income for a new state. From the time Saddam invaded Iran in 1980 to the war of 2003, all of Iraq's oil revenue flowed either to the Iraqi military or into Saddam's pockets, and little money was left to repair and update the complex system of pipelines, pumping stations, refineries, and port facilities. Without constant and expensive maintenance, any oil infrastructure will fall into ruin. And that's precisely what happened in Iraq. Just after the fall of Baghdad, I was interested in assessing the postwar conditions in Iraq. So I contacted a retired senior engineer from a major oil corporation, a man who had spent most of his working life in the Middle East. He told me that, as early as the 1990s when sanctions were first applied to Iraq following the invasion of Kuwait, the oil infrastructure of Iraq was already limping along, dependent on Bulgarian pumps and all manner of cheap improvisations to keep the oil flowing at a moderate level. By the run-up to the 2003 Iraq War, the whole system had continued to decline and was, by then, a wreck. The engineer believed that Iraq could pump some oil, but just barely. At best, only a fraction of the nation's potential output could be exploited. From his own studies, plus information from his colleagues still active in the oil industry, the retired engineer estimated that the infrastructure would require several years of rebuilding before oil could flow in quantity. He was astonished that the DOD had been surprised by the poor condition of the Iraqi oil infrastructure when Saddam Hussein was overthrown. He commented: "If the CIA had called me up, I would have been happy to brief them. But no one ever asked."

Another assumption is that, while the United States carried on the heavy lifting of the warfighting, other nations would gladly contribute substantial forces for postwar security and rebuilding operations. Before the war, an estimate of 150,000 Coalition troops for the postwar security of Iraq was bandied about the Pentagon, but the Pentagon was disappointed with the level of international support it actually received. The UN generally opposed the war, and the only U.S. ally to contribute substantial forces was Britain, with thirty other allies, including Italy, South Korea, Japan, and Australia, sending smaller forces. At their peak, the total Coalition forces amounted to fewer than 40,000 men. Yet this was, by historical standards, a fairly strong response from America's allies and about as much as anyone familiar with the recent flabby NATO response to the Bosnia and Kosovo crises could reasonably expect. Even now that Iraq has had fair, democratic elections and established a democratic government, few

Western nations are willing to provide any significant forces to assist in the counterinsurgency battle.

The final, and most astounding assumption of all, was the Pentagon's position that once Saddam was deposed, the Iraqis would be able to create an effective government on their own, with minimal involvement from the U.S. forces, and transition from totalitarian dictatorship to a Western, liberal democracy in a matter of months. While the Pentagon believed that some U.S. troops would be needed to keep order and provide humanitarian assistance in the immediate aftermath of the war, there was an optimistic view that only a small force would be needed to help secure Iraq a year after the victory. In this scenario, the follow-on U.S. troops would not be required to run Iraq, but rather to defend the new democratic regime from any outside interference by the Iranian and Syrian regimes. Shortly before the war began, in late 2002, a retired army general, Jay Garner, was named by the DOD to be the civilian administrator responsible for directing U.S. reconstruction operations in postwar Iraq. Certain of his senior staff, some of whom had been planning for the occupation of Iraq for months, argued for the need to take firm control in Iraq as soon as the Coalition forces overran Baghdad and the major cities. Garner's staff argued that the United States needed to set up a full occupation administration—something along the lines of the U.S. occupation of Germany and Japan after World War II—and be prepared to provide security and supervise all functions of government for a period of years to carefully direct an orderly transition to democracy. His staff proposed numerous plans and concepts for setting up and supervising a new Iraqi government, but, according to some of his staff, Garner seemed strangely disconnected from it all. He wanted to limit his own involvement, and the level of any U.S. administration of postwar Iraq, to a bare minimum of emergency humanitarian assistance and governmental advice. He and other senior officials believed that, somehow, the Iraqis would sort it all out.

Some fairly detailed planning for postwar Iraq was carried out by midlevel officers at the State and Defense Departments that took into account the supposedly "unforeseen" circumstances that the Bush administration officials and senior military alluded to in postwar testimony. James Fallows in an article for the *Atlantic Monthly* ("Blind into Baghdad,"

January/February 2004) recounted in detail the prewar planning efforts of several groups and agencies within the State and Defense Departments that, largely on their own initiative, put together plans to occupy Iraq at the end of the conventional war phase. Their goal was to plan to establish order, stability, and the conditions to carry out the president's primary objective: creation of a peaceful and democratic Iraq. The primary planning group in the DOD, a group that evolved into General Garner's staff and then into the more formally named "Office of Reconstruction and Humanitarian Assistance–ORHA," included a variety of experts on aspects of military occupation. For example, Garner's staff included midranking officers with extensive civil affairs experience as well as recent experience in the Bosnia and Kosovo operations.[12] The ad hoc planning group, coordinated by Army War College faculty Dr. Conrad Crane and Dr. Andrew Terrill (Terrill is an expert on the Middle East and fluent in Arabic–albeit with a noticeable Lebanese accent), formally came together in October 2002. This was only five months before the war started, although some planning studies had been going on for months beforehand. The planning group worked quickly and, in January 2003, presented a study to the army staff that challenged several of the core assumptions of the DOD senior leadership.[13] First of all, the planning group doubted that Iraq's oil wealth could pay for the cost of reconstruction. They estimated the cost of rebuilding Iraq to be between $30 and $100 billion–not including the cost of occupation troops.[14] The planning group looked carefully at the sociology of Iraq and conditions for indigenous and outside terrorism and resistance to the occupation. They concluded that, under a variety of likely scenarios, the initial Iraqi gratitude for their liberation could sour and become an active insurgency against the United States and Coalition forces.[15] The planners were not worried about an insurgency defeating the American forces. They instead feared that the postwar upheaval in Iraq could turn Iraq into another Lebanon, a nation embroiled in civil war engendered by the long-suppressed competition between Iraq's three main ethnic groups. The planners also directly challenged one of the primary assumptions of the DOD leadership: that Iraqi exile groups, most notably the faction headed by Ahmad Chalabi, could immediately take over leadership of Iraq, establish a popular government, and spare the United States

the trouble of governing the country. "It is doubtful that the Iraqi population would welcome the leadership of the various exile groups after
Saddam's defeat. Many Iraqis are reported as hostile to the external Iraqi
opposition groups despite the fact that a post-Saddam power struggle has
yet to take place. According to former CIA analyst Judith Yaphe, 'Iraqi exile
leader Ahmad Chalabi and the INC (Iraqi National Congress) are known
quantities and extremely unpopular in Iraq.'"[16]

The most important part of the Army War College group's report was a
mission matrix of 135 essential tasks in occupying and rebuilding a defeated Iraq. The 135 tasks, grouped into twenty-two mission categories and
based on a broad historical study of lessons from military occupations that
included recent operations in Bosnia and Kosovo, made it clear that the U.S.
military would have a vast, costly, and complex undertaking on its hands
AFTER the war, if the war to depose Saddam went forward. The report,
Reconstructing Iraq, took a long-term view of creating a viable, stable, and
democratic Iraq, a process that would likely take several years at least. As far
as the military was concerned, 32 of the essential tasks required the immediate attention and resources of the military commander, including reestab-
lishing basic human services and basic security for the population. The
other tasks could be approached with deliberate planning and directed primarily by civilian agencies and included restoring the economic infrastructure, reforming the government institutions, and establishing a broad and
fair electoral process.[17]

Implicit in the Army War College report was that, in order to do it right,
the occupation of Iraq would require a LOT of manpower—far more troops
than the Pentagon wanted to deploy. The manpower requirement was based
on a considerable amount of historical experience. To establish security and
stability in a country in the wake of a major conflict, you need to go in
heavy, with enough troops to saturate the major population centers, quickly squelch any resistance, and let the defeated and occupied population
know that you are in full control. Historically, once initial stability is
achieved, the bulk of the forces can be quickly withdrawn and the work of
reconstruction carried on by civil affairs, administration, and logistic units.

Military planning for the 2003 war had not occurred in a vacuum. The
plans to fight Iraq had been evolving ever since the 1991 war, and there

was a broad understanding within the military that we would probably have to fight Saddam again. When the Bush administration first looked at Iraq following the September 11, 2001, terrorist attacks, the CENTCOM plan called for a force of 400,000 troops to take down Iraq. This was derided in the Pentagon as being a holdover from the "old way of war," and seen as completely unnecessary under the new theories of high-tech warfare.[18] But Marine Corps General Anthony Zinni, CENTCOM commander in the 1990s, pointed out that there was a sound reason for planning for such a large force: "The reason we had those two extra divisions was the security situation. Revenge killings, crime, chaos—this was all foreseeable."[19] The DOD did not buy into this reasoning and ordered the force for invading Iraq to be pared down to its essentials. In revising the war plan in 2002, the army proposed a force of 250,000 for a war with Iraq. In November 2002, at a discussion of the current army plan for Iraq, an army colonel on the joint staff made it clear that 250,000 men were not needed to defeat the Iraqi army. Every intelligence assessment of the Iraqi forces indicated that they wouldn't fight much and, if some units did, they would suffer quick destruction due to their poor training and leadership. The colonel insisted, however, that 250,000 ground troops would be needed to establish firm control in Iraq *after* the Iraqi army had been defeated. It seemed to me like pretty sound thinking. But as soon as the discussion was over, a U.S. Air Force colonel (a long time Pentagon insider, a great fan of Deputy Secretary of Defense Paul Wolfowitz, and a true believer in the new, high-tech way of war) ridiculed the concept of using 250,000 men to occupy Iraq as "dinosaur thinking." He insisted that Saddam could be whipped with a small force of 80,000 troops supported by airpower and high tech. If the air force colonel had been listening, he should have understood that the army colonel had agreed with him about the troop numbers needed for the combat phase of the war. What failed to get through is that there is more to winning a war than beating the enemy army. Indeed, the ultimate purpose of any war is to establish peace favorable to your national interest.

Throughout the planning for the Iraq War, Army Chief of Staff General Eric Shinseki and Army Secretary Thomas White (a retired army general), fought with the DOD civilian leadership over the force requirements. In hard Pentagon infighting they were defeated at every turn and marginalized as the war drew closer. In the end, the army leadership was beaten down, and a relatively small force of 130,000 ground troops became the final figure for the Iraq War plan. The army feared—correctly—that at the end of the war they would be the service left with a mess in Iraq and too few troops to deal with it. So far, their prewar fears have been amply justified. General Shinseki got in one last blow when he testified before Congress in February 2003, admitting that an occupation of Iraq might require hundreds of thousands of troops and take several years. This was challenged the next day by Paul Wolfowitz, one of the primary strategists of the DOD's war policy. Testifying before Congress, Wolfowitz asserted that Shinseki's estimate of troops required for the occupation of Iraq was "wildly off the mark" and also argued that the United States would not likely have to foot the bill for the occupation and reconstruction of Iraq thanks to Iraq's oil reserves and frozen assets. As Wolfowitz noted, "There's a lot of money there, and to assume we're going to pay for it is wrong."[20] The historical record of the ongoing Iraq War and the costs incurred to date provides a very eloquent commentary on the soundness of Wolfowitz's strategic thinking.

THE REALITY OF IRAQ: THE START OF THE INSURGENCY
When the American forces liberated Baghdad from the tyranny of Saddam Hussein in April 2003, there was general rejoicing from the majority of the population who had suffered through decades of dictatorship, fear, brutality, and mass murder. However, in the wake of Saddam's fall, the situation quickly turned sour. This is what decades of emphasizing the "new way of war" led to: a military that could take down Saddam's armed forces in rapid order and with few casualties but was almost totally unprepared to handle the postwar tasks of controlling a large country and dealing with the inevitable disorder that follows a war and the collapse of a totalitarian regime. The assumptions that the Iraqis would quickly sort themselves out and fashion a democracy, that large-scale international aid would restore Iraq, and that large numbers of international peacekeepers would soon arrive under the UN's auspices proved false. Nor was Iraq in any condition to quickly pay for its own rebuilding. The U.S. military took over a large nation of 25 million people, without a plan and without a

clear policy. The results have been glaringly obvious since 2003. Lieutenant General William S. Wallace, one of the senior Army commanders in Iraq during the first months of the occupation, admitted that the U.S. military leadership was surprised by the level of looting and disorder in Iraq. "There was a point when the regime was no longer relevant, no longer running the country. We were slow to pick up on that." Wallace also admitted that "The complexity was much greater than what we trained and exercised for prior to this campaign."[21]

General Anthony Zinni, CENTCOM commander from 1997 to 2000, has repeatedly discussed the American blunders in Iraq after the war. In 2004 he asserted that the U.S. leadership had underestimated the reconstruction risks, relied too heavily upon the Iraqi exiles and their promises to lead the country, and failed to develop a coherent plan: "I think that the lack of planning—the idea that you can do this by the seat of the pants: reconstruct a country, make decisions on the fly, with just a handful of people at the last minute—was patently ridiculous." Most important, according to Zinni, the DOD failed to provide adequate forces to secure the country.[22] "The extra divisions we wanted ... were to freeze the security situation because we knew chaos would result when we uprooted an authoritarian regime like Saddam's." Zinni noted other mistakes, including the ad hoc nature of the postwar administration and the disbanding of the Iraqi army.[23] General Tommy Franks, CENTCOM Commander during the 2003 Iraq War, admitted that his warplanners expected 150,000 additional international troops to help with peacekeeping operations, but they never materialized. He said in 2004 that the United States should have thought in terms of a five-year timeline for Iraq occupation. "It takes time to solve problems when you're talking about twenty-five to twenty-six million people."[24] L. Paul Bremer, who served as the head of the civilian administration of Iraq from May 2003 to early 2005, pointed out that the planning for the postwar occupation was inadequate. The only deliberate planning had been to deal with a possible refugee crisis and postwar famine. But those situations did not arise. On the other hand, there had been no planning for the postwar disorder. "There was planning, but planning for a situation that didn't arise."[25]

The greatest strategic error, however, was simply having too few troops on the ground in Iraq to establish firm control in the country and create a secure atmosphere in which the business of rebuilding a shattered economy and creating a new democracy could take place. The failure to place enough troops into Iraq after Baghdad fell was not due to any lack of American manpower or resources. U.S. National Guard and Reserve units could have been called up and rushed to Iraq. An even better solution would have been to have troops already mobilized and ready to move to Iraq if the situation warranted it (and it did). But the U.S. military leadership chose to try controlling a heavily armed and disorderly country the size of California with 25 million people, many of them hostile, using a minimal force of 160,000 U.S. soldiers. Most of the subsequent problems that arose in Iraq were due to this one, grand, strategic mistake. The consequences had a cascading effect that America is living with today. With too few troops, the rule of law never took hold in Iraq, and the loose control imposed by the Americans offered criminal gangs, radical Islamic groups, and well-armed factions and militias the opportunity to organize and begin an insurgency. With too few troops in Iraq, the borders remained wide open, and thousands of foreign *jihadists* flocked to Iraq to fight the Americans. L. Paul Bremer outlined the consequences of the decision to not stop the looting in Baghdad and establish U.S. authority, "We paid a big price for not stopping it (the looting) because it established an atmosphere of lawlessness." He added, "We never had enough troops on the ground."[26]

With no plan, little guidance from above, and far too few troops and resources to do the job, the U.S. soldiers tasked with policing their sectors, rebuilding the infrastructure, and getting the economy moving again did a superb job. They helped to quickly restore basic services and infrastructure, as well as the foundations for a civil society in many regions of Iraq. Little if any credit for the many U.S. successes in Iraq can be given to the top leadership. Time and again it was the middle-level army officers—the lieutenants, captains, majors, and colonels—who simply took charge and went to work. Many had no training in this kind of operation and quickly proved they could learn on the job. One of the most successful and innovative programs was carried out by U.S. Army civil affairs officers in the south of Iraq. From 1991 to 2003, Saddam had waged a nonstop war against the Shiites living in the marshlands of the Tigris and Euphrates

Rivers in southern Iraq near the Gulf Coast. As part of a deliberate policy to suppress the Shiites, Saddam had allowed the extensive canal and irrigation system that serves the vast farmlands of southern Iraq to go to ruin. U.S. officers, without guidance from above and using their own initiative, found various humanitarian funds and former Iraqi regime funds and quickly put tens of thousands of Iraqis to work repairing and clearing the silted-up canals and repairing the irrigation system. The work continued for months and provided immediate employment for many Iraqis who otherwise would have been jobless and dependent upon foreign aid for food rations—a perfect breeding ground for discontent and anger against the occupation forces. Instead, the infrastructure for a large proportion of Iraqi agriculture was restored as was the local economy, and the formerly impoverished people could look forward with hope. All thanks to a handful of American officers who showed what a little imagination and drive can accomplish.

In the first months of the occupation of Iraq, the CPA (Civilian Provisional Authority—the Coalition governing authority in Iraq and successor to ORHA) was so disorganized and the top U.S. military command, CENTCOM (headquarters for all U.S. military forces in the Middle East) so unprepared for occupation duties, that these top commands could provide little clear guidance for the soldiers in the field. In the spring of 2003, the UN arrived briefly in Iraq but quickly left after a bombing at the UN headquarters killed the senior UN representative. One U.S. Civil Affairs Command in southern Iraq actually sent officers over the dangerous roads on weekly trips to Baghdad to see if they could pry some guidance on policy out of the CPA, but their trips were in vain.[27] Other windows of opportunity opened up in the immediate aftermath of the fall of Baghdad. As Iraq dissolved into looting and disorder, one U.S. colonel who served as the strategic policy director for ORHA was contacted by an Iraqi army major general and several other Iraqi officers who offered to mobilize ten thousand trained Iraqi military policemen in two days, place them under American command, and use the Iraqis to help Americans end the looting of Baghdad. The U.S. colonel thought this was an excellent idea, and such an offer also opened the way to place more than one hundred thousand Iraqi army soldiers and officers under clear control of the Coalition. The colonel passed the Iraqi and his proposal for cooperation up through the chain of command with a strong recommendation that we take up the offer. But the top commands either ignored or rejected the idea and the disorder in Baghdad continued.[28]

Throughout 2003, in the messy aftermath of the Coalition invasion, U.S. Army and Marine civil affairs officers and local unit commanders lacked anything resembling long-term plans and direction from the CPA—which operated in an ad hoc and crisis management mode for the first months of the Iraq occupation. Since the CPA was unable to look more than a week or two ahead, midranking army and marine officers simply took whatever resources were at hand and developed their own programs to rebuild and restore Iraq. The most positive aspect of the occupation of Iraq was the high degree of initiative, imagination, and competence demonstrated by the junior and midlevel officers who saw a job to do, figured out what needed to be done, and simply went ahead and did it. The story of the restoration of agriculture in southern Iraq was repeated on a small scale throughout the country. Ironically, while the senior officers in the U.S. military proved themselves masters of the tactical battles, it was the junior and midranking officers who consistently showed a solid grasp of strategy. Strategy implies the politics of war and looking to attain the national objectives. American officers, many of whom had just commanded tank or infantry units fighting the Iraqi army, showed considerable talent for learning to deal with local tribal sheikhs and figuring out the local power structure as they worked with Iraqis to rebuild the nation. It must be remembered that in most of Iraq, outside the three provinces of the Sunni triangle of central Iraq, the occupation went smoothly and U.S. forces, undermanned and underresourced as they were, adapted effectively to do the job. Ironically, we now have an army in which the generals understand and concentrate their energies on the tactical level of war and the immediate conventional war battle but demonstrate little interest in the long-term strategic goals, while the captains and majors have learned to understand the strategic and long-term effects of their local actions and think about their work in terms of the national strategic objectives.

One of the most consistent and serious problems with planning and executing the occupation of Iraq—and in fighting the insurgencies there and in Afghanistan—has been the inability of major U.S. government agencies to work effectively together. Suppressing the insurgency in Iraq, as well as fighting a global war on terror, requires not just the DOD but extensive cooperation between the Defense, State, Justice, and Treasury Departments. As history shows, fighting insurgencies and rebuilding countries require a large amount of civilian expertise. An impressive amount of this necessary expertise already resides within the branches of the federal government, including Treasury Department experts to rebuild the economic system in Iraq, people in the Justice Department to reform the national legal system and train a police force, and State Department regional and development specialists to direct foreign aid. Unfortunately, interagency cooperation throughout the Iraq occupation can be rated from poor to dismal. However, this is not just a problem that originated with the Bush administration. Poor interagency cooperation has been a consistent problem with U.S. nation-building and counterinsurgency operations for decades—and it has undermined the strategy of Democratic and Republican administrations alike. Senior U.S. officials noted the interagency problem when they crafted a national strategy for El Salvador in the 1980s. Studies published by the DOD have also noted the poor level of interagency cooperation in the operations of the 1990s that included the conflicts in Somalia, Bosnia, and Kosovo. For her 2004 book, *Interagency Fratricide: Policy Failures in the Persian Gulf and Bosnia*, U.S. Air Force Major Vicki Rast interviewed numerous major and minor Washington players who "agree that the policy-making system is personality-driven, especially at the upper levels."[29] Rast details the complexity of U.S. government agencies trying to negotiate and communicate with each other. Rast cites a top State Department official on the issue, "It is usually the fault of leadership, not the process, that impedes policy from energizing."[30] Another senior leader interviewed noted, "More than anything else, the lack of a coherent policy at the highest level is the problem [in generating interagency conflict]. From the very top, there must be articulated a vision and a policy. In their absence, these fiefdoms will always push their agendas [e.g., human rights, energy]."[31] Most of the people who have studied the issue of interagency cooperation, or lack thereof, insist that the root of the problem lies in the strategic culture of Washington, D.C.[32] Large-scale reorganization of government agencies is sometimes useful—but it is not a means that addresses the core problem of poor interagency coordination. Fixing the interagency process cannot be done through a periodic restructuring of government agencies. This can only be fixed through good leadership at the top levels of the federal agencies.

However, in the absence of clear guidance from the top, junior and midlevel U.S. Army and Marine leaders are quickly learning to deal with the minutia of occupying a country and fighting an insurgency. In the lower leader ranks, the army and marines have proven to be healthy institutions, capable of rapid adaptation and improvisation and able to carry out a vast array of missions—building schools, running public works programs, managing police forces—that they were never trained for. Still, all of those admirable qualities cannot compensate for the military's failure to have a long-term plan, or enough soldiers to carry out the mission.

The impact of too few ground troops can be seen in fighting the insurgency in one of the toughest sectors of the infamous "Sunni Triangle." The vast Al Anbar Province, which reaches from the outskirts of Baghdad to the Syrian border, has been a hotbed of Sunni and foreign insurgency since the beginning of the occupation. Yet, U.S. Marine Corps officers in 2005 frankly admitted that there were far too few troops to police a vast area. In 2005, just three marine battalions covered the whole province, down from four the year before. And in 2005, each battalion was smaller by one company. Al Anbar Province was described by Marine Corps Lieutenant General James Conway as "a region in turmoil." Officers fighting insurgents told the press that, "commanders in Baghdad and the Pentagon have denied their repeated requests for more troops." This means that when marines conduct effective sweep operations that destroy or drive out Iraqi and foreign insurgents in a sector, the marines must withdraw and move to fight in the next sector—and the troop shortage means that neither the marines nor the Iraqi government have enough forces to leave behind to maintain a credible government presence.[33] In short, the United States carries out combat sweeps but is unable to support a pacification program. Such a policy is a violation of the most basic rules of conducting a successful counterinsurgency campaign.

In another tough sector of northwest Iraq, the army could provide only four hundred soldiers to control a vast border region covering ten thousand square miles. Like the marines in Al Anbar province, the army could carry out successful sweep operations, but was unable to provide any consistent government presence in the region. "Resources are everything in combat. . . . There's no way four hundred people can cover that much ground," said Major John Wilmerding of the 3rd Armored Cavalry Regiment, which is responsible for the northwest tract that includes Tal Afar.[34] Like the marines, after successful sweeps there were too few army troops or police to pacify the cleared areas and the rebels moved in behind them. In May 2005 in the border city of Tal Afar, a major center for smuggling weapons, money, and foreign insurgent fighters into Iraq, the police—with only 150 officers left in what had been a 600-man force—were holed up in the only remaining police station, unable to exert any effective government control in a consistently lawless region.[35] As of this writing (mid-2005), little progress against the insurgents is being made in many sectors of Iraq.

THE WEAKNESS OF THE U.S. STRATEGIC APPROACH

The U.S. military could have done a far better job of planning for postwar Iraq and Afghanistan simply by looking to its own very impressive strategic tradition. A good first step for any American strategist would be to examine how two of America's greatest strategists, Generals George Marshall and Dwight Eisenhower, handled the incredibly complex strategic issues of World War II coalition warfare and planning for the occupation of Germany and Japan.

In the weeks following Pearl Harbor, when American forces were suffering a series of painful defeats at the hands of the Japanese and the U.S. Navy was barely holding the Atlantic lifelines open, Marshall might well have been excused if he had concentrated the efforts of the U.S. Army staff on dealing with the crises at hand. But even in the early days of the war, when things looked darkest for America, Marshall had the strategic foresight to look ahead to the political requirements of the eventual Allied victory. In early 1942, Marshall ordered the army to train a corps of specialists to prepare for the postwar occupation of Germany and Japan. Moving with a rapidity that would astound the current Pentagon culture, in May 1942 the army opened the School of Military Government in Charlottesville, Virginia. There, soldiers and civilian specialists began training and planning for the postwar occupations.[36]

After the Allied grand strategy conference at Casablanca in January 1943, planning for the postwar conditions entered high gear. In early 1943, a combined U.S./British staff, under the capable leadership of British Lieutenant General Frederick Morgan, began planning for the occupation of Germany.[37] When General Eisenhower took over as Allied Supreme Commander in late 1943, the occupation staff was already working out many of the details of the military administration of postwar Germany, including plans for denazifying the country and building a democratic civil order.[38] Eisenhower, like Marshall, might have been excused if he had ignored the postwar political aims in favor of dealing with planning for the largest combat operations in American history. Despite crises such as the Normandy battle, the airborne attack on Holland, and the Battle of the Bulge, Eisenhower nevertheless refused to ignore the political element of strategy, remaining closely involved in the planning for postwar Germany.[39] Thanks to the strategic vision and leadership of Marshall and Eisenhower, the occupations of Germany and Japan were not ad hoc affairs, but part of a well-conceived and thoroughly planned program to fulfill the long-term political goals of the Allied leadership. By any measure, U.S. and Allied planning for postwar Europe was highly successful.[40]

We can contrast the inspired strategic leadership of Marshall and Eisenhower with the American theater commander for the Iraq and Afghanistan campaigns, U.S. Army General Tommy Franks. Although faced with an enemy hardly as dangerous as Nazi Germany, Franks still concentrated his efforts almost exclusively on the tactical and operational issues of the conventional war, putting only a few members of his large staff to work on postwar strategic planning. Essentially, he concentrated on fighting the battles while he ignored the strategic context that emphasized not only taking out the Taliban and Baathist dictatorships but also replacing them with functioning democracies. Still, Franks' failure to act or think strategically is not unusual for modern U.S. military leaders. One commentator, Army Lieutenant Colonel Tony Echevarria, wrote a monograph after the Iraq and Afghanistan invasions in which he argued that, while the U.S. military has a way of battle (i.e., fighting the big conventional war), it has no genuine "way of war." He pointed out that the American military, and the army in particular, now sees the combat phase as the whole thing and has taken war out of its political and strategic context.[41] From my own experience of twenty-eight years in the army and fourteen years teaching in military staff colleges, I believe that Echevarria's critique of the U.S. Army strategic culture is spot on.

There are several causes for the current confusion within the U.S. military in dealing with occupations, nation-building, and fighting nonstate enemies. The problem is, above all, a cultural one. First of all, there is little study of basic military history at the U.S. military's institutions of higher learning. The preference for a methodical and high-tech approach to war was always there, but since 1991 this cultural preference has become extreme. Across broad sectors of the U.S. military, the belief that technology has made history irrelevant predominates. One senior academic who served for many years on the faculty of the U.S. Air Force War College, the Air Force's premier school of strategy, told me, "We have to fight in this place to get any history prior to 1990 taught at all." The point is quite simple: American officers are unable to model the strategic performance of Marshall and Eisenhower because they know little, if anything, about it. Furthermore, they have been advised that such things have no relevance to the modern world.

At the center of modern U.S. military culture lies a belief in technological determinism: that technology is a central factor in warfare and that the country with the best technology is bound to win. This is an exceptionally dangerous concept because it's simply wrong—and there is a vast amount of historical data, and recent cases, which disproves such theories. For example, the United States had a vast technological superiority over North Vietnam. We even dropped over two thousand precision-guided bombs on North Vietnam in the 1970s. Nevertheless, the North Vietnamese won the war. The French Army of 1940 was, in many respects, technologically superior to the German army. The French had far more tanks and artillery—and better tanks—than the Germans, who handily defeated them with a combination of better training, tactics, and leadership. In short, technological determinism is a concept that may prove to be the undoing of American strategy and military effectiveness.

Another root cause of the current problem with our strategic approach is the popularity of several new theories of conflict developed by political scientists in military/academic circles. After the Gulf War, various branches of coercion theory postulating that whole nations could be controlled and coerced by precision firepower, applied at long range and requiring few or no ground troops, became highly popular in the staff colleges and military think tanks. These concepts supported the neoconservative view that wars could be quick, decisive, and cheap. The main problem with these theories is that they are either thin on historical evidence or based on a gross misreading of historical evidence, or sometimes employ no evidence at all to support their conclusions. Notably, two of the central figures in the tactical and operational decision making through the current Iraq War, Deputy Defense Secretary Paul Wolfowitz and Undersecretary Douglas Feith, both had political science backgrounds and both approached the problem of the occupation of Iraq through the lens of their neoconservative concepts. Remarkably, for men involved in operational military decisions during wartime, neither Wolfowitz nor Feith had ever spent a day in the armed forces. Such aspects of the decision-making process of the Iraq War hearken back to the Vietnam era, when civilian political theorists such as McGeorge Bundy involved themselves in tactical decisions and helped President Lyndon Johnson choose bombing targets during White House lunch sessions, while the Joint Chiefs of Staff were largely cut out of the process.

The political goals of the neocons were fairly sound. They recognized Saddam as a long-term threat. They also understood that establishing a moderate, democratic government in Iraq would be a positive development for bringing long-term greater peace and stability to the Middle East. Where the neoconservative concepts went wrong was the assumption that a democracy could be quickly, cheaply, and easily created out of the ruins of a nation with no tradition of democracy and governed by a totalitarian ruler for decades. From the viewpoint of history, even recent history, such a notion is ludicrous. Yet in 2003, pure theory trumped centuries of experience when minimal planning for postwar Iraq was decreed. And we have seen the result in the postwar chaos and disorder. The events in Iraq since 2003 have simply conformed to historical reality. Nations are controlled and insurgencies are fought not with machines, but with human beings. To be effective in occupying countries and suppressing insurgency, you need plenty of well-trained people with appropriate plans and adequate resources. Those fundamental aspects of conflict and politics remain unchanged.

CHAPTER FOUR

INTELLIGENCE: HOW TO REFORM A DYSFUNCTIONAL CULTURE

The importance of intelligence in such a campaign as we are conducting cannot be over-emphasized. Everything depends on it.
— Unnamed British officer, *in Malaya*, 1954

Good intelligence does not win wars—at least the conventional state-on-state wars. In conventional war, the combat troops on the front line win by defeating the enemy armies. A nation can win battles and the war without a good intelligence system if it has the ability to apply overwhelming military power. In World War II, if the Allied coalition had not broken the Enigma code and won direct access to German military orders, plans, and strength reports obtained by intercepting and decrypting German communications, they still would have beaten Nazi Germany on the battlefield. America, Britain, and the USSR had such a margin of resources and personnel over the Germans from 1943 on that Allied victory was inevitable. However, without the superb intelligence system, defeating Nazi Germany would have taken much longer and cost many more American and British lives.

It's different in fighting insurgencies. One can bludgeon one's way to victory in conventional war. While materiel and manpower superiority are decisive elements of conventional warfare, they provide no assurance of victory in fighting irregular forces and insurgents. There are many historical examples of nations with vast military, economic, and equipment superiority that were defeated by insurgent forces far inferior by any measure of military or economic power. Without an effective intelligence system to provide accurate, timely, and useful information to the military and government, conventional forces and institutions are virtually blind in a counterinsurgency campaign.

Clausewitz did not talk much about intelligence because it was not a key element to fighting the wars of his day. The conventional states of the Napoleonic era had a very good idea of the strength, organization, equipment, and capabilities of their opponents. In the early nineteenth century there was little notable difference in the effectiveness of the equipment or weaponry of any of the warring powers. For most of the era of modern warfare, an army commander didn't need an intelligence officer to tell him what his opponent's options were to move, supply, and attack his forces. The transportation net was limited and there were only a few roads or rivers that could handle the passage of a significant force. Twenty miles a day, often less, was the top speed that a corps or army could move on Europe's road net. It took time to bring up and sort out armies for a battle and, unless a commander was especially dim-witted, cavalry scouts could locate and plot enemy movements within a 20-mile radius of his own forces. For most of the nineteenth century, surprise was rare in war and battles fought virtually by the consent of both sides.

The ability of forces to move rapidly by rail, and later by motor vehicle and by air, changed the tempo of war and those factors changed the intelligence requirements of the commander. With increasing disparities in technology between powers and more means to move forces to battle, intelligence became far more important. With large armies spread over a large area, good communications became essential for a senior commander who might have his forces stationed hundreds of miles from his headquarters. Radio and telephone communications also increased the opportunities for an enemy to intercept and decode the most secret military communications, and a large part of the ever-increasing intelligence apparatus was devoted to signals intelligence and electronic warfare. The advent of the airplane as a reconnaissance platform, followed by satellite imagery, pushed the military and national intelligence organizations toward a cultural preference for the high-tech end of intelligence. Yet the conventional state-on-state wars are still fought on a linear battlefield, and conventional armies are still limited by fairly traditional supply, movement, and terrain considerations. In addition, any moderately bright commander can figure out the likely landing places or probable routes of advance for a conventional army without too much trouble. And if a commander in a conventional war is still unsure of the enemy positions and strength, he can send out light forces to make contact with the enemy and at least ascertain the position of the forward enemy forces—a staple of basic intelligence collection that remains from Clausewitz's era.

Today we have an impressive tactical and operational intelligence system built primarily around air reconnaissance, unmanned aerial vehicles (UAVs) and space surveillance systems that can go deep behind the enemy lines and use a variety of means (imagery, heat sensing, etc.) to locate the enemy's vehicles, larger units, aircraft and depots, and the like. American tactical units have radars that can spot the movement of enemy heavy equipment at a distance or locate the firing point of an enemy artillery battery. Although the high-tech assets can bring in a lot of intelligence, they are also exceptionally expensive and have routinely failed to provide the level of intelligence that was promised or expected (see Chapter 2). However, in a conventional war, the senior ground commander can still find a conventional enemy force even if all the high-tech assets break down. He only needs to send his light screening forces up to the front line. Eventually he'll locate some enemy forces and then, with a superb communications net, he can call an impressive array of aerial and artillery firepower down upon the enemy. When the enemy retreats, he can advance again, locate him, and bring down more firepower.

None of the above applies to a war against the insurgent. First of all, the conventional army has to defend its rear area—its headquarters, supply depots, fuel storage, barracks, military industries, and so on. No conventional army can fight without these things. If an enemy gets through the front lines and gets into the rear and destroys these assets, it's all over for the conventional army. The insurgent rarely has a front line or industrial assets or complex logistics to defend. He'll have arms caches and headquarters— but these are normally carefully hidden and indistinguishable from any local business or farm. The insurgent's protection lies in cover and concealment and dispersion. He scatters his stock of weapons, ammunition, and explosives in numerous small caches and he expects to lose a few of them. His headquarters has basic communications equipment—perhaps just a few computers and mobile phones—things that can be spirited away or quickly destroyed if the army or police raid the building. Unlike the conventional army, the insurgent is usually in the enviable position of being able to pick and choose his battlefield and his targets. If you come down the highway with a heavily armed convoy, the insurgent will likely let you pass and wait to ambush the lightly armed supply trucks coming along an hour later—after the highway has been "cleared."

In this type of war, it's normally the insurgent who has the intelligence advantage versus the high-tech, conventional Western army. The insurgent, hidden as he is in the guise of an innocent civilian, refuses to present an easy target to the high-tech surveillance and reconnaissance assets. Moreover, he has a host of other advantages. The insurgent is on his home turf and is completely at home with the terrain, language, and local customs. If the insurgency has strong popular support, then a large part of the population becomes a direct intelligence asset. The insurgent has the opportunity to keep the military and police under constant close surveillance. Perhaps the shoeshine boy is counting vehicles and troops and providing detailed reports to local insurgent commanders on the daily routine of the military. Perhaps the local street vendor is notifying the insurgents of the route and composition of every convoy that leaves the military compound. How do you spot the sinister cell-phone conversation among the others on the street talking interminably on their cell phones to pass the time of day?

Count on the insurgent to plant sympathizers and even active agents among the local police and military forces. This means that if more than a couple of people know of an impending operation or raid by security forces, then the insurgents will probably have the plan before your own troops and will slip away or even use their intelligence to ambush you. Insurgents often operate highly effective counterintelligence programs to prevent the security forces from slipping agents and informers into their ranks. Let only a few, highly trusted colleagues know of the whereabouts of the insurgent leaders. Carry out attacks with unemployed teenagers hired by lower-level insurgent officers who simply pass out the weapons, put a few hundred dollars up front, and tell the kid to fire a few rounds at the sentry post at midnight or to set up a rocket pointed at the security forces' base and set a timer for five minutes—enough time to get away. Such rank-and-file insurgents have little idea who hired them and have almost no information to provide if captured. Finally, if the insurgents catch a government informer or agent, they can execute him and display the body in the middle of town so that everyone gets the message about what happens to informers. Insurgents only need to publicly kill a few of the population who collaborate with the government to cow the overwhelming mass of the population. Carefully applied terrorism doesn't win support for the insurgent, but it is an effective means of protecting their core fighters and ensuring that the mass of the population will be reluctant to provide any information to the government.

If the insurgents are smart, and they usually are, they can plan terrorist attacks or raids on government forces for maximum effect and maximum publicity. Bin Laden is famous for cautiously and patiently planning his attacks over a period of months or even years and then letting only a few of his closest followers know the outlines of the attack plan. In attacking the World Trade Center in September 2001, in attacking the USS *Cole* in the harbor in Aden in 2000, and in carrying out raids and attacks on U.S. troops and Iraqi security forces in Baghdad and Mosul, the terrorists and insurgents have shown a distressing tendency to find the weak spots in government or military security and effectively attack them—and it's impossible to be strong at all times and places. This intelligence superiority gives the insurgent a notable advantage and also allows him a flexibility that is denied to the government forces. It also means that a relatively small insurgent group can inflict heavy casualties and cause a great deal of mayhem.

THE AMERICAN MILITARY CULTURE AND INTELLIGENCE

In a campaign against insurgents and terrorists, the primary means of collecting intelligence is through direct contact with people—in military terminology called "human intelligence" or simply HUMINT. The vast array of high-tech and high-cost intelligence assets possessed by the United States, such as our space surveillance capabilities, are of marginal use against insurgents. Unfortunately, for more than a generation, the U.S. government and military emphasized building a high-tech intelligence system geared for the

Cold War and largely ignored the requirements for HUMINT. Now, fifteen years after the collapse of Communism in Eastern Europe we are still putting the budget dollars and primary effort into intelligence collection systems and failing to adequately address the deficiencies of decades of neglect of human intelligence. If anything can cause America to fail in the Global War on Terror, the lack of effective HUMINT is it.

The U.S. military went into Iraq in early 2003 supported by superb high-tech intelligence assets useful for finding and targeting conventional military forces. However, even improved high-tech assets did not live up to the breathless expectations of the post–Gulf War I era when it was predicted that commanders would soon have a near-perfect vision of the enemy forces and that commanders at all levels would be networked together and have immediate access to all information and imagery about his immediate battle zone and a broad area around it. Although hundreds of space vehicles, aircraft, and drones hovered over Iraq with an impressive array of motion and heat sensors, and U.S. forward commanders and intelligence units networked together, some of the units at the tip of the spear advanced blind with no information on the Iraqi defenses in front of them or, even worse, of large Iraqi formations massing to attack them. One armor battalion commander recalled that his forces were repeatedly ambushed on the approaches of a vital bridge before Baghdad. "There is zero information getting to me. Someone may have known above me, but the information didn't get to me on the ground."[1] This was not an unusual occurrence in Iraq. Many army and marine commanders at the battalion level fought and moved almost blind—with little information about what was ahead of them. Indeed, this theme is repeated often in several military chat rooms where soldiers on the ground relate their experiences of the campaign. Apparently it was an old story—the higher headquarters, division and above, had a good view of the battle space and were getting good information, but disseminating the mass of imagery and information and getting it to the front commanders fighting the battle proved extremely difficult, if not impossible. Luckily, the Iraqi army was so badly trained and incompetently led that U.S. forces could still fight with an information disadvantage and win. In conventional war, a lack of a clear picture of the battlefield is inconvenient but not fatal. In counterinsurgency, the lack of a clear picture means defeat.

126

The lack of accurate human intelligence since 9/11 finds its roots in the military, more specifically the U.S. military culture. The U.S. military leadership is technologically oriented, and has been for so long, that there is very little understanding of the capabilities of, requirements for, and limits of HUMINT. High-tech intelligence has appeal for several reasons. Senior officers, mostly trained as engineers or managers, have difficulty appreciating any insights at all from the "soft" subjects such as history, sociology, or psychology. If you can give them some hard data—exact enemy locations, strength reports, and so on—they're happy. But more commonly when an intelligence analyst briefs a senior officer about an insurgency he will be dealing with estimates of political attitudes among the population, estimates of insurgent morale, and judgments about which way certain political leaders might bend. All very important stuff—but it all sounds pretty vague to an officer with engineering and management degrees. Many senior officers show open irritation at listening to what is, essentially, an interpretation based on very limited and inexact data. Contrast this with the intelligence officer who specializes in space and surveillance imagery. Unlike the HUMINT specialist, the imagery specialist can put some very impressive aerial images on the PowerPoint screen. He can pinpoint locations, houses, and vehicles while the Air Force's aerial surveillance assets such as the joint surveillance target attack radar system (JSTARS) can also track vehicles and provide precise information about movement patterns over time. This is hard, clear data—just what most senior officers are conditioned to accept. Whether it really means anything is beside the point. The HUMINT officer with his estimates and vague judgments looks pretty weak and ineffective in comparison to the intelligence office with the high-tech data.

During the Cold War, faced with Soviet numerical advantages that would have been virtually impossible to match, the U.S. military consciously decided to play on the American advantages in technology and meet the Soviet conventional force threat with smaller but technologically superior conventional forces. It was a sensible decision, and relying on technological strengths became a core part of U.S. military doctrine and personnel policy. In the mid-1980s, under General Max Thurman, the army's personnel chief, the army wanted an officer corps heavy in engineering, science, and management degrees. Thurman had an engineering degree himself and had a low opinion of officers not trained in the hard sciences. In the mid-1980s, the goal for army ROTC commissions was to have 40 percent of the new lieutenants with engineering degrees and 30 percent with management degrees. The army wanted no more than 5 percent of the new lieutenants to have degrees in the humanities or social sciences, which included history and foreign languages. ROTC scholarships, designed to attract high-quality students into the army's junior leadership ranks, were set on a strict quota with priority going to students who declared for an engineering degree (no matter that the student might have low test scores and have a mediocre academic record) and very few scholarships allocated for liberal arts majors—no matter what the student's academic performance showed.

The idea was that with a high-tech, equipment-oriented army, engineers would make the most effective warriors and commanders. There's no doubt that in some highly specialized branches of the army, notably the Engineer Corps and the Ordnance Corps, an engineering degree would be especially useful. But no one ever provided evidence that engineers made better infantry or tank platoon commanders. Looking back, it all seems somewhat absurd. If operating the latest equipment in the field required having trained engineers and scientists at the lowest level of command, then the army was in serious trouble as there would never be enough trained engineers for army needs. Although the army showed a great preference for officers with engineering and science degrees, it couldn't come close to meeting Thurman's quotas. On the other hand, the policies of the Army leadership and of the Army Personnel Command hurt the army. With 40 percent of the U.S. Army stationed overseas and any likely enemies not likely to speak English, penalizing ROTC cadets who majored in foreign languages made little sense and certainly hurt the effectiveness of the Intelligence Corps.

The preference for engineers and high-tech personnel in army policy also meant that the U.S. Army had the only Intelligence Corps of any major power that did not require its officers to speak a foreign language. Speaking foreign languages was seen as a function of enlisted men who were sent off to special language schools. From the 1980s through the 1990s and to the present, the way ahead for any career-minded officer in the intelligence branch who wanted to get to the top was to master the high-tech side of intelligence—electronic warfare, signals intelligence, imagery intelligence, and so on. People who specialized in human intelligence such as interrogation and counterintelligence operations could have a nice career, but HUMINT was basically seen as a career-killer. The army, at least, tolerated some HUMINT specialists, but intelligence in the U.S. Air Force and Navy was overwhelmingly of the high-tech variety.

Another thing that works against the United States having good human intelligence is politics. The best human intelligence comes from spies, informants, agents, and prisoners, in that order. The problem for spymasters and agents who collect intelligence is that they have to deal with a host of very shady characters, and many American politicians express a moral revulsion at the idea that the U.S. government should regularly find, seduce, exploit, blackmail, and pay large bribes to foreign officials and even criminal types to get good information. There's an old American tradition that our nation, with its idealistic traditions, ought not to do that kind of thing—the kind of behavior that ought to be left to dictatorships and decadent old European nations. The United States came very late to the game, taking its time setting up the spy agencies and covert operations organizations that are de rigueur for any great power. Indeed, we still tend to be very uncomfortable with the whole idea. For example, in the late 1920s when the Secretary of State found out that his department sponsored a highly successful code-breaking operation that could read the diplomatic correspondence of the Japanese—then our most probable major enemy—he disbanded the whole operation stating, "Gentlemen don't read other gentlemen's mail!" It was seen as a noble act at the time, in keeping with the tradition of American idealism in foreign affairs; it also crippled U.S. intelligence efforts for several years.

Just after the Vietnam War, a similar wave of idealism swept through the U.S. Congress. Every mistake and minor abuse of the CIA and other covert intelligence agencies was magnified and held up for public hearings. As a result of the political fallout, the U.S. Congress and government gutted the human intelligence and covert operations establishment, purging a large number of highly experienced operatives. While retaining a limited spying capability, covert operations were put under close congressional oversight. This led to the deaths of some U.S. covert agents in the 1970s and 1980s, when they were publicly identified through congressional leaks. Suddenly, doing human intelligence was not only bad for your career; it was now even more dangerous. The dislike of human intelligence operations was notable in the Clinton administration in the 1990s, when the CIA was strongly rebuked for having as a paid informant a Guatemalan colonel who was suspected to be a human rights violator. When the matter was raised before Congress, regulations were passed that forbade U.S. intelligence agencies from using suspected human rights violators as paid informants. Few in the intelligence community were willing to challenge a few congressmen to point out the ridiculousness of such a policy. It's awfully hard to find officials in the third world with access to the kind of information we need who do *not* have a poor human rights record, or at least a reputation for corruption. If the United States wants to get information about money laundering, drug trafficking, and international crimes—including international terrorists—we will have to pay out some large sums to some pretty nasty people. For a good analogy, try to prosecute some Mafia family bosses while excluding all evidence from paid criminal informants or Mafia small fry who might seek a plea bargain for criminal acts in exchange for testimony.

Rather than fight the trend and take on some powerful politicians, the intelligence community simply went along and accepted the severe limitations on human intelligence and covert operations, eliminating some of our most cost-effective intelligence sources. In the great scheme of things, good spies are very cheap. In one notorious case in the 1980s, Soviet intelligence paid the Walkers, U.S. Navy communications personnel, a measly couple of million dollars in return for access to U.S. military secret communications. The damage to the United States was enormous, and it cost a few billion dollars to revamp and resecure our communications systems. Now that the Cold War is over, we have learned that a few well-placed spies in the Warsaw Pact military provided the West with Soviet war plans and accurate accounts of strategic discussions. That valuable information all came at a very low price: we needed good spymasters and we had to provide a covert means for our agents to escape when things got hot. Even multi-billion-dollar technology cannot provide this type of inside, strategic information. The only drawback is that good spies, covert agents, and competent spymasters take a long time to develop—even longer than a new technical system. When you lose a good spy or spymaster, you lose an invaluable asset. In the atmosphere of the 1970s to the 1990s, however, few people in the U.S. government were willing to stand up for human intelligence because of the bad publicity generated by operations that went wrong.

On the other hand, high-tech intelligence, while extremely expensive and often very limited as to the kind of strategic intelligence it provides, carries none of the moral baggage and consequent political fallout of the human intelligence field. In fact, the very expense of high tech is an advantage in the Washington culture. Low-cost operations don't get you much respect in Washington. Indeed, no one is going to lobby very hard for a program costing a few million dollars. But a $2 to $3 billion upgrade to a space surveillance satellite system that will only marginally improve the enormous capability we already have will attract a host of major contractors and congressmen, all pushing hard for the program. A $30 million program to train three hundred area experts and linguists at American graduate schools, however, is not likely to attract the attention of any politicians or senior defense officials.

INTELLIGENCE REQUIREMENTS FOR COUNTERINSURGENCY

In a military oriented toward conventional war, the midlevel unit intelligence officer must have a solid understanding of tactics, be able to manage a variety of technical assets, and perform a basic analysis of the enemy forces and intentions, based on a solid understanding of the enemy organization and doctrine. The Army Intelligence Corps, and intelligence officers of all the services, are well trained and qualified to perform these tasks. However, when the U.S. military is fighting terrorists or insurgents, or performing peacekeeping duties among a foreign population, intelligence officers need to be competent in a wide variety of subjects largely irrelevant to conventional war if they are to be effective.

For fighting insurgents and terrorists, the intelligence officer needs a basic understanding of the history, sociology, culture, and politics of the country in which he is operating. A basic knowledge of the local language is also important. However, it is not necessary for an intelligence officer to be expert in all the fields mentioned. There have been a few gifted renaissance warriors such as T. E. Lawrence, who was effective as an advisor and leader of insurgent forces because of his intimate knowledge of the local languages and dialects, as well as the traditions and history of the Middle East. But one cannot require or expect this level of genius to be common in the armed forces, or anywhere else for that matter. What the army can reasonably expect is that a unit intelligence officer will have enough knowledge of the local sociology, culture, and politics to be able to ask the right questions, set the right information-collection priorities, and to place the human intelligence he receives in its proper context. Almost all the vital information received about insurgents and local conditions will be colored by the social background and political allegiances of the local sources. Much of the effectiveness of intelligence is dependent upon the personality of the intelligence officer. He needs diplomatic skills and the patience to develop relationships with local leaders, indigenous military, and police. Yet even the most capable intelligence officer needs time to build up an accurate intelligence picture of the local area of operations to effectively serve the unit and commander. One of the first requirements is to collect as broad and accurate a database on the local region as possible, including population, social, economic, and political profiles. This database must be constantly collected and updated. At the same time, the intelligence officer has to develop his personal relationships with local figures. In time—maybe a few weeks, maybe months—a good intelligence officer will be able to assess the reliability of information that he gets from local figures and indigenous forces.

In this situation, intelligence is truly an art rather than a science. U.S. intelligence officers, used to operating in a Cold War/NATO environment and trained to operate for the NATO-type war, have little reason to question the accuracy or credibility of intelligence that comes from Western European armed forces or police. In my own experience operating with British and German forces and coordinating with European police forces, I have found that you can normally expect a high degree of professionalism from the armed forces and security forces of the Western nations. They are usually as good as the American professionals and often better. On the other hand, information provided by third world security and military forces ranges from highly accurate to utterly unreliable—with the "unreliable" being the most common description. Even in third world countries with something of a professional military tradition, the politicization of the military and police forces can be quite extreme, and intelligence and information from those sources liable to be colored by very specific party, group, and faction agendas. This is where the art of intelligence analysis comes into play. Intelligence officers need to have enough knowledge of the local and national politics to recognize the biases of the sources and weigh the information accordingly. To do this well depends partly on the natural ability of the intelligence officer, and partly on his training and education. It's largely a matter of experience. Some people have a knack for high-tech intelligence, and others for human intelligence. Both types are needed in the intelligence community, and intelligence personnel ought to be identified for one track or the other early in their careers and allowed to operate primarily in their specialty. Unfortunately for the U.S. military today, the human side of intelligence has been so undervalued for so long, there is a serious shortage of specialists in tactical and human intelligence with the necessary degree of training, skill, and experience to meet the demands of fighting insurgents or terrorists on the ground.

As an army intelligence officer in Honduras in the 1980s, I witnessed several serious problems with our military intelligence collection and analysis system at that time. All the same problems were evident in Iraq almost twenty years later, with lethal consequences for U.S. soldiers. In the 1980s, as intelligence officer for a 1,100-man task force building roads and carrying out construction programs in the hinterlands of Honduras, my primary concern, and that of U.S. forces operating in the country, was the terrorist threat posed by extreme leftist groups (which was, thankfully, fairly low). I worked with, and came to appreciate, some of the officers of the regular Honduran army and police. Some were very bright and highly professional, and could be relied on to provide a very accurate assessment of the local politics as well as the threat posed by extremist groups. In contrast, most of the information and analysis provided by officers connected with the Honduran military intelligence corps, or intelligence that originated with the special intelligence branch of the national police, was thoroughly and consistently unreliable. To a degree far greater than the regular armed forces or police, the Honduran intelligence agencies were highly politicized, and all information from those sources had to be weighed against the political agendas of those services. Indeed, they routinely inflated some threats to justify their own power in the government and to justify the dirty tactics they employed against domestic enemies.

All of the incoming information had to be evaluated against our own data and understood in the context of the local and national political scene. I acquired some understanding of these things by subscribing to all four of the national newspapers (I paid out of my own pocket—the army doesn't provide funds for anything as basic and sensible as this) and talked a good deal with local leaders and the Hondurans working with us. Many of the Hondurans frankly discussed the local and national political scene and provided a far more accurate picture of conditions than the Honduran intelligence. In time I was able to provide my unit with a fairly accurate assessment of the local threat. However, any effectiveness I had as an intelligence officer came largely from my age and experience. I had worked with German police and intelligence experts on terrorism issues for a couple of years as a junior officer and, as a captain in my thirties, I had enough education and on-the-job experience to understand how to analyze human intelligence information in circumstances where the threat was an unconventional one (terrorists and insurgents).

Most U.S. military intelligence personnel in Central America in the 1980s were far too inexperienced and poorly trained to be effective in collecting and analyzing human intelligence. The soldiers at the core of the collection effort were usually junior NCOs or warrant officers in the counterintelligence branch. They were very bright, for high test scores are required to enter the intelligence field. Most had been to language school and could speak passable Spanish. However, they lacked operational experience and had little preparation in the culture and politics of Honduras and Central America. Some were incredibly ignorant of the Honduran social and political scene. Well out of their depth, they relied on information and analysis from the Honduran intelligence agencies—the same groups that I (and most Hondurans) found utterly unreliable because of their highly political agenda and reputation for corruption.[2] In short, the analysis coming from our own intelligence services was consistently poor—something that ought to have been expected from young, inexperienced, and low-ranking personnel, sent to a region with little background training.

Some of the senior officers in the intelligence chain ought to have quickly spotted the problems, but the mid- to higher-level intelligence officers were usually specialists in the technical side of intelligence and didn't have sufficient understanding of human intelligence to correct the deficiencies of their own personnel. When the information and analysis of the counterintelligence personnel were criticized, the natural reaction of the regional senior intelligence officers, in the tradition of the military bureaucrat, was to circle the wagons and deny any failings in the competence and training of their subordinates. This was routine in the 1970s and 1980s army, in which "zero defects" was an official slogan. Problems were meant to be ignored, covered up, or explained away. Rather than recognizing systemic problems and trying to correct them, it was more practical to avoid bureaucratic battles and simply develop ways to work around a badly functioning intelligence system. We could do that and get away with it in Honduras because the threat wasn't high—but the consistent failure of the military to correct such basic deficiencies in its HUMINT personnel has proved to be much more lethal in Afghanistan and Iraq.

TACTICAL INTELLIGENCE IN AFGHANISTAN AND IRAQ

Since the Vietnam War, the U.S. military has emphasized technical intelligence at the expense of human intelligence. What had been the weakest part of our military intelligence system during the Cold War was weakened further in the post–Cold War cutbacks of the 1990s. HUMINT took the brunt of personnel and funding cutbacks. By 1997, in fact, more than 70 percent of the army's human intelligence capability had been moved into the reserve forces, or eliminated entirely.[3] One area of human intelligence especially hard hit by cuts was the small corps of trained interrogators. At the start of the Afghanistan war, the entire U.S. Army—including the active forces, National Guard, and Army Reserve—had only 510 trained interrogators, and only 108 of these spoke Arabic.[4] It's interesting to contrast the treatment that high-tech intelligence received during the 1990s. Certain sectors of the intelligence community, such as space surveillance, saw increased funding and manning in the 1990s. The air force added brand-new units to manage space assets, with mostly intelligence duties, to its force structure in the wake of the Gulf War. The human intelligence assets that were cut actually cost the services very little, only a small fraction of the high-tech assets. But HUMINT requires a high degree of training and, once these units are eliminated, they are far harder to reconstitute and replace than equipment. However, under heavy pressure from the president and Congress to cut the budget in the 1990s, the weak HUMINT structure was further gutted for minuscule budget gains, while the high-tech intelligence budget was carefully protected.

We are paying a high price today for the failure—over three decades—of the senior military leaders to understand the value of human intelligence. The ongoing campaigns in Afghanistan and Iraq prove that basic human intelligence is now one of the weakest parts of the U.S. military force structure and operational effectiveness. A blunt report by the U.S. Army Center for Lessons Learned in October 2003 assessed the effectiveness of U.S. tactical intelligence operations in Afghanistan and Iraq. The report showed that deficiencies in the military HUMINT organization, most of which were clearly evident in the 1980s, were seriously undercutting our efforts to fight insurgents in Afghanistan and Iraq. The report further noted that junior intelligence officers and NCOs were poorly prepared to carry out HUMINT operations and that many had "very little or no analytical skills." Civil Affairs and Psychological Operations reserve troops deployed to Afghanistan had only "marginally effective" training before deployment, even though the mission had been going on for more than a year and a half.[5] The report identified a shortage of HUMINT specialists in Iraq. While sixty-nine tactical teams were deployed by the summer of 2003, there was a requirement for at least fifteen more. Moreover, the intelligence teams that were deployed worked inefficiently. With sixty-nine teams operating in the country, the HUMINT Operations Cell expected at least 120 intelligence information reports daily. Instead, they received an average of only 30 reports a day. The problem was mainly rooted in the inexperience and junior rank of the soldiers manning the intelligence analysis effort. The army report noted that the intelligence operational management teams and the HUMINT operations cell at higher headquarters were both manned by relatively inexperienced junior warrant officers and NCOs. The army assessment team pointed out the obvious: that more senior, and experienced, intelligence operators were needed to make the system work effectively.[6]

The 3rd Infantry Division—the unit that took Baghdad in April 2003—reported that a lack of trained HUMINT personnel was a serious problem in conducting the combat operations in Iraq, especially in the attempt to establish order in Iraq at the end of the war. A year before the Iraq War, when it was clear that war was likely, the division staff had argued that the recent Bosnia and Kosovo experience had proven a clear need for a much larger military intelligence HUMINT staff and for a new staff position, chief of counterintelligence. Despite the request for additional HUMINT personnel, the division's 103rd Military Intelligence Battalion received only partial personnel augmentation shortly before the campaign commenced.[7] The lack of trained HUMINT personnel meant the division in the thick of the fight lacked the capability to man a prisoner of war cage, to "surge collection" (have full intelligence manning for periods of high-intensity operations), or "provide experienced and comprehensive analysis and guidance to operational teams."[8]

Another problem noted in reports from Afghanistan and Iraq has been the poor flow of intelligence information between units and down through the chain of command. One cause lies in technical glitches. The computer nets and communication systems did not work as well as advertised, and these took a long time to sort out. However, the major fault lies with the intelligence culture itself. Knowledge is power, and since the early days of the Cold War, the national and service intelligence agencies have been reluctant to share information. This is generally rooted in the desire to underscore the importance of their own agencies and budget needs, as well as to prevent other agencies from taking credit for intelligence coups. The failure of U.S. intelligence agencies to spot the terrorist threat to America before September 11, 2001, revealed the lack of intelligence or information sharing between federal agencies. As Bill Gertz has outlined in his book *Breakdown*, policy and regulations before 9/11 actually forbade the FBI from sharing information with the CIA, customs agents, and immigration officials in order to coordinate operations. Some of the legal and bureaucratic hurdles that prevent agencies from talking to each other are slowly (very slowly) being addressed. However, the problem of information and intelligence sharing is rooted more in the bureaucratic culture and politics of the armed forces than in legal restrictions. One consistent complaint from the troops in the field is that high-priority or national intelligence assets—the most prestigious intelligence operators—are reluctant to share any of their information with the lowly units in the field. General Franks, who served as the CENTCOM commander and led the U.S. forces through the 2001 Afghanistan campaign and the 2003 Iraq campaign, noted that White House counterterrorism czar Richard Clarke had never provided him with "a single page of actionable intelligence" and had engaged mostly in wishful thinking as his contribution to the war on Middle East terrorist groups.[9] Information is collected by field units and tactical intelligence officers and sent up the chain of command, but little comes down from the top in the form of feedback. As a result, the units who do the grunt work of collecting information have no idea whether their effort is effective, or even useful. In Iraq, one complaint about the army's notorious intelligence interrogation center at Abu Graibh made by the units in the field was that the special interrogation center became a kind of "black hole" for prisoners and information. One army intelligence officer in Iraq commented, "Most of our useful intelligence came from battlefield interrogations, and at the battalion, brigade, and division-level interrogation facilities." The intelligence officer went on to say that once prisoners were sent on to Abu Graibh, "We got very little feedback."[10] Indeed, the most important intelligence success in Iraq—the capture of Saddam in a rural hideout in December 2003—was based on intelligence sources developed outside the special Abu Graibh Center.[11]

The failure to establish an intelligence feedback loop flowing from the top to the lower echelons was also a common complaint in Vietnam, and the situation is not much better today.[12] Withholding information might seem sensible for large-scale, high-intensity conventional war operations, in which the higher headquarters would not want to overload the tactical units with extraneous intelligence in the middle of a battle. Information overload is something to think about in the middle of intense campaigns. But for the day-to-day work of controlling a country, suppressing an insurgency, or carrying out small-unit combat operations, such concerns about information overload do not apply. In the lower-intensity forms of combat, the main problem is finding the enemy. If you know with some certainty where the enemy is, defeating him in battle will not be the major problem for a highly trained and well-equipped conventional army. Therefore, you need as much information as you can possibly get. If a unit is constantly sending information, documents, and prisoners to higher-level intelligence units, but getting no feedback regarding the usefulness of their information or prisoners, they will have little incentive to continue passing information up the chain. At the very least, such a system encourages a spirit of distrust among the units and higher staffs. At its worst, tactical units develop an active dislike and mistrust for military intelligence personnel.

The most basic intelligence deficiency for the wars in Afghanistan and Iraq has been a shortage of linguists. When it comes to providing language-qualified personnel to carry out intelligence, civil affairs, psychological operations, or liaison with foreign forces and governments, the U.S. military leadership solemnly says one thing but does very much the opposite. The need to have military personnel available who can speak the languages and dialects of the third world regions that are the focal point for the Global War on Terror ought to be fairly obvious. Numerous recent strategic and armed forces policy documents have stressed the importance of linguists in the armed forces and the need for a broad range of language capabilities.[13] The reality on the ground, and in budgeting for the force structure, demonstrates a very different picture of the DOD and armed services' true priorities for providing adequate linguist support to the troops on the ground. Public statements by service chiefs on the importance of language-trained personnel have not translated into actual funding support, and a large percentage of the stated linguist requirements remain unfunded to this day.[14] Beyond the very small base of soldiers in 2001 who were capable of speaking Arabic, Pushtun, Tagalog, and other languages of regions where we are conducting active operations, there has been only very limited progress in increasing linguist support or in adding linguist positions to the military force structure. Yet the demand for more linguists has been a feature of virtually every after-action report coming out of the combat zones.[15]

The military could be excused for underestimating the need for qualified linguists before September 11, 2001. But four years after the start of the Global War on Terror, the military has yet to realistically assess its language requirements or modify its force structure. It's a superb example of the power of bureaucratic inertia in the DOD and in the armed services. One might expect to find some dramatic expansion of language training within the reserve forces, but that is not the case. Before 9/11, the U.S. Army National Guard's 300th Military Intelligence Brigade was the only operational unit in the DOD where linguists were concentrated in large numbers. That is still the case today.[16]

The U.S. military's persistent shortage of qualified linguists for intelligence, civil affairs, and liaison support illustrates the military's cultural attitude toward liberal arts skills versus technology skills. The situation is deeply rooted in the military personnel system in which speaking a foreign language fluently is considered a skill for low-ranking personnel, undeserving of significant extra pay, bonuses, or rapid promotion opportunities. Trained army linguists complain they spend more time sweeping the motor pool than honing their skills. The reenlistment rate for linguists is low, as one might expect.[17] For U.S. military officers, there are few career incentives to becoming fluent in a foreign language, or serving as a foreign area officer, as opposed to serving in a technological career field. Language-qualified personnel in the reserve forces have to spend a great deal of their own time and money, to study in their free time, or take courses at a local college, if they want to stay proficient. For a high-tech warrior, the situation is completely different. Air Force pilots, for example, receive huge bonuses, accelerated promotions, and thousands of dollars in flight pay per year. To keep their proficiency high, no expense is spared for refresher training and special courses in operating new equipment. This costs billions of dollars a year—but no one questions the necessity to do this. On the other hand, to keep reserve component linguists fully proficient by paying for extra days of training, or for language courses at a nearby university, might require a few thousand dollars per soldier per year—minuscule sums compared to the money spent on technologically oriented personnel. Yet for decades before 9/11—and even since 9/11—there have been no major initiatives to solve the linguist shortage. A study of the DOD linguist programs published in late 2004 bluntly concluded, "Services do not consider language and regional expertise as critical warfighting skills."[18]

The DOD's own report has pointed out that the DOD currently lacks a coherent system to identify and track linguists through the personnel system. Each service has a different way to identify and track linguists, and no comprehensive oversight of linguists exists in the personnel system. Language skills are immediately transferable to other services and, theoretically, if the army had a dire shortage of linguists, navy linguists could easily be loaned to the army. But under the current DOD personnel system this is not easily possible.

The current fix to the linguist shortage has been to hire large numbers of linguists on contract to serve with the U.S. forces in Iraq and support intelligence and civil affairs operations. This is in keeping with the DOD's consistent policy of no significant increases in the personnel strengths of the armed forces, even in wartime. While programs to hire contract linguists in low-risk peacekeeping operations, such as Bosnia, have worked adequately, accounts of operations in high-risk combat zones such as Afghanistan and Iraq indicate that the practice of using contract linguists is not working well. First of all, contract civilian linguists are just that—civilians. Many of the contract linguists hired to support army intelligence operations in Iraq were unwilling to endure the hardships of war and did what civilians have a right to do: they quit. In other cases, the contract linguists were poorly qualified to support military operations. Many of the military contract linguists were immigrants with low-paying jobs and poor educational levels, lured into a contract for $100,000 a year pay—a far higher salary than a language-qualified U.S. lieutenant colonel. However, intelligence and interrogation work requires a specialized military vocabulary, and many of the civilian linguists have had difficulty dealing with this. There have been other problems with hiring local people as interpreters. In Iraq, many were forced to quit due to terrorist threats to themselves and their families if they continued working for the Americans.[19] Finally, there is a well-grounded suspicion that some locally hired interpreters are insurgent spies. Their position in the middle of a U.S. headquarters provides the insurgents with superb intelligence. For this reason, local contract civilians have only limited use because they can only be assigned to the lowest-level unclassified liaison duties, and cannot be permitted to translate any intelligence material or operational documents. To use contract civilians in classified work requires a lengthy and complicated security clearance process. Currently, there is a backlog of personnel security investigations in the DOD (482,000 waiting for DOD security checks in August 2004) and other agencies, and eight months is needed before a basic clearance can be granted to a civilian.[20] Of course, military personnel already have clearances and undergo security checks as a routine part of their military service—another argument for preferring military personnel as linguists.

THE ARCANE ART OF INTERROGATION

The stories about widespread torture and abuse at the U.S. military interrogation center in Iraq that appeared in 2004 were a shock, but should not have been a surprise to anyone familiar with the history of counterinsurgency. Few experiences upset and frustrate a conventionally oriented army more than to find itself in the middle of a war in which the enemy wears civilian clothes and might be friendly one moment and shoot soldiers in the back the next. Insurgents commonly use terrorism as a primary tactic, and attack not only soldiers. The soldier sees the carnage or the insurgent's handiwork—the women and children blown up by a randomly placed bomb. He is likely to see his comrades not just killed, but mutilated if their bodies fall into insurgent hands. The moral instinct of the soldier is to show no mercy to the merciless. Granting the insurgent the same rights and privileges as a soldier, honorably captured in war, goes against the soldier's sense of justice. So, when a Western army is confronted with this situation, somewhere in the force a breakdown of discipline will occur, and soldiers will abuse and torture prisoners in an attempt to break the insurgency by the most rapid means possible. From the viewpoint of military psychology, it's an understandable phenomenon—but one that senior officers must guard against, lest a breakdown in discipline affect the whole force. Whatever useful information might accrue from the torture and abuse of suspects is more than canceled out by the inevitable leak of the stories, and the tremendous propaganda value that the insurgents get from being able to honestly characterize their foreign enemies as barbarians and hypocrites.

The problem of abusing prisoners and detainees in counterinsurgency operations is certainly not limited to the U.S. military or to recent Middle Eastern operations. In the confusion and frustration of fighting an enemy who wears civilian clothing and uses terrorism as a primary tactic, discipline will break down even in well-led and well-trained professional armies. There were several prisoner torture and abuse scandals in the British army and security forces during the Malayan emergency of the 1940s, especially in the early stages of the conflict.[21] The early stages of the Mau Mau rebellion in Kenya in the 1950s also saw numerous incidents of abuse and cruelty toward detainees and prisoners carried out by British army and local security units. Some of the British army units committed crimes, including murder, against suspected IRA sympathizers in Northern Ireland in the 1970s. In Iraq in 2003 and 2004, there were incidents of prisoner abuse that led to the arrest and trial of several British soldiers. For the French Army in Algeria in 1954 to 1962, torture and abuse of prisoners and civilians was not confined to a few isolated units or explained by any local breakdown in discipline. In Algeria, it became a standard policy of the French Army to torture and murder people suspected of membership in the National Liberation Front (FLN, from the French *Front de Libération Nationale*) insurgent bands. Human rights abuses were widespread, and were carried out through the entire period of the counterinsurgency campaign, although some French commanders and units resisted the practice.

The most serious human rights abuses by the U.S. Army in Iraq occurred at Abu Graibh prison, which also served as a special interrogation center for suspected terrorists and insurgents. The abuse and torture were originally documented in an investigation by U.S. Army Major General Antonio Taguba, and led to the court-martial and conviction of several soldiers, the relief and reprimand of several senior officers, and a series of ongoing trials for U.S. personnel stationed at Abu Graibh prison.[22] According to statements from many of the soldiers stationed at Abu Graibh, the justification for the abuse and torture of prisoners was to assist in the interrogation of insurgent suspects carried out by military intelligence personnel. According to some of the military police guards who participated in the abuse, torture of prisoners was encouraged by some of the intelligence personnel as a means of "softening them up" so they would talk freely for the interrogators.[23] Ironically, torture of suspects did not lead to any useful intelligence information being extracted. The abusers couldn't even use the old "means justifies the end" argument because, in the end, there was nothing to show but a tremendous propaganda defeat for the United States and a specific incitement of the insurgents to carry out a spate of kidnappings, brutal murders, and terrorist acts as "retaliation" for the crimes committed against Iraqis.

The prisoner abuse scandal is partly the result of the poor state of training for the military police and military intelligence personnel involved in prisoner handling and interrogation. The 800th Military Police Brigade and some of its battalion cited in the abuse scandal were National Guard units that had been poorly prepared for the Iraq mission. Many of the soldiers did not even know the basic procedures for the proper handling of prisoners, nor did the brigade commander make a serious effort to improve the training level of her military police when they did arrive in the country. Several officers I know saw the 800th MP Brigade in action when they were first deployed in Iraq, and told me it had a reputation as a poorly disciplined "bad unit." For example, after the fall of Baghdad the main job of the brigade was to hold and process a large number of Iraqi army prisoners. These men had surrendered willingly, were out of the war, and posed no threat to Coalition forces. Indeed, many if not most of them would have willingly worked with the Coalition in rebuilding the country. In the opinion of my colleagues, these military police treated the Iraqi prisoners with unnecessary harshness, making them sit or squat in the sun for long periods and holding them under strict guard routines. Since most of these prisoners were soon released, it is likely that some of them joined the insurgency, as their first direct contact with the Americans had been so decidedly unpleasant.

Another major cause for the torture scandals seems to have been the poor standard of training of the military intelligence personnel. The director of the Joint Interrogation and Debriefing Center at Abu Graibh, Lieutenant Colonel Steven Jordan, was a military intelligence officer with no training or background in interrogation. Due to the shortage of trained HUMINT personnel in the armed forces, the army deployed a variety of civilian contract personnel for very sensitive positions as interpreters and interrogators at Abu Graibh. Two civilian contractors, an interrogator and an interpreter, were specifically cited in the Taguba report of April 2004. Apparently, with no one at the top who understood the art of interrogation and some of the contractors unqualified for the job—one contractor didn't even have a security clearance—discipline and normal procedures broke down.

Iraq is not the only place where a connection can be made between poor intelligence collection and contract interrogators and interpreters. In a frantic search to find intelligence personnel for the interrogation and detention center in Guantanamo, the U.S. Southern Command contracted with an information technology company in 2002 to provide interpreters and interrogators—although the company (CACI) had no experience whatsoever in recruiting, evaluating, or training such personnel. The military is now evaluating whether the civilian contractors were able to do the job. Surprisingly, the government told the company that it would NOT be barred from further government contracts.[24] Apparently, the interpreter and interrogator shortage in the armed forces is so extreme that even companies with no expertise are kept on the approved contractor list. Without its own interpreters and trained interrogators, the army has to take whatever contract people come along, and pay top dollar for them.

What military intelligence specialists have known for many years is that abusing prisoners rarely gets you good information, as people under torture usually tell the interrogator what the interrogator wants to hear. Moreover, the negative aspects—such as a propaganda coup for the enemy, generating mistrust in the populace, and making prisoners more hostile—outweigh any positive aspects, such as ending the conflict quickly by a brilliant intelligence coup. Few prisoners know anything of immediate and decisive value, such as ongoing plans for major attacks or the location of major insurgent figures. Still, under the hands of a skilled interrogator, prisoners and detainees can yield bits of useful information that, in themselves, are not of great import but, when added to many other bits of information such as other interrogation reports, captured documents, and police records, they can build a comprehensive picture of enemy organization, tactics, training, and intentions.

A legendary Marine Corps intelligence officer of World War II, Major Sherwood Moran, in a 1943 memo for other interrogators, outlined the highly successful interrogation techniques he used to get Japanese prisoners taken on Guadalcanal to provide information to their captors. His memo is divided into two sections: the attitude of the interrogator toward his prisoner and the interrogator's knowledge and use of the language. First of all, the prisoner was removed to a safe location, away from the front lines, in order to make it clear that the war was over for the prisoner. Once away from the battle, the interrogator would get the best results by treating the prisoner humanely—making sure he was fed, had wounds treated, and was treated with sympathy. At this point, the interrogator was to interview the prisoner. Ideally, the interrogator should not only be fluent in the prisoner's language but also should know a great deal about the prisoner's country and culture. Moran himself had lived in Japan and was fluent in Japanese. The interrogator was to develop a friendly approach while conversing with the prisoner, then proceed to talk about the current conflict, and the prisoner's recent experiences. Most people—especially soldiers recently in battle—have a story to tell and desperately want to tell their story, but need a sympathetic audience—and that the interrogator provides. Given the well-deserved Japanese reputation for toughness and fanaticism, many marines were surprised that Moran was able to get Japanese prisoners to talk at length about their experiences, gleaning a great deal of valuable information for the intelligence analysts, without using strong-arm methods.[25] One advantage for the marine and army interrogators in the Pacific War was that the Japanese soldiers were completely untrained in what to do if they were ever taken prisoner, for the Japanese military simply assumed that no soldier would ever permit such a thing. Well-trained interrogators, fluent in Japanese, were able to rapidly exploit the prisoner's psychological vulnerability—and no torture was required. U.S. Marine Corps interrogators, trained in an intensive one-year language course that included a great deal of Japanese culture, proved to be exceptionally effective intelligence gatherers in the great island battles of 1944 to 1945. Marine interrogators were deployed to the Marianas in June 1944, and through prisoner interrogation, were able to provide their commanders with the complete Japanese order of battle within forty-eight hours of landing on Saipan and Tinian.

The United States has not been the only nation to use the sympathetic approach to prisoner interrogation with great success. One of the "cult books" for intelligence officers is the story of Hans-Joachim Scharff, one of Germany's expert interrogators, who specialized in interrogating captured American and British pilots during World War II. Scharff, a *Luftwaffe* NCO, had lived in South Africa before the war and was exceptionally fluent in English. He treated recently downed airmen in a friendly, straightforward manner and, due to his warm personality, got them to converse. Armed with extensive cross-referenced material from other interrogations and captured documents, as well as the known details of the pilot's shootdown, Scharff would take the "we already know everything approach" and tell the pilot about his unit, his recent deployment, and recent operations. Although the pilots had been trained to avoid discussing anything of value if captured, they found themselves telling their story to Scharff. In this manner, Scharff was able to pick up bits of information—the range of fighter fuel tanks, standard formation procedures, and so on—which, when added to the rest of the data base, provided the German fighter and flak force with valuable tips on opposing the Allies in the air.[26]

Many HUMINT specialists know this approach to interrogation still provides highly useful and accurate intelligence. In the recent campaigns in Afghanistan and Iraq, our intelligence personnel have noted that the Taliban militia fighters and the Iraqi insurgents are good subjects for classic, sympathetic interrogation techniques because they have no training on how to behave if captured. Captured al Qaeda fighters or foreign members of radical Islamic factions that have infiltrated Iraq have proved to be a different matter. Not only are such opponents ideologically committed because of years of intensive indoctrination in radical Islamic schools, they also tend to have a high degree of special training in tactics and terrorism, as well as special training on how to resist interrogation if captured.[27] Al Qaeda even developed a sixty-page special training manual describing all the tricks and procedures of interrogators and circulated it among their fighters.[28] One of the endless frustrations for American intelligence officers since 9/11 has been the inability to get many of the highly trained al Qaeda fighters to talk. When dealing with well-trained and well-prepared members of international terrorist groups, one of the most useful interrogation techniques is the same approach the FBI uses to get lower-level Mafia figures to testify against the big shots: threaten a long prison term or even the death penalty for prisoners against whom there is a clear material case—taken in arms while fighting the government or clearly implicated by captured documents—and then offer to reduce the sentence or drop charges based on the degree that the prisoner is willing to provide information.

The Geneva Convention clearly states that POW status is not granted to insurgents who are not members of recognized national armed forces, and who do not fight in uniform. While the Geneva Convention and other international protocols require that prisoners be treated humanely and fed, given medical care, and so on, international law also clearly allows terrorists and insurgents to be treated as criminals, and subject to trial and punishment for criminal acts. Membership in a terrorist organization, murder, terrorism against civilians, and attacks on the police or military are criminal acts. What is necessary in an insurgency is to ensure that military tribunal systems or local special courts are set up by the local government, with American and Western assistance, that provide a rapid and fair means of trying, convicting, and punishing members of terrorist groups. Such special courts would provide for counsel and allow the prisoner to speak in his own defense. However, various special procedures can be allowed due to the nature of terrorism and the need to protect the members of the court from retaliation. Courts could consist of three to five judges in closed session, with procedures to classify some evidence and proceedings if necessary. The identities of the special court judges would not be released to the public to prevent terrorist retaliation against them and their families. What is important is that the courts have credibility with the populace, and are able to act swiftly to convict prisoners against whom there is clear evidence of participation in terrorist acts. The special courts should be able to sentence convicted terrorists to twenty to thirty years of imprisonment, and even issue a death penalty in the case of captured terrorist leaders. The special court judgments and sentences should be imposed quickly and given full publicity. Once word gets out of the government's hard-line policy of treating insurgents as criminals, the job of the interrogator becomes much easier. Imagine a twenty-year-old insurgent, taken in arms and brought to the interrogation center. He may be highly committed to the cause, and even well trained in what to do if captured. However, he will also be upset at the probability of spending the rest of his life in a criminal prison. The interrogator, using the sympathetic approach, offers a plea bargain in which the prisoner might spend only a few months in detention rather than thirty years in a criminal prison, but only if the prisoner cooperates fully with the interrogator and provides a full account of his insurgent group and cell. Some of the insurgents might be strong-willed enough to refuse to cooperate, but many will cooperate if faced with a sufficiently dire alternative.

ORGANIZING THE INTELLIGENCE EFFORT

General Frank Kitson, a British counterinsurgency specialist who served in Malaya, Kenya, and Northern Ireland, advised that no single interrogation could be expected to provide the intelligence coup leading to the capture of the insurgent high command or some other dramatic event. Even the best interrogations might add just bits of data to a large database. The important consideration at every level is that the military intelligence and police build up a comprehensive data base, and be able to cross-reference material about local businesses, local family relationships, political groups, and suspected insurgent supporters with the bits of information provided by interrogations, captured documents, or conversations soldiers have with local civilians on patrol. The most serious intelligence problem early in most insurgencies is the lack of an accurate database, as well as the lack of cooperation and coordination between intelligence agencies, government agencies, military, and police. Developing a comprehensive database and establishing effective interagency cooperation normally requires a great deal of time. Patience is therefore one of the traits required of any intelligence officer or commander who has to fight insurgents. Unfortunately, there are no quick fixes to intelligence collection and analysis, although creating an effective organization for handling information can speed up the process considerably.

Problems in developing an effective information and intelligence gathering and analysis effort seem to be almost universal for conventional armed forces faced with fighting an insurgency. In Malaya in the first years of the insurgency, the police and military had little data to work with. Moreover, the police and military forces were reluctant to share what little information and intelligence they did have. Eventually, the British worked out an effective system in which police and military intelligence personnel colocated their operations, coordinating their collection and analysis at every level.

When Rhodesia was first faced with an insurgency in the late 1960s, the police and the military again went their separate ways for the first few years. When the Rhodesians finally created a joint intelligence center in 1973 to serve as a clearinghouse for information and intelligence from all sources, the effectiveness of the military and security forces in combating insurgents increased significantly and immediately.[29] When insurgency exploded in El Salvador in 1980, there was no tradition of military services and the police cooperating in intelligence collecting or military operations. From 1981 to 1985, the government campaign against the insurgents proceeded slowly, with few successes and numerous setbacks. With American advice the Salvadoran security forces set up a joint intelligence center in 1986.[30] In addition to improved training for the police and security forces, the establishment of a joint intelligence center as a clearinghouse for intelligence collection and analysis provided much better support to the planning and operations staff, and can be credited with a notable turnaround in the success of the government's anti-insurgent campaign.

The British counterinsurgency campaign in Malaya is a useful model for establishing effective intelligence coordination to fight a third world insurgency.[31] For the first two years of the conflict, 1948 to 1950, the government effort against the insurgents muddled along with little focus or direction. The police, largely disbanded during the 1941 to 1945 Japanese occupation, were still rebuilding and lacked any comprehensive database on the local population. With minimal training in managing intelligence, the police had little idea of how to use the information they did have. There was no tradition or clear procedure for sharing information and intelligence with the military, so the military reinforcements that poured into the country operated almost blind at first. Whatever cooperation existed between military and police was informal, and any information sharing occurred at the initiative of individuals in the police forces.[32] Knowing that the Communist guerrillas had numerous base camps in the deep jungles of Malaya, the army attempted grand, battalion-sized sweeps of the areas where there was insurgent activity. These big sweeps, conducted by soldiers poorly trained in jungle warfare and with little knowledge of how to deal with the local population, yielded few contacts with the enemy and few results. The rebels were highly mobile; when rebel camps were found by the army, they were usually found abandoned by the rebels who had been alerted to the clumsy army way of operating.[33] Operating in small bands, the rebels were able to routinely strike at weakly defended targets such as rail lines and tin mines. Many of the insurgents could operate with relative impunity in the towns, carrying out an assassination program for civilians who were known as supporters of the British/Malayan government. This, in turn, intimidated local civilians and kept them from providing information to the security forces.

In April 1950, with little progress made in fighting the insurgents, Lieutenant General Sir Harold Briggs was appointed British military commander, and he initiated a program to establish joint military/police headquarters at every level, and made the creation of a competent police/military intelligence organization his top priority.[34] Building an effective intelligence organization went slowly, largely due to the shortage of well-trained police and intelligence personnel. To coordinate the counterinsurgency effort, a committee system was set up at the district, state, and national level. Typically, a district committee would include the local military commander, the police commander, the chief local civilian administrator, and a representative from the military intelligence. In rural areas, important members of the civilian administration, such as the district agriculture director, might be brought in. The civilian, military, and security aspects of combating insurgents were coordinated and directed together. Priorities of effort were set, and resources allocated so the police and military were given clear directions for concentrating their intelligence and security efforts. This level of guidance also provided the intelligence services with an idea of focusing their collection and interrogation efforts. Instead of the haphazard arrangements for intelligence collaboration that had existed previously, the police and military now maintained constant contact through liaison officers located at the military headquarters and police district headquarters.[35]

Central to the intelligence effort was building up a police "special branch," a small corps of the best-trained, most experienced policemen, carefully screened for loyalty and reliability. The special branch concentrated on studying and analyzing the insurgent organization. A broad range of information about the population, and about insurgents, was collected and circulated at all levels. To maintain security, however, the higher-level analysis and information, such as interrogation reports, was held closely, shared only among police commanders, the special branch, military intelligence, and senior commanders. Due to poor health, Briggs was relieved in late 1951 and Lieutenant General Gerald Templer was brought to Malaya in 1952 and given full control of both the civil administration and all military forces in Malaya. Throughout his tenure as high commissioner in Malaya (1952–1954), Templer built on the policies that General Briggs had set in motion by giving intelligence the top priority, and by stressing cooperation among police, civil administration, and military at every level. It took time for Briggs' and Templer's organization and doctrine to kick in, but by 1954 the tide had clearly turned in favor of the government, and the insurgency was in the process of being broken.

SOME LESSONS FROM PAST COUNTERINSURGENCY OPERATIONS
In almost every insurgency, one of the best intelligence sources against insurgents has been former insurgents who have "turned" and thrown in their lot with the government. No one knows the insurgent leadership, membership, organization, or tactics better than a former insurgent. Turning members of the leadership is especially valuable because it is especially demoralizing for the insurgents and lends credibility to the government forces. The U.S. forces fighting the Filipino *insurrectos* in the early 1900s made rapid progress breaking the insurgency in some provinces when they convinced some insurgent leaders to switch sides and surrender their troops and weapons. Often the ex-insurgents became some of the staunchest government supporters. The U.S. forces arranged the surrender of Juan Cailles, one of the most dangerous insurgent leaders on Luzon. Cailles was given amnesty and a large cash reward, and made a district governor. He then became one of the most pro-American of the Filipino leaders, and took to hunting down the remaining insurgents with enthusiasm.[36] In Malaya and Kenya, the British were able to convince a significant number of the insurgents to change sides and join the government forces. This played a key role in defeating both insurgencies.

Convincing insurgents to change sides requires a combination of attractive incentives to support the government, and some harsh punishments for remaining with the insurgency. Distasteful as it may be to us, an amnesty program for some insurgents and terrorists who change sides is necessary, combined with effective protection for the former insurgent's family. Cash payments—dependent on the insurgent's rank, degree of support, and value of the information he provides—are an essential part of a program to undermine the insurgents. The Marine Corps *Small Wars Manual* of 1940, built on the experience of fighting insurgents in Central America and the Caribbean in the first half of the decade, speaks matter of factly about the need for a special intelligence fund, under the control of the intelligence officer and used for paying secret agents and informers among the population and insurgents. The *Manual* warns that many agents will have their own political agenda, and are likely to provide inaccurate or highly biased information. To prevent this, "it is often advisable to pay them low regular wages and to reward them with bonuses for timely and accurate information... Liberal cash payments for information that proved correct and timely have sometimes brought excellent results."[37] Of course, agent and informer networks have to be carefully managed, and only a small number of intelligence personnel and police special branch allowed access to information about the informers and intelligence they provide. As embarrassing as this might look in the military budget, unit intelligence officers down to a fairly low level need to deploy with a cash fund, immediately available, for paying local informants and rewarding insurgents who offer to change sides. The amounts don't have to be large by U.S. standards. An immediate $200 to $300 provided to a third world person as a first payment—providing that some intelligence of real value is turned over at first as a token of good faith—combined with assurances of much larger sums for reliable and valuable intelligence, provides a far higher return for the investment than most of the high-tech intelligence gadgets currently being promoted within the defense establishment. The U.S. Marine Corps intelligence officers of the 1920s to 1930s understood this well, which is why the marines were highly effective in counterinsurgency and suffered very few casualties. However, for this approach to succeed, a corps of junior intelligence officers who understand human intelligence needs to be trained and carefully developed.

FIXING THE INTELLIGENCE SYSTEM
The first step in dealing with the intelligence requirements for fighting insurgents and terrorists is simple: significantly increase the numbers of military servicemen assigned to the human intelligence fields, and provide

for many more officers to become qualified as foreign-area experts. This should be done across all the services and new specialist HUMINT units in both the active and reserve forces established. In Iraq, the shortage of competent HUMINT personnel and interpreters has been repeatedly identified as one of the most serious obstacles to fighting the insurgency. In November 2003, while visiting the 1st Armored Division, responsible for the security of Baghdad, experienced security analyst Anthony Cordesman commented, "The unit feels that intelligence is the key to success. It was slow to organize and create suitable databases, learn how to run sources, find out what sources were reliable, and what sources work. A lack of translators and trained intelligence personnel was and is a problem."[38] It takes years to develop a properly qualified HUMINT specialist, thus a major, and permanent, expansion of our HUMINT personnel cannot wait for the usual Pentagon approach of studying the subject endlessly and fighting over budget slices. Moreover, the costs for training HUMINT operators, as opposed to high-tech intelligence personnel, are actually much lower. Contracting area studies instruction or language training to academic institutions is generally far cheaper than providing for high-tech simulations equipment or training. It is important to recognize that contracting out highly sensitive intelligence work, including interrogations, to civilians—who are likely to not have security clearances and be minimally qualified for the work, if qualified at all—is not an effective solution. The military often fails to see the future hidden costs of such quickie solutions. Not only are contractors expensive at $100,000-plus a year but, as civilians, they also need to have personal security provided by trained soldiers—thereby thinning an already thin force and taking soldiers off of direct counterinsurgency duties. If the interpreter and intelligence personnel are American military personnel, they will be armed and able to provide their own personal security. Finally, there is the psychological aspect of dealing with an insurgent or civilian. Making a "plea bargain" or amnesty deal in return for information on terrorists and insurgents will have a good deal more credibility if made with a uniformed U.S. officer than with a civilian contract employee.

Unfortunately, the need for major changes in funding for HUMINT and in providing HUMINT personnel does not seem to be getting through in a

Pentagon culture that emphasizes high-tech and rapid, decisive operations. After analyzing future requirements in the light of operations in Afghanistan in late 2001and early 2002, the initial Pentagon requests for the FY 2003 budget included $2 billion for improving satellite communications, as well as requests for numerous, expensive improvements in high-tech assets such as space-based radar and imagery systems, airborne acquisition and targeting systems, and improvements in sensors and electronic warfare assets. The acceleration of the multibillion-dollar program to build the airborne laser theater missile defense system was included as well, and increased procurement of UAVs was requested.[39] Against a laundry list of these requests, improving the HUMINT capability urgently needed by the troops on the ground amounts to small change.

There are several very effective models for building up a competent force of linguists, experts, and interrogators within the armed forces. With war looming in 1941, the U.S. Army set up the Military Intelligence Service Language School in November of that year with mostly *nisei*—first-generation Japanese-Americans—as students. While only a few of these soldiers were truly fluent in Japanese writing and speaking, most had a basic knowledge of Japanese language and culture learned from their parents and relatives. As the war raged, the need for interpreters and interrogators intensified. By cutting the language course from one year to six months, the army was able to deploy the first sixty graduates in time for the 1943 Aleutians and New Guinea campaigns. Eventually, six thousand linguists were trained by the army during the war, and they served with such effectiveness that our Allies in the Pacific clamored for U.S. language support. U.S. Army Japanese-language teams were deployed to support British, Australian, Dutch, and Chinese forces. At the end of the war, these soldiers played a major role in the occupation of Japan and deserve considerable credit for making the American occupation go quite smoothly.

The U.S. Navy and Marine Corps also had only a handful of Japanese speakers available at the start of World War II. In 1942 they set up their own Japanese/Oriental Language School in Boulder, Colorado, to train interrogators. The marines recruited a mix of students with strong language and academic skills from a broad variety of backgrounds—even waiving some of the age and physical requirements of the U.S. Marine Corps—and put them through an intensive yearlong language course taught by Japanese-Americans from California who had been interned early in the war. While only some of the students attained a high degree of fluency, it was good enough, and the graduates still functioned effectively as interrogators and interpreters throughout the Pacific Campaign.[40]

A great deal of language training can be accomplished simply through command emphasis. From 1912 to 1938, the U.S. Army stationed the 15th Infantry Regiment in China to help guard the embassy, and to protect American nationals from the almost nonstop civil wars that raged. In the 1920s, the army hired Chinese teachers and made instruction in Chinese mandatory for officers. Five hours a week were set aside for language instruction, and exams in Chinese conversation were set. Later, Chinese-language training became mandatory for the NCOs as well. Although most soldiers did not become fluent, the Americans were better at speaking Chinese than any of the other foreign nations with troops stationed there. On several occasions, the language training paid off handsomely. In 1924, small units of U.S. troops had to act as peacekeepers and diplomats as the warlord armies approached Peking, threatening to attack foreign concessions and citizens. During tense negotiations between the warlord troops and the foreign military detachments, the American officers played the key role in preserving the peace since they were the only officers of the foreign troops who could make themselves understood in Chinese.[41] In peacekeeping, insurgency, or low-level conflict, one doesn't have to be a highly fluent linguist to make a big difference. In the 15th Infantry even a very basic, and low-cost, local language program significantly enhanced the effectiveness of the U.S. troops in a dangerous situation.

Although the United States has many good venues for training military linguists and regional specialists, including top university programs and the DOD's own language school (Defense Language Institute at Monterrey California), the problem is more likely to be recruiting the right people and finding enough of them to serve as language-qualified interpreters, interrogators, and civil affairs officers. The old military intelligence culture that placed little value on language skills will have to be discarded and linguists given the same treatment as if they were technical specialists. This means a program of monthly extra pay for maintaining language proficiency—something in the $700 or so range that pilots get—and hefty special bonuses as well as an accelerated promotion program. Being a competent linguist should be a great enhancement to one's military career—not as it is today: a neutral or even negative factor.

One could reasonably argue that the U.S. Air Force could save many billions of dollars in training, personnel costs, retirement costs, and so on if it just got rid of all its transport pilots and relied on contracting transport pilots to fly its planes in wartime. After all, there is a large pool of trained, fully qualified multiengine pilots available who could be hired to support U.S. combat operations. By current DOD reasoning, contracting this mission makes perfect sense, and it has the advantage of freeing up a lot of money for space technology. Of course, if such a plan were seriously proposed, the outcry from the military would be pretty loud. The air force would point out, quite rightly, that they would not want to depend on contract personnel who might not be trained in specialized military transport operations and would be liable to walk off the job any time things became dangerous. The air force makes a huge investment in transport pilots to ensure that essential support for the combat forces is maintained in the toughest situations. Going to war without assurance that essential personnel will be available puts the national interest and the lives of our troops at stake.

The same arguments that the air force leaders would make about pilots can be made to support increasing and maintaining a large corps of HUMINT and language-qualified intelligence specialists. In short, in the case of military intelligence, we not only need more personnel and funding for HUMINT but also a cultural change in the military at the top levels, to improve the current faulty personnel system and to understand the proper role of HUMINT as well as its value and its limitations.

Fixing intelligence at the national level requires more than increasing funding and expanding the training programs. In contrast to the military's support for human intelligence, the overall support and funding for national intelligence programs in the United States is fairly strong. The question is not about spending or even personnel levels—it's whether we are getting the right kind of intelligence and analysis for all the money and effort. We should also ensure that U.S. troops who deploy to fight insurgents and terrorists have a legal apparatus available that can provide for quick trials with long and severe punishments meted out to irregular enemies who pose as civilians but are caught bearing arms or captured in combat. Having such a system in place when we go to war or intervene as part of a peacekeeping operation would be of inestimable value in getting reluctant prisoners to talk and cooperate.

When huge bureaucracies are faced with a crisis, such as the intelligence system has faced since 9/11, one of the most common responses is to reorganize. Sometimes this is the correct response. Bill Gertz, in his analysis of the intelligence failure of 9/11, makes the case that the Defense Intelligence Agency (DIA) duplicates most of the same analysis functions as the CIA and argues that its role as a national-level agency is redundant. He proposes that the DIA be dissolved, and its personnel and resources deployed in support of the major military commands.[42] Gertz further points out that the problems of poor intelligence analysis made so evident in 9/11 were much more than a problem of organizational disconnects that prevented the intelligence agencies that dealt with foreign terrorism from communicating with each other. Gertz and several other commentators have pointed out that intelligence analysis at the national level tends to be on the basis of consensus, and in reaching a bureaucratically "safe" conclusion that can be passed to the president and national civilian and military leadership.[43] Analysis that sharply dissents from that of the senior intelligence leaders is often toned down or even deleted. Dissent from the mainstream can hinder one's career in intelligence.

The Bush administration's proposal to reorganize the American intelligence system and place all the intelligence agencies under the direction of a single intelligence head, does not directly address the problem of analysis by bureaucratic consensus. It may even exacerbate the current intelligence analysis problems by placing yet another level of bureaucracy between the president and policymakers, and the professional intelligence analysts. Analysis does not necessarily get better as it is handled by more people. Indeed, a new level of bureaucracy, manned with ambitious Washington players, is likely to further slow the process of forwarding information and analysis up the chain of command, and in providing direction for the collection effort down the chain. Bill Lind, a respected writer on defense issues, has proposed that competition between agencies and sections, something now an anathema to the system, be allowed and encouraged. "The process should be reformed so that end users, policymakers, get not a single, consensus agreement, with all dissenting views sanitized, but a summary of disagreements and agreed points. The policymakers, in turn, need to be able and willing to be able to explore the disagreements themselves, rather than simply deferring to 'the experts' and their compromise consensus."[44]

Fixing the intelligence collection and analysis system for military and civilian agencies will take much more than laws, resources, or new organizations. In the end, making the system work and reforming the system will require old-fashioned leadership.

CHAPTER FIVE

WINNING HEARTS AND MINDS: THE MEDIA AND COUNTERINSURGENCY

War is a thinking man's game. A military too used to solving war-fighting problems just with technology alone should begin to realize that war must also be fought with the intellect."
—Major General Robert Scales, U.S. Army, 2004

Guerrilla war is far more intelligent than a bayonet charge.
—Colonel T. E. Lawrence, 1929

The shooting side of this business is only 25% of the trouble and the other 75% lies in getting the people of Malaya, behind us.
—General Sir Gerald Templer, 1952

The idea that an insurgency wins or loses by its ability to win the hearts and minds of the people is an old cliché. However, like so many clichés, it happens to be true. While some insurgencies might be defeated by sheer brute force, this option is ruled out by any Western democracy today on the grounds of morality and practicality. Maintaining American legitimacy while waging war, as viewed in the eyes of the world and under our own laws, requires that we adhere to the high standards of behavior demanded in the Western democratic tradition. It also makes practical sense to help allied governments fighting insurgents to win the active, or at least passive, support of the greater part of the population.

Max Manwaring, one of America's top counterinsurgency theorists, points out that in a case of revolution or revolt, the insurgents and the government have the same center of gravity: the support of the civilian population. Insurgents might carry on for a long time, but they can rarely win without the active support of at least a significant proportion of the population, and usually the neutrality of another significant portion. If a government is seen as illegitimate in the eyes of most of its own people, no matter how strong it is in military terms, it will eventually collapse. For a government to establish its legitimacy in the eyes of the people, it must be effective not only in fighting insurgents, but also in providing fair elections, competent administration, a fair justice system, and economic progress. Not only must the government do these things at least moderately well, but it must also present its case convincingly before the whole population. This requires a well-planned, fully resourced media campaign in which every form of popular and mass media is harnessed to win the support of the mass of the population. In short, an effective media campaign is central to an effective counterinsurgency strategy.

WAR AND MEDIA IN INSURGENCY—THE EARLY AMERICAN EXPERIENCE

The idea of battling for the hearts and minds of the population is nothing new. Indeed, the war for public opinion was a major factor in the American Revolution. In the 1770s, the printing press was the mass media of its day. The American patriots used the press to devastating effect, to undermine loyalist sympathy and to win support for the cause of independence. In the 1770s, America was a highly literate nation for its time and had a very active intellectual life centered around the seven universities—England, by contrast, had only two universities in 1776. In America, a variety of newspapers, journals, and pamphlets that discussed political issues sold briskly, and new systems of courier mail carried news quickly from one colony to another.[1]

One of the greatest advantages the American patriots had in mobilizing public opinion as conflict with Great Britain brewed between 1763 and 1776 was the support of the newspapers and the major centers of learning.

For a decade before the Revolution, most of the American newspapers waged a constant crusade criticizing the British government's policies concerning America. The press covered the debates and resolutions of the First Continental Congress (1774–1775) in detail. American universities became hotbeds of anti-British sentiment as student idealists, such as Columbia University's Alexander Hamilton, published essays critical of British policy in the newspapers. Pamphleteers and engravers carried on a propaganda campaign against the British Empire. Paul Revere's sensational, and highly inaccurate, print of the British soldiers shooting unarmed American civilians during the Boston massacre was widely circulated and made for superb visual propaganda. While many Americans, perhaps even a majority in 1776, did not demand independence from Britain, the Loyalist position still went largely unheard. There was little effort by the British government to meet the hostile American press with a campaign of its own, and the efforts of the few Loyalist newspapers and pamphleteers could not compare with those who favored independence. There was never any British equivalent to Thomas Paine's eloquent, impassioned argument for American independence as presented in *Common Sense*, a pamphlet printed in early 1776 and circulated not only throughout America, but also abroad. Paine followed up his brilliant revolutionary piece by publishing a journal called *The Crisis* to inspire the Continental soldiers by explaining the principles they were fighting for.

Once war began, the American colonies ruthlessly suppressed any Loyalist press or open supporters in their territory—as the Loyalists suppressed pro-American sentiments in territories under their control. Since the British controlled only that part of the population under their direct military occupation, a minority of the population, the American revolutionaries had the advantage in being able to reach a far larger audience.

The churches were very much the center of social and intellectual life in the American colonies, and many of the churches weighed in firmly and publicly in support of a war for independence. The most popular Protestant churches, especially the Presbyterians and Congregationalists, had been persecuted in Britain and had a long heritage of conflict with the British crown. When the time came to choose between Britain and independence, it was a simple choice for many of the most influential church leaders of the day. In consequence, many of the Protestant churches lent their moral authority to support the American cause.

Overseas, the leading American representative to France, Benjamin Franklin, carried on a magnificent propaganda campaign to win French support for the American cause. Franklin, as clever, sophisticated, and well educated a politician as America has ever seen, brilliantly played the role of the simple, virtuous American man of the people to adoring crowds of French aristocrats. Although personally a worldly man of fairly sophisticated tastes, Franklin eschewed the wigs, fancy clothing, and elaborate manners common to his era, visiting the French Court dressed in a simple suit, and carried on with American informality. He became the first media celebrity of his age, as his *Almanac* filled with simple American sayings was published in French and became a best seller. Simply put, to the French he personified the American spirit and skilfully maneuvered the French intellectuals and court leaders into an open alliance with America.

The American Revolution was very much a war in which the mass media of the day—the newspapers, engravings, and pamphlets—played a central role in the prosecution of the war, and in determining its outcome. During the darkest days of the American cause, the message of the Continental Congress and the advocates of independence was presented and disseminated as a means to rally the people. The media campaign in Europe waged by Franklin and the American representatives was successful in convincing the anti-British powers that not only could the Americans win the war, but that their cause was reasonable and just.

War, Media, and Insurgency in the Twentieth Century
World War I saw the evolution of large, government-sponsored propaganda campaigns, designed to influence both domestic and international opinion. Years of grueling warfare at the front and the hardship of rationing and shortages at home meant that the government of every combatant power had to pay close attention to the morale of their own civilians, as well as the morale of the enemy nations. Governments organized war information offices and generously funded programs to influence public opinion by newspapers, books, journals, posters, speeches, and patriotic rallies. Government public-relations offices worked hard to influence the public

opinion of the neutral nations. Events such as strikes by war industry workers in Britain, the widespread mutinies in the French army in 1917, and the collapse of morale on the German home front in 1918 dramatically demonstrated the power of public opinion and propaganda in warfare.

The post–World War I era saw the development of new media, especially radio broadcasting and the cinema (with sound), that were revolutionary in their ability to reach and influence mass audiences. Combining highly advanced new film and radio media with modern mass marketing revolutionized both economics and politics. Revolutionary new movements such as Communism, Fascism, and Nazism became especially adept at using the new media to propagate their ideology, both domestically and overseas. All of the dictatorial powers before World War II put significant resources into propaganda campaigns. Western democratic nations such as the United States and Great Britain, with a tradition of free press and open debate, generally disliked the idea of a government-sponsored propaganda campaign. Then the war started, and propaganda programs and the mass media were recognized by the democratic powers as yet another weapon to be employed to support the war effort. America and Britain used radio, press, and film campaigns to encourage the morale of their own people. The Allies also created media campaigns to broadcast to the citizens of occupied countries to encourage resistance movements. The Allies bombarded the soldiers and civilians of the enemy countries with leaflets and radio propaganda, as well as bombs, to undermine enemy morale. It is difficult to gauge things as amorphous as "morale," and the role of media in either supporting or undermining it. Yet, although no measurements could be made at that time, when the war ended, all the victorious powers were convinced that some of the media campaigns had worked effectively. In any case, the media campaigns had clearly been worth the money and effort devoted to them.

This new and more sophisticated understanding of the role of media and public opinion was sufficiently developed by 1945 to play an important role in the post–World War II occupation and reeducation of Germany and Japan. In the 1940s, public opinion polling had developed to the point that it could be relied upon as a fairly effective means of measuring the political and social views of a population. When the U.S. forces occupied their zone of western Germany in 1945, they brought with them a special office staffed with experts in Gallup-type public-opinion monitoring. Using the same methods and mathematical models of opinion sampling as in the United States, the occupation administration's public-opinion specialists immediately set up a program to carefully monitor German public opinion—and provided the U.S. commanders an understanding of German opinion on diverse issues such as the U.S.-imposed government reforms, the attitude of Germans on the behaviour of U.S. troops, and the public's views of the state of the economy as well as general attitudes held by the Germans toward the Americans. Throughout the American occupation of Germany, public opinion was carefully monitored by state and district and the results, which were classified, provided an exceptionally useful tool for the U.S. commanders in shaping their public-relations and media campaign, and in explaining the occupation policies in terms that the Germans would understand and support. Since the political objective of the U.S. and British occupation was to turn Germany from a totalitarian state into a democratic one, a broad media campaign was an invaluable tool for the occupying powers, a means to educate Germans in the benefits of democracy, and to monitor German opinion.[2]

COUNTERINSURGENCY IN MALAYA AND THE MEDIA CAMPAIGN
In the wake of the nationalist and Communist insurgencies that swept through Europe and Asia in the wake of World War II, some of the threatened nations employed and refined many of the propaganda and media methods developed during the war as tools for counterinsurgency. The powers that employed such methods, especially the British, found that the media had become a very important part of counterinsurgency strategy. However, the learning curve in counterinsurgency is often a slow one, and it took considerable time for colonial governments and counterinsurgency commanders to understand how to effectively employ the media to generate support for the government among indigenous populations.

The British counterinsurgency campaign in Malaya (1948–1960) is considered a model of a successful counterinsurgency campaign. The British government, over time, turned a large, popular insurgent movement into a tiny, isolated force. In the end, Malaya made the transition from a colony to a peaceful and stable democracy. To achieve this end, the British strategy employed a full range of counterinsurgency tactics, including the large-scale resettlement of part of the rural population, the deployment of large numbers of troops and police, and the establishment of an extensive civic action program to improve the lot of the disaffected people. A key feature of the British strategy was the development of a comprehensive media campaign to undermine the rebels and win popular support for the government. By any reckoning, the government media campaign deserves a good deal of the credit for defeating the insurgency. However, it was developed only through a long trial-and-error process. In the first years of the insurgency, the media campaign would have been best described as amateurish and ineffective. The British media campaign in Malaya is an example of getting it wrong at first, then learning from mistakes.

One of the features of the British rule in Malaya before World War II was the government's preference for the ethnic Malayan population. The nine Malay states and two British settlements were all ruled by ethnically Malayan rulers and councils. The Chinese, although the largest ethnic group, had long been ignored. The Chinese were disliked by the Malays, and many of the older British officials took up this prejudice. While the Malaya Security Services kept tabs on Chinese labor union leaders and leftist politicians, their general knowledge concerning the Chinese community was poor. The government had only a few officials and policemen who spoke Chinese, although many of the British officials and police spoke Malay. Due to this lack of basic knowledge of the language and culture of more than 40 percent of the population, early government media operations were clumsy and ineffective.

During the first stage of the counterinsurgency campaign in 1948 to 1951, the government's media offensive was run by the public affairs directorate of the colonial government. The initial campaign consisted mostly of distributing leaflets filled with very British slogans such as a "redeeming friendship" and "The only good bandit is a dead one." The latter was not very reassuring to the Chinese, many of whom had relatives involved in the insurgency. In other cases, British expressions such as "sitting on the fence" were literally translated into Chinese—much to the confusion of the Chinese, to whom such English phrases and sentiments were meaningless.[3]

Aside from confusing and irritating the Chinese population, the leaflets were distributed in the urban areas, rather than in the rural areas, where the insurgency had its primary support. In any case, leaflet campaigns could only be marginally effective in rural areas, where most of the population was illiterate.

In 1951, the government began to develop a coherent counterinsurgency strategy, bringing in a senior BBC official, Hugh Greene, who had been a propaganda expert for the BBC during World War II. Greene frankly assessed the government's propaganda campaign and rated the insurgent propaganda to be much more effective than the government's for dealing with ideas and themes designed to win popular support. Up to this point, the government had failed to make effective use of film and other media to support the government position. Greene crafted a new government media strategy with three primary aims in mind: 1. Raise the morale of the civilian population and encourage confidence in the government with the view to increase the flow of information from the public to the police. 2. Attack the morale of the insurgents and drive a wedge between the insurgent leaders and the rank and file. This would encourage defections and undermine the determination of the Communists to continue the struggle. 3. Create awareness of the values of a democratic way of life and contrast these with the threat of Communism.[4]

Finally understanding the need to appeal to the Chinese in their own cultural terms, each state and district information officer was provided with an ethnic Chinese assistant. Also, the local Chinese affairs officers were expected to provide input into the local counterinsurgency propaganda. In 1951, the government started to make effective use of surrendered guerrilla fighters as a centerpiece of their own propaganda campaign. The assumption was that the converted guerrillas would have the greatest effect upon their former comrades, and it was a sound assumption.[5] Through a program of leaflets, now distributed in the rural areas, that featured photographs of the former guerrillas, now established on their own farmland provided by the government, and testimony of their families receiving government-provided medical care, and of their children attending government schools, the material benefits of supporting a democratic system were made evident to the rural Chinese community. The leaflets and photographs, as well as numerous public appearances by former insurgents, began to take a toll on insurgent morale.[6]

After 1951, the number of cinema projectors available in the villages was doubled, and the Malayan government film unit began to produce a large number of feature-length and short films featuring insurgent outrages, as well as the testimony of former guerrillas. Films also publicized the success of government land reform and civic action programs.[7] Announcements concerning the program of large rewards for rebel leaders were broadcast on the radio and from village loudspeakers to reach the whole population. In the battle for hearts and minds, the insurgents were soon put on the defensive, their own propaganda trying without great success to undermine the new government campaign. As insurgent strength declined, the government was able to bring ever-increasing resources against an ever-decreasing insurgent force. Small local bands and even individuals were targeted by the media campaign. RAF aircraft equipped with loudspeakers flew over jungle areas where guerrilla bands were known to operate, broadcasting messages from converted guerrillas to their former comrades by name.[8] The loudspeaker broadcasts would even tell the rebels where to go to surrender.

As more of the direction of the government propaganda campaign passed into the hands of the Malayans themselves it became more effective. Local officers imaginatively used every form of media to reach the rural population, including printing photos of wanted guerrilla leaders on the wrapping paper used in village general stores. The insurgency slowly died out as more and more rebels came in from jungle hideouts and surrendered to the police. Many insurgents who surrendered carried leaflets, dropped by RAF aircraft, which promised amnesty and good treatment for insurgent rank and file who were willing to support the government and provide intelligence about the insurgent movement. After 1951, increasing numbers of guerrillas specifically cited the government media campaign as the main reason for their loss of faith in the insurgency.

One disadvantage faced by the insurgents in Malaya is that they did not have a correspondingly large and coordinated international media campaign carried out on their behalf by sympathetic powers. There was some propaganda put forth in favor of the Malayan insurgents by the Red

Chinese government, but it wasn't a large effort and may have even been counterproductive. Red China at the time was engaged in an aggressive war against UN forces in Korea, and propaganda support for the Malayan rebels reminded people that communism as practiced in the USSR and China—and would be practiced in Malaya—was a dangerous and ruthless international movement.

The Role of the International Media in Algeria and Cyprus

In contrast to Malaya, other nationalist movements that opposed colonial rule received considerable support in terms of propaganda and political support from outside nations. During the 1950s, the FLN rebels in Algeria and the rebel National Organization of Cypriot Fighters (EOKA, from the Greek *Ethniki Organosis Kyprion Agoniston*) in Cyprus both benefited from well-crafted, international media campaigns that put the colonial governments on the defensive from the start. These media campaigns played a large role in the success of both insurgencies.

In the 1950s, the majority Muslim population of Algeria, a French colony for over a century, was rife with discontent over French rule. Several major violent incidents, motivated by Algerian nationalism, occurred in 1945 and had been ruthlessly suppressed by the French military and police. Nationalist sentiment continued to grow, and in early 1954 a small group of nationalist activists formed the FLN with the intention of fomenting a national revolution to drive the French out and win independence. As anti-Western nationalists and Muslims, the FLN could count on the political support of the new Egyptian regime of President Gamal Nasser, who was an outspoken advocate for social, political, and economic revolution in the Arab world. The governments of Tunisia and Morocco, former French colonies recently granted independence, were also sympathetic to the Algerian cause. As soon as the FLN was formed, its leaders approached Nasser's Egypt and other independent Muslim states, hoping for military and financial aid. Nasser was encouraging but wanted to see the revolution start before he committed himself. When the FLN began its insurgency with a wave of attacks on government and police centers across Algeria on November 1, 1954, they proved that they had indeed managed to muster considerable public support for a revolution. True to its word, Egypt—then seen as the leading Arab state—began sending money and arms to the Algerian rebels. More important, Nasser initiated a major press and media campaign in favor of the Algerian nationalists and led the other Arab states to bring the cause of Algerian independence before the UN.[9]

In the first years of the insurgency, the French saw the problem as a military one. They enjoyed considerable success against the insurgents, thanks to a massive deployment of police and military forces. However, the French were slow to develop the psychological operations and civic action side of the campaign. In 1956, two years after the start of the insurgency, the French began to deploy small groups of Arab-speaking, culturally sensitive French soldiers and civilians to organize and direct government relief and jobs programs as well as staff new schools and clinics for the benefit of the Algerian rural population, most of whom were desperately poor and illiterate. Part of the civic action program was to organize village self-defense forces in an effort to mobilize the rural population against the FLN and in support of the French government.

Although it started relatively late, the combination of civic action programs and self-defense forces was remarkably successful. By 1959, there were 4,868 French officers, NCOs, and civilians taking part in the civic action program. By a decree of September 1959, they were made responsible for coordination between the local Algerian officials and the French government.[10] The self-defense program in the villages increased from 9,100 Algerians under arms in January 1957, to 85,000 villagers enrolled by June 1960.[11] On the military side, the French army managed to close the Algerian borders to arms smuggling and the infiltration of rebel bands trained in sympathetic Arab nations. Through 1958 and 1959, only a trickle of arms and reinforcements managed to get into Algeria to support the FLN fighters. Militarily speaking, the combination of civic action, relentless military operations, and interdiction of arms and reinforcements broke the FLN as an effective revolutionary force. By early 1960, with most of the FLN bands on the run from overwhelming French forces, the morale of the FLN revolutionaries was at rock bottom.[12]

Though they won on the battlefield, the French lost the media and propaganda war. The excessive use of force against the Algerian rebels played into the hands of the world media. In February 1958, the French handed the FLN a huge propaganda victory by bombing the Tunisian border village of Sakiet with a squadron of B-26 bombers. Since Sakiet was a known base for FLN rebels trying to infiltrate into Algeria, it might have been considered a legitimate target. The bombing took place on market day when a large number of civilians were present, however, and the French managed to hit a school during the bombing run. At least eighty civilians, many of them women and children, were killed, and hundreds more wounded. This French approach to counterinsurgency became world news as dramatic pictures of the wrecked school and injured children were published. The action of the French in bombing a target in another country became an issue in the UN and helped mobilize international efforts to provide political support for the FLN.[13] Thanks largely to the relentless efforts of Nasser's press and radio on behalf of the FLN, what the world saw was not the successful French civic action campaign in Algeria, or the broad support the French government had among the Algerian population (in fact, far more Algerians fought for France than fought for the insurgents). Instead, the world witnessed the heavy use of French force against civilians.

As the FLN effort largely collapsed, the insurgency was kept alive by the strong international media effort on its behalf, as well as the political pressure of Egypt and other Arab governments in bringing the issue before the UN. Faced with fighting a war that was increasingly unpopular at home and abroad, the French government decided to grant Algeria independence in 1962—after having essentially won the war.

Cyprus had been a British colony since the 1870s and, as Britain pulled out of most of its colonies and protectorates in the Middle East after World War II, the island assumed an increased importance for British strategy. Cyprus became the vital base for British forces in the Middle East as well as its regional center of influence. Even though the overwhelmingly Greek population was in favor of uniting with Greece, the idea of granting union or independence was unthinkable for the British government. Given the high level of political intransigence on the part of the UK, Cypriot political leaders quietly imported arms, organized themselves, and plotted revolution. In 1955 the island blew up in a wave of terrorist attacks against British police and military installations, and the insurgency began.

Seen as a military and police operation, the Cyprus insurgency saw the most lopsided ratio of police and military forces to rebel forces ever seen in insurgency. At the height of the insurgency in 1956 to 1957, the British government deployed forty thousand military and security personnel to Cyprus to control a total population of four hundred thousand Greek Cypriots—one British soldier or policemen for every ten Greek Cypriots. The total number of active insurgents was never more than a few hundred so, if one views counterinsurgency as a mathematical model of force application, then the Cypriots never stood a chance. Yet the Cypriots basically won the conflict. Although the Cypriots did not get the hoped-for union with Greece, the British did grant Cyprus independence in 1959, with the government of the island passing to the same Cypriots who had mounted an insurgency against them. A primary reason for this victory against overwhelming force was the effectiveness of the Cypriot media and propaganda campaign versus an ineffectual British media response.

From the start, the Cypriots were well organized and prepared for an insurgency. Archbishop Makarios, head of the Greek Orthodox Church on Cyprus and a charismatic leader, served not only as the spiritual leader of his people but also as the political and ideological leader. The Orthodox Church served as the cultural center for the Cypriot Greeks and employed its priests and pulpits to oppose Britain and argue for *énosis* (union with Greece). Not only did Makarios and the Church justify violent rebellion against British rule, they were willing to decree excommunication for Greek Cypriots who supported the British. The small band of trained rebels who led a terrorist campaign against British rule, led by retired Greek army Colonel George Grivas, could rely on the full support of the church and population—including hiding arms in Orthodox monasteries.

The other great advantage of the Cypriots in the propaganda war was the staunch support of the Greek government and media for the cause of union with Cyprus. The Greek government committed itself to support the Cypriot Greek cause in the UN, in European diplomatic forums, and in direct negotiations with Britain. While the British could place the island's press under strict censorship and control, they couldn't shut out the nightly broadcasts of Radio Athens that encouraged the Cypriot insurgents in their struggle.[14] The British also couldn't control their own journalists, whose reports to the press in Britain and the West became increasingly critical of Britain's Cyprus policy and the misbehavior of the British security forces on Cyprus. When the British arrested and deported Archbishop Makarios from Cyprus for incitement to violence, he reappeared in Greece, constantly talking and preaching on Radio Athens and encouraging the Cypriot Greeks to hold firm as he solicited support from the mainland Greeks to support their brothers in Cyprus. The action of the British government in deporting the archbishop was one of the "lose-lose" propositions often faced by a government defending itself against an insurgency. At home, Makarios had been a powerful leader. Outside of Cyprus, he became a living martyr and an international rallying point. His deportation brought protests from many sectors of British society, including the Archbishop of Canterbury and other leading British churchmen.[15] Britain's heavy-handed approach to suppressing insurgent leadership had backfired.

In drawing up his "General Plan for Insurrectionary Action" to drive the British out of Cyprus, Colonel Grivas intended to institute a campaign of violence and terror specifically directed at the British in order "to draw the attention of international public opinion, especially among the allies of Greece."[16] When Grivas and EOKA started the insurgency, they had no intention or expectation to win militarily. Grivas argued, "It should not be supposed that by these means we should expect to impose a total defeat on the British forces in Cyprus. Our purpose is to win a moral victory through a process of attrition, by harassing, confusing and finally exasperating the enemy forces ..."[17] By proving the Cypriot will for self-sacrifice, "we are prepared to continue until international diplomacy exercises through the United Nations, and the British in particular, are compelled to examine the Cyprus problem ..."[18]

At the outbreak of the insurgency, the British reacted by sending in a distinguished army officer, Field Marshal Sir John Harding, to serve as governor general. Harding, who used his ample forces to saturate the island, tried to suppress the insurgency with a heavy hand. On several occasions, British troops reacted to Cypriot terrorist outrages with out-bursts of violence against Greek civilians. On one notable occasion whole battalions rioted, smashing Greek shops and beating Cypriot civilians.[19] Such actions undermined the legitimacy of the British position, as the British and Greek media quickly broadcast images of such actions around the world. Indeed, enough abuses occurred that the British newspapers began to routinely criticize the Harding regime—and with good cause.[20] While there were some cases of police abuse and torture during interroga-tions of Cypriot terrorist suspects, accounts were certainly exaggerated. However, broad claims of British police abuse were made by the Greek newspapers and radio and brought to world attention with the support of the Greek government. There had been enough credible incidents of police and military intelligence brutality to give media credence to many false charges. In 1956, the Greek government brought the issue of British abus-es before the European Commission and forced an international investiga-tion of British police and military actions.[21] Although many allegations were later refuted, the damage to the British position was severe. Indeed, Colonel Grivas declared that the first act of the new government after Cypriot independence should be to raise a statue to Field Marshal Harding, "since he had done more than anybody else to keep alive the spir-it of Hellenic resistance in Cyprus."[22]

The vast resources of the United Kingdom were seemingly powerless to confront an international media campaign against the continued British rule of Cyprus. The Greek government was of great help in bring-ing the insurgents' position before the UN and European governments. The UN remained noncommittal about the issue, calling only for a peaceful, democratic, and just solution. Even this minimal acknowledge-ment of the issue helped to legitimize the insurgents' cause in the eyes of the world.[23]

The British approach to the media failed to take advantage of some nonviolent factions in the Greek Cypriot community. Many Greeks, while supporting *énosis*, were willing to take a more moderate, nonviolent approach and were uncomfortable with the terrorist acts committed by Grivas and the insurgents. It is possible that the British might have used a media campaign to pull some Greeks away from a violent, revolutionary approach to settling political differences. But, unlike Malaya, the British had no coherent media strategy for dealing with the rebellion. An illustration of Harding's incompetence in handling the media is seen in the intercommunal rioting between the Greek and Turkish communities of Cyprus that erupted in 1957 to 1958. The Cyprus police, by this time overwhelmingly recruited from the minority Turkish community, routinely stood by and watched, failing to intervene as Turkish mobs ransacked Greek Cypriot shops and assaulted Greeks. These incidents were witnessed by news correspondents, who reported them in the international media. The automatic response of the British administration was to automatically deride any criticism of the police and characterize accusations of misconduct by the security forces as part of an orchestrated insurgent plan to discredit the security forces.[24] These confrontational tactics didn't go over well with British journalists, especially those who had personally witnessed such incidents. The failure of the British government to respond to credible allegations haunted the debate over Cyprus policy. In time, criticism of the Cyprus administration found its way to the House of Lords, as well as the UN and European Civil Rights Commission.[25]

In the end, the British negotiated and agreed to grant Cyprus independence in 1959, with majority rule by the Greek Cypriots. It was not the full union with Greece that the majority of Cyprus desired, but it was at least an end to British rule. The end of British rule was brought about by international political pressure more than anything else, fueled by the effective use of the media by Greek Cypriots and the Greek government. Grivas' long-term strategy of simply staying in the field, harassing the British with small attacks, did not inflict significant losses to the British, but it kept the attention of the international media focused on Cyprus. In the end, it was a successful strategy for insurgency.

THE MEDIA AND THE MILITARY FROM VIETNAM TO THE 1990S

One of the best examples of the use of the international media as part of the insurgent strategy is the Vietnam War. As America entered the war in Vietnam, the Viet Cong and North Vietnamese developed the *dich van* program (action among the enemy). *Dich van* was a sophisticated psychological warfare program directed against the civilians of South Vietnam and America, and toward the international media. *Dich van*'s goal was to present an idealized version of North Vietnam and the Viet Cong to the world, while undermining the international perception of the legitimacy of the South Vietnamese government.[26]

In a carefully rehearsed program to present several themes to the international media, the North Vietnamese emphasized the "David versus Goliath" nature of the war in Vietnam. For example, the U.S. bombing campaign against North Vietnam from 1965 to 1968 was carefully limited to only a few areas, with the major urban areas of Hanoi and Haiphong off-limits to U.S. warplanes, and American rules were set to minimize civilian casualties. This, however, did not keep the North Vietnamese from over-stating the damage to North Vietnam and grossly inflating civilian casualties in their presentations to a largely credulous and anti-American international press corps. In fact, for all the bombs dropped on North Vietnam, the collateral damage to civilian targets and civilian casualties was very low. From 1968 to 1972, there was an American bombing halt for all of North Vietnam north of the 19th Parallel, which excluded all of the major population centers. However, the North Vietnamese civilians, most of whom were scarcely affected by the air war, were portrayed as a valiant people under relentless bombardment by a large, aggressor nation.[27] The leftist European media, many of whom possessed a strong strain of anti-Americanism, put out a consistent message largely orchestrated by the North Vietnamese. By 1968, much of the U.S. media was following along the same path, and opposition among the European and American elites grew notably.

Surprisingly, the U.S. government and military failed to mount any media campaign of their own to counter the constant drumbeat of North Vietnamese propaganda in international forums. Indeed, the biggest loser of the media war was the South Vietnamese government, which had its legitimacy questioned and publicly derided by most of the international media from the beginning of the war. While unable to defend its own policies effectively, the United States also failed to finance and support a coherent South Vietnamese government effort to bring its view of the conflict, and also the views of the majority of South Vietnamese, who had no great love for the Viet Cong or North Vietnamese either, before the international media.[28]

The Tet Offensive of 1968, which destroyed the Viet Cong as a military force and was, in reality, a notable military victory for the South Vietnamese and the Americans, was portrayed in much of the international and American media as a U.S. military disaster. The deliberate mass murder of thousands of South Vietnamese civilians by Viet Cong terror squads during the Tet Offensive was one of the most grisly and brutal episodes of the entire war—but the carnage received little play in either the international or American media in comparison with the coverage of the U.S. bombing campaign in North Vietnam.

From 1965 to 1975, the North Vietnamese *dich van* campaign to delegitimize the South Vietnamese government in the eyes of the world and brand the Americans as ruthless aggressors worked exceptionally well to create sympathy for the North Vietnamese and Viet Cong cause. *Dich van*, by all accounts, played a major role in setting the conditions for the American withdrawal from South Vietnam and, in 1975, the complete cut-off of military aid to that government. For South Vietnam, the *dich van* program was fatal and for America, the fallout from the Vietnam War was severe. For decades after Vietnam, there existed a high degree of distrust between the U.S. military, and the United States and international media. Unfortunately, the reaction of the American military was not to learn from mistakes made in Vietnam but rather to bury the issue. By refusing to make a detailed study of Viet Cong and North Vietnamese propaganda techniques during and after the war, the U.S. military would be again put in the position of facing a hostile international media without an effective media campaign of its own prepared.

In the post–Cold War era, the United States had new security concerns to worry about, most of them dealing with various multinational interventions. The new conditions required imposing some kind of peace and order in countries that had imploded and faced civil war between violent factions. In a busy decade, the United States took part in interventions in Somalia, Haiti, Bosnia, and Kosovo. In Somalia, Bosnia, and Kosovo, the conflicts were essentially ethnically driven, placing the U.S. and multinational forces in the uncomfortable position of standing between large irregular forces, each eager to destroy the opposing ethnic community. It wasn't the kind of conventional war that the U.S. military was comfortable with—but it certainly wasn't a "peace operation," either.

One important lesson that should have been learned from these conflicts was the central importance of a thorough, properly managed psychological operations campaign to be carried out by the peacekeeping force, targeting the population and combatant factions. In peace enforcement operations it was usually the case that several of the factions did not want any peaceful settlement, perceiving the multinational peacekeepers as a hostile force. The factions opposed to multinational intervention routinely carried out propaganda campaigns among the local population and spread disinformation about the peacekeeping forces to turn the population against the peacekeepers. This happened during the U.S. and multinational intervention in Somalia in 1992 to 1994.

The U.S. and UN force that intervened in Somalia in December 1992 preempted the hostile Somali factions by arriving with overwhelming force. The multinational force initiated a widespread information campaign using leaflets, radio, and loudspeakers to inform the Somalis of the international mission, and to provide information about relief aid to the Somalis. The media program to calm the population was successful. During the first six months of the operation, the Somali population accepted the U.S./UN operation with little difficulty.

Since Somalia had quieted down by the spring of 1993, the United States decided to withdraw most of its troops and turn the operation over to the UN. A fundamental mistake was made when the U.S. psychological operations detachments were also withdrawn from Somalia. At the very moment the mission was being changed from a humanitarian support mission to a conflict between the UN and Mohammed Aideed's faction, the specialist troops who could have mounted a campaign to educate the population about the UN mission were no longer there. The cutback in U.S. forces coincided with a vehement anti-U.S./UN campaign mounted by Mohammed Aideed's radio station. No action was taken in the spring of 1993 to shut down or jam Aideed's radio station. By June, predictably, the UN and Mohammed Aideed were in open conflict, and through his media campaign, Aideed had won the support of many Somalis by portraying himself as a nationalist leader working against foreign oppressors. The UN had no effective counter-propaganda against Aideed. Of course, once Aideed took open military action against the UN forces, the supporting U.S. airpower would have been justified in bombing Aideed's radio station and putting his primary means of public propaganda off the air. Yet, in a manner characteristic of UN operations, the UN troops were cautioned to use minimal force at the same time that Aideed and allied factions were urging their followers on to open war.[29]

The conflict intensified until a U.S. raid was ambushed and shot up in the famous October 1993 incident in Mogadishu, in which two helicopters were destroyed and more than one hundred Americans were killed or wounded by Aideed's faction in a battle that raged through the city. In the end, the UN forces quietly withdrew from Somalia in 1994 in what was correctly perceived by third world nations—and especially by radical Islamic factions such as Osama bin Laden's—as a notable lack of will by an American government that failed to maintain an intervention policy when confronted with light losses and weak, irregular forces. Bin Laden would remember Somalia.

THE MILITARY, THE MEDIA, AND THE IRAQ WAR

One of the greatest assets of democracy is a free and healthy mass media, dedicated to democratic principles and able to communicate effectively with the public. If the legitimacy of the government is the center of gravity—as almost every successful counterinsurgency theorist and practitioner will agree—the effective use of the media is a key tool to establish control in an occupied country or suppress an insurgency. One of the primary goals for fighting the Iraq War in 2003 was to help the Iraqis build a stable and democratic society. The failure to plan before the war to build a democratic mass media in Iraq in the early stages of the occupation was one of the most grievous mistakes of the American military leaders and policymakers.

The Arab world is relatively devoid of anything resembling the free press and media that are the sine qua non of a healthy, democratic society. The greater part of the media in Arab states is government controlled, and often publishes what one can only generously describe as crude propaganda. Peaceful, reasoned debate on public issues, or responsible criticism of the government, is not part of the tradition in the tightly controlled media of Arab nations. In the days after the 9/11 attack, the media in the Arab world was filled with wild stories charging that Israel and the Zionists were behind the attacks on the United States—not Islamic radicals. Indeed, when it comes to commenting on U.S. government policy, America is routinely denounced in terms that would have seemed embarrassingly vicious, violent, and crude compared to the speeches and writings of Josef Goebbels. America is often described as a Zionist nation, under secret control of the Jews. Ironically, American films and television programs are extremely popular in the Arab world, and the preferred place of university study for upper-class Arab youth is the United States.

This bizarre, love/hate view of the United States in the Arab and Islamic nations leads to a broad cynicism toward the press. At one level, many educated Arabs simply ignore their own government media. At another level, the extremes of opinion and the routine calls for violence against Zionists and their allies find a ready audience among many poor and middle-class people—especially those educated in the *madrassas* (Islamic schools), where the concept of *jihad* is glorified.

In Iraq under Saddam, though, the population was not subjected to a similar barrage of Islamist propaganda. Iraqis were presented with a constant program of Baath Party ideology and anti-American rants. As is typical in dictatorships, the general attitude of the Iraqi people was simply to distrust everything that was presented by the government-controlled media.[30] Owning a satellite television in Iraq was a criminal offense under Saddam's rule; internet correspondence was monitored and foreign news journals prohibited, so news from the outside world was circulated in garbled form. Considering its pervasiveness and crudeness, Saddam's propaganda machine did not inspire many Iraqis to fight to the death for Saddam. On the other hand, even the well-educated Iraqis who yearned for the fall of Saddam and the chance for a democratic Iraq had little idea how to go about organizing and nurturing the kind of free, responsible media that a democracy needs to function. One key problem was that although most educated Iraqis, and even the people who worked in the Iraqi government media, wanted a democratic Iraq without Saddam, none had the kind of journalistic training for operating in a democracy or understood the Western model of a democratic media.

The U.S. Army's prewar planners placed the restoration of media communications in Iraq and establishing a free media high on their list of priorities as a means to establish stability in Iraq after the fighting.[31] The planners for General Garner also insisted that a media campaign geared toward the Iraqi people would have to be coordinated with the U.S. forces and the authorities of the new Iraqi government.[32] One proposal made in the prewar planning process was to place strict controls on political and media activity by Iraqis in the immediate aftermath of the invasion and to ban antidemocratic sentiments and incitements to violence by Iraqi media organs. These proposals were recommended to prevent a resurgence of the Baath Party and to inhibit the formation of parties that preferred a violent path to power.[33]

Unfortunately, the U.S. military failed to follow any of the common-sense proposals of the prewar planners, or to realize the value of a mass media program in occupying and democratizing Iraq. A group of specialists from twenty media organizations that supported the creation of a modern, democratic media network in Iraq met in late April 2003, shortly after the fall of Baghdad, expressing concern at the chaotic state of the Iraqi media. They outlined the problems faced in Iraq and pointed out that "the fall of the Iraqi state media has left a huge void."[34] When the Coalition forces took over Iraq, they failed to establish any regulatory structure for the distribution of frequencies or licensing media. Groups and factions of Iraqis simply seized the assets of the old regime and set up their own newspapers, radio, and television stations. The situation was described as a "free for all—if you have enough armed men."[35] Since the Coalition forces at first did not place any controls or censorship on the newly liberated Iraqis, some of the Iraqi factions used their new media outlets to demand the violent suppression of their opponents as they openly opposed the new Iraqi Governing Council, which was composed of the more moderate and democratic elements in Iraq who were working with the Coalition forces. With the situation clearly out of hand, the CPA finally issued Order Number 14, prohibiting media activities against Coalition forces and the CPA. However, neither the CPA nor the Iraqi Governing Council were able to take quick action to suppress the newspapers and radio stations calling for violence.[36] Because of the belated action by the Coalition forces in controlling the media, the radical elements in Iraq had several months to organize their supporters and get their message out. One of the most proviolence television stations broadcasting to Iraq, Al Arabiya (largely Saudi-owned and broadcasting from the Emirates), unfortunately became one of the most popular stations. In the fall of 2003, it even broadcast an audiotape, purportedly of Saddam, urging Iraqis to attack the Coalition forces and their Iraqi collaborators. Only in November 2003 did the Iraqi Governing Council move to shut down the Baghdad bureau of the station. The CPA only closed down the Al-Hawza newspaper of the rebel cleric and militia leader Muqtada al-Sadr in March 2004.

The lack of an effective mass media hampered the Coalition effort to organize postwar Iraq and to build a democratic Iraqi government. The Iraqi Media Network was established by ORHA in April 2003 and set out with few resources and little support from America to get a radio station up and running. In the postwar chaos, a small band of dedicated volunteers managed to cobble together some old equipment in a studio in Baghdad and begin broadcasting. The problem of old equipment and damaged studios was compounded by the shortage of trained Iraqi media professionals willing and able to work for the new Iraqi government. Immediately after Baghdad was occupied, the major networks of the Arab nations hired many of the best-known and most experienced Iraqi media specialists to manage their reporting and broadcasting in Iraq, for salaries five times what ORHA was willing to pay them. Unfortunately, many of the Arab networks took a generally anti-American position on the Iraq War and employed their Iraqi correspondents to criticize every action by the Coalition forces, magnifying every perceived mistake. In July 2004, the Iraqi Foreign Minister accused some regional satellite channels of inciting violence, complaining specifically of Al Manar (owned by Hezbollah), Al-Alam (the Iranian government's Arabic channel), Al Arabiya (mostly Saudi-owned), and Al Jazeera (independently owned). Instead of news getting out that conditions were quickly improving in Iraq—which, in fact, was the case—the Arab world and the West were presented with repeated messages depicting a chaotic and failing Iraq. It was largely an untrue picture, spread by groups openly hostile to the idea of a democratic Iraq who had well-supported, professional media operations at their disposal. The small, idealistic band of amateurish Iraqis working for ORHA and the Iraqi Governing Council tried their best to present their side—but their resources were far more limited than those of the more radical networks.

By not planning for media operations before the war, the U.S. and Coalition forces set themselves up to lose the postwar battle for the hearts and minds of the Iraqis. General Jay Garner, who headed the first civilian administration in Iraq in 2003, admitted after his dismissal that he should have done a better job communicating with the Iraqi people.[37] The United States belatedly poured in millions to help the Iraqi Governing Council establish a center for public diplomacy and also established an Arabic language television station, Al-Hurra, geared specifically to Iraq and following the model of the BBC. Unfortunately, the more radical regional stations had already won the audience share in Iraq. Al-Hurra was able to make little inroad into the popularity of the anti-Coalition stations such as Al Jazeera and Al Arabiya.[38] James Schlesinger, former U.S. defense secretary under presidents Nixon and Ford, commented that Al Iraqiya, the television station set up by the Iraqi government, "has not been well-designed to attract an audience and has thus been peripheral for Iraqi viewers." Summarizing the approach of the U.S. government in Iraq, Schlesinger concluded, "We have failed to convey to the Iraqis what our intentions are—or belatedly conveyed them. Consequently, all too many excellent and well-intentioned actions on our part have not gotten through to the Iraqi public. It is almost as important that such plans or such actions be understood, as that they be executed."[39]

The first budget of the Iraqi government in 2004 had little money to support its media and press operations, allocating only $1.57 million. Luckily, groups in the West, private citizens, and even U.S. soldiers began raising money to finance and support Iraqi-owned television and radio stations that would be committed to a democratic Iraq.[40] In 2005 the new Iraqi government was able to allocate more funds to train the personnel of the government-operated Iraqi Media Network.[41] These efforts will, in time, help the government of Iraq. In terms of fighting the onset of the insurgency and reestablishing order in Iraq, however, the creation of a coherent media program came much too late, while the factions opposed to the Coalition forces and the new Iraqi government showed an impressive ability to step in and employ the mass media effectively as a weapon to undercut the Coalition and the Iraqis attempting to build a democratic state.

COMBATING RADICAL ISLAM AT THE STRATEGIC LEVEL

The U.S. government has repeatedly stated that the threat of radical Islamist ideology in the third world needs to be opposed with a media campaign to support democracy, peaceful reform, and moderate Islamic values. The 9/11 commission argued, "If the United States cannot act aggressively to define itself in the Islamic world the extremists will gladly do the job for us."[42] The U.S. 2002 National Security Strategy also noted the importance of a strategic media campaign when it urged "supporting moderate and modern governments, especially in the Muslim World, to ensure that the conditions and ideologies that promote terrorism do not find fertile ground in any nation" and "using effective public diplomacy to promote the free flow of information..."[43] This sounds like the right approach to deal with the strategic problem.

However, some analysts have noted that little real progress to implement a strategic media campaign has been made in the sluggish culture of the Washington bureaucracy. James Carafano and Paul Rosenzweig, authors of a book on strategy to oppose terrorism, wrote in 2005, "The bad news is that U.S. public diplomacy has been ineffective and unimaginative." After 9/11, the State Department hired some Arabic speakers to handle media and produce some television commercials to promote religious tolerance toward moderate Muslims, but the whole effort was "too small a scale to make a difference."[44] For example, Carafano and Rosenzweig noted that the Middle Eastern Broadcast Network, supported by the U.S. government, had been exceptionally slow to launch. The new Arabic radio network was still not broadcasting even six months after the 9/11 attacks. In contrast, the Voice of America, a radio network to promote democratic values overseas during World War II, was on the air in

February 1942—only a few weeks after Pearl Harbor.[45] It is astonishing that the nation that invented the modern mass media and enjoys enormous financial and technical resources still has so far to go in putting together a coherent and comprehensive message that will appeal to the average citizens of the Islamic states, who are bombarded daily with anti-Western and anti-American messages.

WHAT SHOULD HAVE BEEN DONE IN IRAQ—AND WHAT SHOULD BE DONE IN FUTURE CONFLICTS

Richard McKenna's novel *The Sand Pebbles* describes the dilemma of a U.S. Navy detachment trying to carry out a peacekeeping and security mission in the midst of chaos and civil war in China in the 1920s. The novel describes the bewilderment of U.S. officers trying to carry out their mission and keep the peace when they are confronted, not with a straightforward military threat, but a mass propaganda campaign conducted by revolutionaries who intend to raise the population against the Western Powers and create political pressure to withdraw the U.S. and Western forces from China. The first step was to blame all of China's myriad problems on the Western Powers. Every legitimate action by the gunboat of the novel was distorted by the nationalist press and agitators and depicted as a human rights violation. When the gunboat fires on river pirates and kills one pirate, the nationalist press reports that thirty unarmed women and children were massacred. The gunboat commander ruefully comments, "We are fighting lies now, not armed men." He reluctantly passes on orders that U.S. operations and even the right to shoot in self-defense will be restricted to prevent further political outcry.[46]

The Sand Pebbles is a great novel about the nature of revolutionary warfare and an accurate picture of decent and honorable American military men of an earlier age who remained unable to comprehend the new mode of political warfare being employed against them. The descriptions of the media tactics employed against the Americans in the 1920s comes very close to the media tactics waged against the U.S. forces in Iraq and Afghanistan and played out in the Middle East and world media. Unfortunately, the American military's lack of comprehension of the media and propaganda side of warfare depicted in the novel is also an accurate representation of the U.S. military in Iraq and Afghanistan. Islamic radicals and other factions opposed to the United States in Iraq have demonstrated no respect for the truth when they manufacture charges of American atrocities. While the U.S. forces take great care to avoid inflicting civilian casualties, such casualties will inevitably occur. A few injured civilians becomes a massacre of innocents, first in the Arab press and then often by the Western media. While the Western media is somewhat more skeptical of allegations leveled at the Americans, such allegations are still respectfully reported. While American forces are generally well disciplined and real instances of abuse or impropriety are rare, such abuses are magnified and depicted as typical American behavior by a largely anti-American European and international media. That a U.S. invasion and occupation of Afghanistan and Iraq would not be acceptable to much of the world and that the U.S. and Coalition forces would face an intensive media and propaganda campaign unfettered by any rules or ethics could have, and should have, been anticipated by the U.S. military and by the U.S. leadership.

Since the start of the Iraq War, the insurgents and radical Islamic factions both inside and outside Iraq have employed a sophisticated and relentless media campaign against the U.S. and Coalition forces. The internet has been a powerful new tool for movements and factions to spread their message and win new recruits. Insurgent and radical factions have also spread their message with posters and leaflets throughout Iraq and can rely on a sympathetic radio and television media in several Arab nations and in Iran to carry stories with an Anti-democracy and anti-American twist. Suicide bombers are characterized as "freedom fighters" and Iraqis working to establish democracy are labeled as "puppets" of the "American occupiers" who are in Iraq to "subvert Islam and steal Iraq's oil." Many of these themes resonate with broad segments of the population, and countering such messages requires extensive planning and a broad media campaign. Unfortunately, the media problems (as with so many other problems in Iraq) were not anticipated and planning was thoroughly inadequate. Even after almost three years in Iraq, the overwhelming consensus of the U.S. officers who have served in Iraq and Afghanistan is that our own information operations are ineffective.[47] Most American officers who have served in Iraq

187

and Afghanistan recognize the vital importance of an effective media campaign in counterinsurgency warfare. The problem is getting a military establishment trained up in the conventional war/Cold War era to understand the central importance of these supposedly "nonmilitary" operations. The U.S. military has a host of lessons to learn from recent operations that it must apply to future conflicts.

First, the U.S. military needs to recognize that a well-planned, fully resourced strategic communications campaign is an essential part of a postwar process and for combating insurgency. In any insurgency there will likely be a minority of the public actively supporting the government as well as a minority trying to overthrow the government. When states collapse and face widespread disorder, most of the population typically remains passive. This was very much the case in Iraq. The vast majority of Iraqis were happy to see Saddam fall but were unwilling to publicly take sides for or against the Coalition until they were sure of the winner. An initial media campaign in Iraq should have reassured Iraqis that the Coalition presence would be temporary; that the nation would be governed by the rule of law; and that Iraqi-run local government, then provincial and national governments, would be restored quickly—if the population cooperated and worked together in a peaceful manner. Criticism of the Coalition could have been allowed, as well as a strenuous and open political debate, as long as newspapers refrained from even implicitly arguing for violence.

Before the war, we should have had a comprehensive plan to get television and radio stations up and running, using the latest equipment and staffed with Iraqis loyal to a provisional government that could spread a message with an Iraqi face. No matter how just our cause, many Iraqis would be bound to resent any rule by foreigners. In order to present the message, well-known television and radio personalities, as well as popular entertainers, such as actors and singers, should be hired and put under contract (with good salaries) to present the message. If we don't hire them, then they'll go to work for Al Jazeera or one of the other anti-American Arab networks.

The presentation of the message is as important as the content. A media message is best presented by people who can use the most advanced techniques, such as marketing surveys, and who can couch the message in terms, images, and music that will have the maximum appeal to the average Iraqi. The only practical way of "selling" democracy to the Iraqis is to rely upon professional salesmen. The people who can best craft the message will be marketing specialists in other Arab lands, people who speak the language and are culturally very close to the Iraqis. Before the war, the Coalition should have hired top advertising and marketing firms in Jordan, Kuwait, Qatar, and the Emirates and had them conduct marketing surveys and analysis of Iraqi advertising and media. Arab firms under contract could have carefully prepared television commercials, television shows, radio programs, and commercials that would use the images, themes, slogans, and music that could "press the right buttons" in the Iraqi psyche. Early in the campaign for Iraq, there should have been a media blitz to the Iraqi people, a blitz to convince them of the friendly intentions of the Coalition forces and to undermine the radical factions and supporters of Saddam. An effective strategic advertising and marketing plan would have to be administered by the Iraqis themselves, and not by the Coalition. The Coalition role would primarily be in financing the operation, and providing technical help and broadcasting resources. In order to support the legitimacy of a new government and democratic Iraq, the message and the messengers must be Iraqis.

When the insurgency began in May 2003, the object of a strategic communications campaign should have been oriented toward the majority of the population that was passive, to convince them that the government is going to win, the government is a good cause, and that their lives will improve if only they support the government. If only 20 to 30 percent of the undecided or passive part of the population can be convinced that the government cause is just and legitimate, then public support for the government can, hopefully, gain momentum. If that can be done, the insurgents will be limited to a small, embattled corps—one that is not going to grow. At that point, it is a matter of mopping up the die-hard enemies of the government.

One important tool for developing and measuring the effectiveness of a media campaign is polling. As noted earlier, public opinion polling was an important tool for the U.S. military forces occupying Germany after World War II. It would not have been difficult to set up a polling organization before the war, staffed by contracted professionals and ready to begin public opinion sampling as soon as the U.S. forces captured Iraq's major population centers. Polling could tell the Coalition commanders what Iraqi attitudes are, district by district. It could also serve as a measure of the effectiveness of the Coalition and Iraqi provisional government's media campaign. General Garner's prewar planning group mentioned polling as a useful tool for an occupying force. Yet, one year into the Coalition occupation of Iraq and well after the start of the insurgency, no systematic polling system for the whole of Iraq had been set up by the Coalition authorities, although some local commanders had conducted polls in their districts. By refusing to employ modern polling techniques, the Coalition forces rejected one of the most basic forms of intelligence required in a counterinsurgency campaign: understanding what the local populace is thinking.

The failure of the U.S. military to seriously consider planning for a media campaign before the war, or to use techniques such as polling in administering a large, complex nation, is symptomatic of the U.S. military's approach to the war in Iraq and subsequent operations. Media campaigns and polling cost money—a lot of it. Providing an Iraqi provisional government with adequate equipment, support, training, and advice would have cost hundreds of millions of dollars. From what I saw before the war, and in Iraq in 2004, the U.S. military is seeking to fight a "war on the cheap" and keep the costs of fighting a major conventional war and occupying a large country at an absolute minimum. Ideas such as providing an Iraqi provisional government with expensive media equipment and support fell by the wayside in the desire to win the conventional victory and get out of Iraq as quickly as possible. Though restraint in spending the American taxpayers' dollars is commendable, this attitude also threatens to undermine the whole strategic objective of the war—building a peaceful and stable Iraq. It's not as if the United States is so strapped for cash that it could not support a sophisticated media campaign.

Spending the money and allocating resources for a strategic media campaign should have a high priority in any future military or peace enforcement operation. The payoff in a properly planned and supported campaign can be winning the support of the population and decreasing the number of attacks on the government and Coalition forces. Increasing the chance for victory is worth spending money on the media. But one cannot expect immediate or decisive results from a strategic or local media campaign, as the effect is generally cumulative. There are seldom quick victories in counterinsurgency. Part of a media campaign would be educating the people in the basics of democracy, and this will take time. Unfortunately, it is the time factor that works against a U.S. military culture that demands visible, immediate, and decisive results.

CHAPTER SIX

TRAINING LOCAL
FORCES

*From now on a claim to officer rank shall in peacetime be
warranted only by knowledge of education, in time of war
by exceptional bravery and quickness of perception... All
social preference which has hitherto existed ceases completely in the army.*
— King Frederick William III, *Prussia,* 1808

*What holds society together is not the policemen but the
goodwill of common men, and yet that goodwill is powerless unless the policeman is there to back it up. Any government which refused to use violence in its own defence
would cease immediately to exist, because it could be overthrown by any body of men, or even any individual that
was less scrupulous.*

— George Orwell, 1941

Not even a great nation with enormous military and economic power
can hope to defeat a modern insurgency in another nation, or even
keep any semblance of order for an extended period, without the active support of an effective, indigenous security force. To defeat insurgents or terrorist organizations, it is axiomatic that the locals need to be able to provide for
their own security if there is to be any hope for establishing a stable and successful government. U.S. or Western forces are likely to be burdened with the
responsibility to provide most of the security forces in the early stages of a

counterinsurgency campaign. But eventually, the local forces must be able to stand on their own feet if the campaign is to be a strategic success. Therefore, building an effective indigenous military and security force is a primary task for any power that intervenes—whether to overthrow a regime and occupy a country, to stabilize an imploded country, to end a civil war through a peacekeeping operation, or to support an allied government threatened by insurgency.

The mission of creating effective local security forces has been around for centuries. One can go back to the Roman Empire for historical precedents. Throughout the Roman Empire, for instance, most low-level police and security operations were carried out by a variety of local forces, raised and financed by the local governors or monarchs loyal to Rome. While the Roman legions dealt with the major threats, the auxiliary cohorts, a branch of the Roman military that recruited from the ranks of noncitizens, were kept busy with a variety of police duties. If we fast-forward to the era of colonial imperialism from the sixteenth to the twentieth centuries, the burden of maintaining stability and suppressing rebellions in the colonies fell mostly on the local forces recruited, trained, and equipped by the major powers. Running and maintaining a successful empire was impossible without effective local forces. First of all, it was simply too expensive to bring out enough troops from the home country to police colonies. Local forces were much cheaper to pay, equip, and maintain. Second, local forces knew the language and culture of the people—a basic requirement for success in apprehending criminal bands or suppressing local insurrections.

Training local security forces should be a major American concern in the global war on terror—whether in nations directly threatened by insurgency, nations that fear another nation's insurgency will spill over their borders, or nations that have all the right conditions for an insurgency to begin. Many small nations that are allies or friends of the United States face a variety of serious threats today—threats ranging from large-scale insurgency in Iraq, Afghanistan, and Colombia to the problem of Chechen rebels slipping over the border from Russia into the territory of Georgia. One of the best ways for any hostile group or power to undermine the United States is to foster insurgencies against American allies. If the United States cannot help build effective police and military forces in small allied countries and countries struggling to build democracies, then our national strategy is doomed to failure over the long term—no matter how powerful our conventional military forces are.

Over two generations, training people to fight their own wars and to provide for their own security has been one of the successful pillars of American strategy. During the Cold War, the United States spent vast sums to support and train allied forces, helping them to set up adequate, and realistic, defense structures through training and advice and providing them with the military equipment appropriate to their defense needs. However, training local security forces to fight insurgency in the Cold War was a more difficult task than that faced by the old colonial regimes because of the touchy matter of national sovereignty. American officers and State Department officials could not directly order sovereign national governments or foreign police and military commanders to create comprehensive strategies, commit themselves to reforms, or establish effective training regimes for policemen and soldiers. Historically, the job of American regional commanders and State Department diplomats has been to advise, cajole, and negotiate with national governments and security forces to find reasonable—and usually compromise—solutions. It has rarely been a straightforward process, and military officers in the position of supporting third world security forces have needed to employ diplomatic, as well as professional, military skills. American advisors often have to use aid and support as a lever, sometimes coupled with the threat of aid reductions, to force countries to accept necessary reforms—especially when they concern their security forces.

The quality and level of professionalism and combat effectiveness of the armed forces of developing countries vary widely. A few small nations, such as El Salvador, have fairly professional and capable armed forces. Moreover, the Salvadorans proved their competence in service in Iraq in 2003 to 2004. However, the Salvadoran forces weren't always that way; the twelve years' large-scale U.S. military aid program during the civil war from 1980 to 1992 made a huge difference.[1] However, a dysfunctional military culture is the most common model in undeveloped nations, and the problems of poor training, low professional standards, and a weak infrastructure remain the primary obstacles to third world nations' ability to conduct effective military and security operations.

An additional obstacle to building effective security forces in developing nations is the standard terrorist and insurgent strategy of specifically targeting the police and military forces and their families, as a means to deter recruitment and intimidate the security forces from operating energetically against rebel elements. Nonetheless, building effective security forces is a mission that must succeed if terrorists and insurgents are to be defeated. Max Manwaring, one of the leading counterinsurgency theorists today, identifies building disciplined and competent armed forces as one of the six key issues that must be addressed to defeat insurgency (see Chapter 1). If the military and security forces of a nation fighting an insurgency are incompetent, or if they have a poor relationship with the people, then the government is on the path to defeat. Thus, one of the essential tasks for the United States and Western nations fighting worldwide terrorism and insurgency is to help small allies and developing nations build effective military and police forces. Transforming largely dysfunctional military cultures is a long and complex process that goes against the current American preference for "quick, decisive warfare." But it must be done to ensure a reasonable chance for success.

EARLY AMERICAN EXPERIENCE IN TRAINING FOREIGN FORCES

When the United States won the Philippine Islands in the war with Spain in 1898, U.S. troops found themselves confronting a well-organized, indigenous independence movement with a large military force determined to assert their recently proclaimed independence. Open war erupted with the Filipino nationalists in February 1899, and with their superior training and firepower, American troops soon beat the rebel armies in conventional battles. Rather than admitting defeat, the Filipino nationalists turned to guerrilla warfare, complete with terrorist acts. The rebels killed U.S. soldiers in ambushes and small raids. Erecting an underground political infrastructure, they waged a relentless campaign to kill and intimidate Filipino officials or businessmen who opted to work with the Americans. The Philippine Insurrection (1899–1902) turned into an ugly war that required tripling the size of the U.S. Army, stationing seventy-five thousand U.S. troops in the Philippines and engaging in a long pacification campaign of endless jungle patrols and skirmishes to find and destroy the rebel groups.

A primary factor in the American success was the creation of Filipino military and police units, loyal to the U.S. regime and under command of U.S. officers and NCOs. From the start, many Filipinos opposed Emilio Aguinaldo and the independence movement and were happy to collaborate with the Americans. Early in the conflict, U.S. Army local commanders started raising local Filipino units to serve as scouts and auxiliaries. By 1901, the situation was formalized with the establishment of an official force of several thousand Philippine Scouts as part of the U.S. Army. At the same time, a U.S.-officered paramilitary police force called the Philippine Constabulary was organized. The Constabulary was officially under civilian, not military, control. In practice, however, Constabulary companies served alongside the army and the Philippine Scouts in active operations. By the official end of the insurrection in 1902, fifteen thousand Filipinos were serving in recognized Scout or Constabulary units. However, the trouble didn't end with the collapse of the nationalist movement, for on several islands, large bandit bands and various rebel groups still terrorized the population. The Scout and Constabulary units played a central role in suppressing these disorders. On the Island of Mindanao, Moro tribes in the hinterlands initiated several rebellions between 1903 and 1914 that compelled the U.S. army and the Constabulary to conduct major counterinsurgency operations. In later campaigns, the Philippine Scout companies recruited from Moro tribes played the key role in defeating their rebellious brethren.[2]

In the early days, the Scouts and the Constabulary were short of uniforms, supplies, and equipment. They were armed with old army surplus rifles and other cast-off items. In short, they were not much better armed and equipped than the rebels they were fighting. However, the U.S. Army ensured that, at least, the Philippine units had good leadership. The army department headquarters in the Philippines carefully examined and approved every officer who served with locally recruited troops. The regular army assigned experienced officers to provide senior leadership. Many of the junior officer positions were filled by experienced NCOs from the volunteer regiments, who were willing to sign up and stay for another hitch in the Philippines. These men, who already had considerable experience in small-unit patrolling and combat, were able to put the Scouts and the

Constabulary through a proper training program. With experienced leadership, the Scouts and the Constabulary soon became highly competent counterinsurgency forces.

POLICE AND HOME GUARDS IN COUNTERINSURGENCY
THE MALAYA CASE

In many counterinsurgency campaigns of the last century, local police and paramilitary forces have played key roles. During the Malayan Emergency from 1948 to 1960, the locally organized forces played the lead role in defeating the insurgents. Under the British and Malayan laws, the role of the armed forces was to support the police and the civil authorities, and the captured insurgents were treated under the criminal code, prosecuted under a system of special courts and tribunals. At the start of the insurgency, the Malayan police were a relatively small force, untrained and poorly equipped for countering an insurgency, and just beginning to recover from the disruption caused by the Japanese occupation. During the war, some of the police had retreated to the hills and become guerrillas. Others had stayed at their posts and been imprisoned. Others had collaborated with the Japanese. In 1948, the police were still reorganizing, so training levels were low in contrast to the prewar police force. Although the Malayan police had been one of the most effective police forces in the British Empire, they still shared many of the characteristics of a third world police force. As in most colonial regimes, there was considerable petty corruption. This was especially prevalent in the lower ranks of the rural police, where there was less supervision. At their best, the rural police units weren't very energetic. In 1948, the strength of the police force was just over 10,000 personnel for a country of 8 million people. Often scattered in small outposts, the police were an easy target for the well-organized insurgents, who could easily raid the local outposts and seize police weapons. In the early stages of the conflict, many of the police refrained from risking their lives, and offered little resistance to the rebels. Low morale also plagued the regular police, for they took the brunt of the government casualties. Another major problem for the police was their ethnic makeup. Almost all the Malayan police were ethnic Malayans, but 90 percent of the insurgents were ethnic Chinese. Although more than 40 percent of the Malayan population was ethnic Chinese, the Malayans had little social contact with the Chinese, did not know the Chinese language, and had little understanding or sympathy for the Chinese grievances with the government. In short, the police had to deal with an essentially alien people in their midst.

The British government responded with a major expansion of the police forces. They created special paramilitary police units, essentially light infantry forces called jungle companies, which were organized and equipped to take the fight to the insurgent base areas hidden in the Malayan jungle. One advantage the British had in 1948 was a large, well-trained corps of police throughout the empire with extensive experience in dealing with local unrest and even large-scale insurgency. The recent end of Britain's Palestine mandate meant that there were several hundred ex-Palestine police available for service in Malaya, and they were sent immediately to bolster the force. There were good and bad aspects to this. On the plus side, the ex-Palestine police had recent counterinsurgency experience and solid training. The downside was that the Palestine police also had a deserved reputation for strong-arm tactics and the use of torture in interrogations that, in fact, led to many substantiated charges of excessive force used against the Chinese population. Indeed, brutal police methods served as one of the best recruiting tools for the insurgent cause in Malaya, as they have in many other insurgencies. Alienation of the Chinese population, coupled with few police officers who understood the Chinese language and culture, meant that even ethnic Chinese who had little liking for the insurgents were reluctant to assist the police and provide information about the insurgents.

The Malayan police force was quickly expanded by creating a force of thirty thousand "special constables": volunteers from the Malayan population formed into "area security units" of about thirty-five men each. Special constables carried out paramilitary duties such as searches, patrols, guard duty, and road checks.[3] Colonel Gray, who had served as inspector-general of the Palestine police and had considerable counterinsurgency experience, was brought in to reorganize and retrain the Malayan police.

One of the greatest problems at the start of the insurgency was the state of police training, leadership, and doctrine. The rapid expansion of the police meant a low standard of leadership and training. Neither the army nor the police knew how to operate in the jungle, so the jungle became a sanctuary for the guerrillas. Lacking an adequate doctrine and experienced leaders, the police and military response was geared to the heavy-handed methods typical of the recent insurgency in Palestine. The army carried out large, firepower-intensive military sweeps of the jungle, and the police conducted cordon and search operations in built-up areas. Both methods resulted in a lot of impressive activity, but inflicted few casualties on the insurgents. Rebels easily retreated, then moved back into areas "cleared" by the police and army. There was no effective coordination of the police and military.

As in many insurgencies, the police and military high commands were slow to adapt.[4] For the first two years of the Emergency, the police and military blundered through the counterinsurgency campaign. Things improved somewhat with the arrival of General Briggs as the operational commander in 1950 and the establishment of a British government commission in 1951 to investigate and report on police performance in the wake of the poorly handled Singapore riots of December 1950. Briggs, given authority over all the security services, began to reorganize the police and military forces. In order to provide for effective intelligence, he created a special branch of the police, separate from the criminal division, which would have special responsibility for intelligence against the insurgents. The weakness of the junior leadership of the police was recognized. The establishment of junior police officers (inspectors) was increased by several hundred, and direct recruitment of police inspectors authorized instead of promotion from the ranks. Police lieutenants, mostly British or Eurasian ex-army NCOs, were recruited on short-term contracts to help lead the force. Efforts were increased to recruit Chinese into the police ranks to improve the poor relations between the Chinese and the Malayan police.[5]

To train the police and army units in jungle warfare, a special jungle warfare course was established, run by a British army lieutenant colonel and veteran of the wartime SAS commandos with a small group of instructors who had experience in jungle warfare from the Burma campaign. Whole units were eventually run through the course. With training in how to operate in the jungle, the army and police were able to employ small patrols to hunt rebels—a tactic that proved far more successful in finding insurgent bands than the large, clumsy military operations that had characterized the first stage of the counterinsurgency program.

Still, by late 1951, the best that can be said is that the British had stabilized the situation and prevented an insurgent victory—but they still weren't winning. Insurgent recruiting remained high, as did the level of violent incidents. New leadership was needed. In early 1952, the British sent out General Gerard Templer to be the new high commissioner, with full civil and military authority. Of equal importance was the appointment of Sir Arthur Young, formerly the head of the London City police, as the new police commander. Young had studied the findings of the 1951 police commission. He realized that the police had plenty of manpower, but lacked effective training and leadership. He immediately set out a long-term program of retraining the police that emphasized developing highly professional commanders and NCOs. Dozens of the most capable Malayan policemen were selected and sent to Britain for the year-long police academy course.[6] Understanding that a shortage of trained leaders was also the major problem in standing up Malayan army units, Templer followed a similar policy. Hundreds of junior officers were sent to new military and police schools established in Malaya, for courses lasting from several weeks to several months. Carefully selected Malayans were pulled from combat to attend the one-year officer course at Sandhurst in Britain, receiving the full, British army professional course. To train personnel for the Special Branch, an intelligence school was created in which police and intelligence officers were introduced to the latest techniques, equipment, and doctrine. The school's scope was expanded to teach a variety of specialist courses on counterinsurgency not only for police and military personnel, but also for civilian government leaders.[7]

Concentrating on leader training slowed the growth of the Malayan police and army. This meant that Britain was required to continue to maintain a large regular army force to fight the insurgents until indigenous Malayan units under good leadership could become available. It was an unpopular course to take, for the British government was clamoring to withdraw regular military forces from Malaya. Templer insisted on his long-term training strategy, and the government reluctantly agreed to keep the military force levels high until more effective Malayan forces could be fielded.

The strategy of training the leaders worked. By 1953, the effectiveness of the Malayan police and army units was improving notably as new officers and NCOs returned from their long training courses. In that year, both Templer and Young could report that the corner had been turned, and the insurgents clearly had lost the initiative.

To assist the regular police and army, several other security forces were formed in Malaya. The largest of these were the Home Guards, volunteers who spent a few hours a week mounting guard at village gates and watch-towers. They normally received no pay for their duty. There were only enough weapons to man one shift of the village guard posts. The weapons would be turned over to the next shift of guards. A small village might have a few dozen home guardsmen armed with twelve rifles. Communications were basic, perhaps a field telephone to the local police headquarters, and training was minimal, amounting to some training in weapons handling and guard procedures. The Malayan Home Guard forces were not capable of doing much beyond guard duty at villages or buildings, or helping to man checkpoints—but it was enough.

Counterinsurgency requires securing government buildings and villages, and protecting vital economic resources such as factories, mines, and large farms. Providing basic security of this nature requires a large amount of man-power and it is, frankly, a waste of resources to use well-trained, well-equipped troops in basic guard and security missions such as this. By using the Home Guards to carry out this mission, the government freed its trained forces for the more complex operations of patrolling and clearing suspected rebel areas. The principle of unity of command was maintained. The Home Guards had their own inspector and training office and the district and national com-manders were answerable to the police chain of command. Some of the states developed special squads from among the most capable Home Guardsmen, and these groups supported the police on one- to two-day patrols, for which they received daily pay. At the peak of the insurgency in 1952, two hundred and fifty thousand men were enrolled in the Home Guards. The Home Guards in Malaya saw little action—but that wasn't important. Their presence alone helped establish a feeling of security among the threatened population. More important, they freed up the regular forces to go on the offensive against rebel concentrations and they cost little money.

The Home Guard was also used as a means of bringing Chinese into the security force structure—an important consideration in view of the highly ethnic nature of the insurgency. Fifty thousand ethnic Chinese were eventually enrolled in the Home Guards as the counterinsurgency campaign progressed. As people with broad connections throughout the Chinese community, the Chinese members of the security forces were invaluable in providing useful information to the Special Branch.

LOCAL FORCES IN ALGERIA

The French developed useful lessons from combating the insurgency in Algeria from 1954 to 1962. Their program to establish home guards in rural villages was one of the most successful features of the counterinsurgency strategy, although it probably began too late to have a decisive effect. In the first three years of the insurgency in Algeria, the government controlled the cities and the areas of heavy French settlement while the FLN had a fairly free run of the rural areas. Although most Algerians did not support the rebels—or were, at best, lukewarm to the FLN—there was little French presence in, or contact with, the rural areas where most of the Algerians lived, aside from heavily fortified local army outposts. In 1957, the French finally instituted a program designed to organize the rural areas against the insurgents. The French army established a new corps called the Special Administrative Service (SAS), composed of small teams of carefully selected, Arabic-speaking French officers and NCOs who would live with the rural population, supervise economic aid and social programs, assist local Algerian officials loyal to France, and, most important, organize a local home guard of Algerians willing to defend their villages from the FLN rebels.

The SAS, nicknamed the "blue *kepis*" by the Algerians, were outside the usual French army command structure and provided a bridge between the French civil administration and the civilian population. The small SAS detachments, commanded by a captain or lieutenant who was fluent in Arabic and who had expertise in Arab culture, usually included several officers and NCOs, some civilian specialists such as a medical team, and fifteen to twenty soldiers for security.[8] The SAS officers were authorized to spend money on public works projects, coordinate jobs programs, and establish schools for the rural populace. One of the most important functions of the

SAS was to run special courses in administration for training Algerian officials. This way, the French succeeded in increasing the number of Muslim functionaries loyal to France. Eventually, four hundred SAS teams operated in the Algerian hinterland.

The SAS helped form small village self-defense forces called *"harkis,"* who were armed with a motley array of hunting rifles and shotguns, as well as some surplus military weapons. The only mission of the *harkis* was to patrol the areas around their own villages and keep out the rebel FLN bands. By all accounts, the program was exceptionally successful from the start. By June 1960, more than 57,000 *harkis* had been enrolled in the home guard programs and another 27,500 enrolled as auxiliary police.[9] The program worked in proportion to the quality of the personnel of the SAS teams and, in general, the quality of the SAS teams was quite high. The *harkis* proved to be exceptionally loyal fighters. Within two years, they had largely driven the FLN insurgents out of many rural areas, with heavy casualties for the FLN. By any account, the French efforts were highly cost effective. At its peak in 1959, the SAS included 1,287 officers, 661 NCOs, and 2,921 civilian specialists.[10] By 1959, the French army and air force, backed up by the home guards in the rural areas, had basically broken the insurgency—with most of the FLN leadership jailed or in exile. The few remaining FLN bands had been harassed and whittled down in a rural environment that was increasingly hostile.[11] However, having won the war, the French government decided that it did not want the expense and trouble of maintaining Algeria as a colony and entered into negotiations with the FLN that led to Algerian independence in 1962.

THE VIETNAM WAR

The Vietnam War provides a useful case study of the effectiveness and limitations of home guards against an insurgency. In the 1950s, as the Viet Cong insurgency was beginning to undermine the U.S.-backed South Vietnamese government, the Saigon government established two home guard organizations: the Popular Forces and the Regional Forces. The Popular Forces were organized into platoons, given minimal pay and a few cast-off military weapons, and assigned to protect only their home villages. The Regional Forces were somewhat better paid and equipped and were organized into companies and battalions for service in their home province—usually no more than twenty miles from their home villages. Through most of the Vietnam War, the role of the home guard organizations was ignored in favor of lavish funding and support for the South Vietnamese regular army. As with most of the Vietnamese military, officer appointments in the Popular Forces and Regional Forces were arranged largely as rewards for political loyalty.[12]

However, despite the mediocre officers, low pay, and poor equipment, the Vietnamese home guard units performed surprisingly well. Despite receiving only 4 percent of the South Vietnamese military budget, they accounted for 30 percent of the Viet Cong and North Vietnamese casualties inflicted during the war. Only after the Tet Offensive of 1968 did the Vietnamese government start to pay more attention to the need to strengthen the home guards.[13]

One of the most innovative and successful home guard programs was supported by the U.S. Marine Corps. Starting in 1965, the marines set up combined action platoons in villages throughout the northern region of the Republic of Vietnam. The combined action platoons were squads of fourteen marines who lived in the villages with the Vietnamese. Each combined action platoon was responsible for a village of about 3,500 people. The Marines organized, trained, and fought with the village home guard platoons of thirty-eight men. The combined action platoons are widely considered to be one of the most effective counterinsurgency programs ever developed by the U.S. military. The Viet Cong were unable to operate in villages protected by the U.S./Vietnamese forces; reassured by the permanent presence of the U.S. forces, the villages were confident that they would not be abandoned. The presence of a few U.S. forces in the villages also assured the villagers that their farms would not become free fire zones for excessive U.S. firepower. At the peak of the program in 1970, the United States deployed 114 combined action platoons, with 2,200 marine and navy personnel. The deployed marine and navy personnel were normal soldiers without special language or culture training, yet they managed to quickly adapt, learning enough Vietnamese to get along, winning the friendship and respect of their Vietnamese comrades. However, General Westmoreland, whose attitude was typical of the army's fixation on large conventional operations and success measured by enemy body counts, did not care for the methodical approach of the combined action platoons. He devoted only one paragraph in his memoirs to the program, arguing that he never had enough troops to carry out such a program in the rest of Vietnam. Actually, to have secured two thousand villages and seven million peasants in this manner would have required twenty-eight thousand U.S. troops—about 5 percent of Westmoreland's total force in Vietnam.[14]

LESSONS FROM OTHER CONFLICTS

In several other major counterinsurgency campaigns, lightly armed home guard organizations have been key elements in defeating insurgents. In Peru, the Sendero Luminoso insurgency of the 1980s to 1990s was largely broken by the creation of village home guard units, in which 300,000 rural peasants were enrolled to provide local security.[15] To combat a Communist insurgency in northern Thailand in the 1970s to 1980s, the Thais raised a force of 170,000 village militiamen supported by 20,000 border police.[16] During the Communist insurgency in Greece (1944–1950), the Greek government raised a 50,000-man home guard force to take over rear area security duties, freeing regular army personnel to go on the offensive against the rebels.[17]

In none of these cases did the home guards take part in major military operations or grand, decisive battles. Many never saw combat; at most, they saw some minor skirmishes. Home guards have normally been lightly armed, with minimal training, and without the expensive, high-tech gear considered essential by the modern conventional military. They are incapable of rapid, decisive combat operations. In many cases, nonetheless, they have provided one of the most essential elements necessary to defeat insurgents: they gave the local people a sense of security and stability, providing clear evidence of government presence in rural and isolated areas. Moreover, they did it for a low expenditure in money and trained military personnel.

MILITIAS AND PARAMILITARY FORCES

One means of combating an insurgency is to raise an irregular militia force. Such forces are essentially private armies, financed or supported by the government with the mission of fighting the insurgents. Employment of militias against insurgents, rather than regular police and military forces, is a very dangerous policy. It has been adopted by governments usually as a desperation measure, either when there were no effective regular government forces, or when the governments were politically constrained from using regular forces.

The most dramatic example of using irregular forces against insurgents is found in the German revolution of 1918 to 1919. With the collapse of the German imperial state in the wake of World War I, a new democratic government was established in Germany—which was immediately confronted by Communist revolutionaries, who seized power in Berlin, Munich, and other major cities in the midst of the postwar disorder. With the army demoralized and fading away, and the police too few and too poorly armed to keep order, the new German government encouraged the formation of irregular army forces, the *Freikorps* (literally: Free Corps), as the only practical means to defeat the revolutionaries and establish the authority of the new state.

The *Freikorps* were organized by professional officers and composed mostly of recently demobilized veteran soldiers, who needed no training to conduct complex military operations. They were essentially a mercenary army, organized and paid by the government on short-term contracts. Within weeks, a force of several hundred thousand men was raised, organized into divisions and brigades and ready to employ tanks, artillery, and machine guns against the rebels. In a series of large operations, the *Freikorps* quickly and ruthlessly destroyed the revolutionaries, who were a poorly trained, poorly led, and poorly armed rabble in comparison. However, after the battle was won, many in the *Freikorps* did not wish to be demobilized or forfeit their status as the primary armed force in the nation. Ideologically committed to counterrevolution, the *Freikorps* tended to support the extreme right of the political spectrum, and once organized, were not to be gotten rid of now that order had been restored. On two occasions, some of the *Freikorps* attempted to overthrow the new German democracy and institute an authoritarian government. The first *Freikorps* attack on democracy was the *Kapp Putsch*, a coup that briefly took control of Berlin in 1920; the second attack occurred when several of the

Freikorps supported Hitler's coup attempt in Munich in 1923. Both coups were suppressed, but at the price of an ugly heritage of bitterness that poisoned the German political life for the next decade and helped weaken the democratic Weimar government.

Using private or tribal armies in counterinsurgency has usually worked out poorly. When the insurgency broke out in Algeria in 1954, the French turned to some dissident Algerian nationalist leaders opposed to the FLN insurgency, authorizing them to recruit their own forces to fight the FLN. One force under Ben Hadj, an Algerian nationalist leader, fought successfully against the local FLN for a while, and the French supplied him with an ample supply of modern weapons. The ranks of Ben Hadj's private army were then infiltrated by FLN nationalists, who assassinated Ben Hadj and led a portion of his force off to join the FLN. Another Algerian nationalist who had split with the FLN, Messali Hadj, was allowed to raise a personal force of 3,300 men, and was again armed by the French. As with Ben Hadj, he proved useful at first, but then his personal political ambitions became evident when he set up his own political network. By 1958, the French administration viewed him as dangerous and untrustworthy, so he was killed by the French forces. Many of his well-armed troops went over to the FLN insurgents, while only 300 joined the government forces.[18]

Another example of using irregular militias to fight insurgents is from Colombia in the 1990s to the present. By the early 1990s, a Communist insurgency had been going on for more than twenty years. An estimated 20,000 armed rebels, in two major Communist groups (FARC and ELN), effectively controlled large parts of rural Colombia. The democratic government of Colombia, which had long been averse to putting the country on a war footing, searched desperately for a solution to the insurgency but lacked the political will to take any concrete measures. The Colombian army of 146,000 troops, 0.5 percent of the population, was too small to provide adequate security in a large country. The military was also bound by numerous political restrictions, such as a ban on using drafted high school graduates in combat units, nor was the government willing to allow the formation of local home guard forces. Rebels operated openly through much of the country, able to pay some police to look the other way, or to kill other policemen who interfered. Finally, the owners of large and medium-sized farms began to ignore the government and hire bands of mercenary soldiers to take on the rebels.

The self-defense groups, later called paramilitaries, were successful in clearing some areas of insurgents where the government forces refused to become engaged. Although they were effective, the paramilitaries' methods were reminiscent of the "no-prisoners" approach of the German *Freikorps*, and numerous summary executions were carried out against rebels and suspected supporters. As the private armies grew to four hundred groups operating by 1994, and began to take control of rural areas away from the insurgents, the government finally authorized their role and provided financial support. In its tradition of half-hearted measures, however, the government also tried to regulate the paramilitaries by forbidding them to carry rifles or machine guns. Per government decree, the paramilitaries were sanctioned to fight—but supposed to fight well-armed insurgents only with pistols. As with all the other attempts to regulate the paramilitaries, such nonsensical rules were simply ignored. The paramilitaries were so effective that in the 2000 peace talks between the government and major insurgent factions, the rebels demanded that President Andres Pastrana stop support for the paramilitaries. The government conceded this issue, officially disbanding the paramilitary groups and cutting off financial support.

However, once organized, the thousands of well-armed paramilitaries, having become a power of their own, refused to quietly disband. FARC, the major insurgent group, had taken over the cocaine trade to finance their insurgency. When the now illegal paramilitaries drove FARC out of a district, they then took over the drug trade to finance their own operations. The once-local self-defense militias had, by 2002, become a major power in their own right in the complex Colombian civil war, ready to take on the government forces in several districts. As of this writing (2005), rural Colombia is now facing a three-way conflict: between the insurgents, the paramilitaries, and the government forces, all trying to establish their authority.[19] Without a real chance to defeat the paramilitaries in battle, the Colombian government will, sooner or later, have to come to some kind of agreement to demobilize the paramilitaries—perhaps with amnesties and large payments for the members—or find a means of regularizing them, and bringing them under government control. Either way, it will be a very expensive proposition. The need to provide security for the rural popula-tion, however, cannot be ignored. The failure of the national government to do this lies at the root of Colombia's current dilemma.

TRAINING ARMIES

The U.S. military has a long and successful history of advising, training, and equipping third world armies, helping them to become effective military forces. In World War II, a small force of trainers and logisticians under General Joseph Stilwell organized, trained, and equipped a Chinese army that played a vital role in defeating the Japanese in northern Burma in 1944. In 1947, Greece was threatened by a major Communist insurgency. The United States initiated a major aid and advisory program for a weak and demoralized Greek military that enabled it to defeat the insurgents by late 1949. The United States carried out an extensive aid and advisory program to help the Philippine Republic defeat the Huk insurgents in the 1940s to 1950s. During the Korean War, the U.S. Army poured in large quantities of aid, advisors, and equipment to rebuild an army shattered by the Communist offensive of 1950. By the end of the war in 1953, the Korean Army was on its way to becoming a formidable fighting force. From 1981 to 1992, American aid and military advisors led a program to expand, retrain, and reequip El Salvador's armed forces, which became an effective force that first prevented a rebel victory and later pushed the insurgents onto the defensive. A regenerated Salvadoran military was able to ensure a peace set-tlement, on the government's terms, in 1992. Against this record of success, the only major failure was the U.S. effort to train and assist the South Vietnamese army from the 1950s to 1975.

A proper account of each of these examples would take at least a volume apiece. For the purposes of this book, a brief summary of the basic lessons learned from this large amount of historical experience will suffice. The problems that armies and security forces of undeveloped nations have expe-rienced, when confronted by war or insurgency, are fairly typical and cross the often-artificial limits of time and geography.

First of all, the military and police forces of many third world states tend to be corrupt, poorly trained, and incompetently led. The officer corps might have a basic professional competence, but with higher appointments commonly made for internal political reasons, rather than an officer's record, there is little chance for improvement. The soldiers might at least be fed and have a basic level of training, but more often soldiers are simply press-ganged peasants led by officers who have little concern for them. The basic elements common to effective modern armies, such as well-trained professional NCOs, are absent. Developing a good NCO corps requires decent pay and conditions—costs that third world military and political leaders are rarely interested in paying.

Third world armies tend to be poorly equipped. Of course, their governments might lay out large sums for impressive modern hardware like tanks and airplanes—the things that impress the neighboring states. The reality is that keeping such equipment repaired and operable requires a lot of well-paid specialist personnel and a considerable outlay for spare parts, maintenance facilities, and the like. As a rule, therefore, most often the heavy weaponry, unless it is especially simple and robust, sits rusting by the barracks or on the airfields for a lack of parts or competent maintenance personnel.

Finally, third world militaries and police faced with an internal insurgency usually have poor relations with most of the population, due to a weak or nonexistent respect for basic human rights. In most cases, these militaries have no strong professional traditions they can look to as a model. Instead, they have existed primarily as forces to enforce internal security—usually at the behest of an undemocratic government. Typically, at the start of an insurgency, the average peasant or poor urban dweller sees the regular police and armed forces more as enemies and oppressors than as friends and protectors. If this weren't the case, an insurgency would have a great deal of trouble getting started.

Throughout the twentieth century, the U.S. armed forces acquired extensive experience in building, training, and remolding ineffective militaries and security forces into effective forces. This experience can be distilled into a several-step process: training the soldiers, training junior leaders, selecting and training senior leaders, and providing effective advice and supervision. Another primary requirement is to provide robust, effective equipment that technologically unsophisticated forces can operate effectively.

Training soldiers to be effective combat troops is the simplest step in the process of building an effective third world military. Training troops in

the fundamental skills of soldiering is something the U.S. Army is exceptionally good at and, although it's hard work, it requires no great degree of
military genius. All that is needed is a training camp with basic infrastructure and a corps of instructors who are competent in their specialities. The
U.S. program under General Joe Stilwell that built several Chinese divisions
for the campaign in Burma in 1942 to 1944 is a good example, having transformed what had been a miserable, badly trained, and defeated army into a
competent and victorious force. In 1942, Stilwell took the remnants of the
Chinese army that had been driven out of Burma, along with new recruits
shipped to him by air from China, and put them into training camps in
India run by U.S. Army instructors. Few of the American NCOs and officers
assigned to Stilwell spoke more than a few words of Chinese at the beginning of the training, so most training was by example and repetition. On vis-
its to training centers, Stilwell himself, the American theater commander,
would get down in the dirt and patiently show the Chinese recruits how to
properly aim and fire a rifle. He did this partly for the benefit of the Chinese
soldiers, to show his personal interest in their training, and partly as an
example for the American instructors in how to teach the Chinese soldiers.
Instruction in more complex skills, such as using mortars and artillery, was
carried out in special courses, and interpreters were hired to assist the U.S.
trainers. Stilwell believed that the Chinese could make good soldiers even
though few others in the West or East thought the Chinese could ever stand
up in battle against the Japanese. Stilwell proved the critics wrong. After two
years of patient and thorough training, his Chinese divisions were able to
take the offensive, defeating veteran Japanese troops blocking the land route
to China through northern Burma.[20]

In the 1960s, the CIA and U.S. military advisors were able to organize,
train, and equip Laotian mountain tribesmen to defend their territory
against Communist Laotian and North Vietnamese incursions. The U.S.
training program in Laos was one of the little-known successes of the
Indochina War. Into the early 1970s, the generally illiterate and unsophisticated Laotians, armed mostly with light weapons, were able to hold their
own—even against well-trained North Vietnamese with far superior firepower. The Laotians were finally forced to flee their land upon the general collapse of Laos and South Vietnam in 1975.[21]

The U.S. Army's first step in combating the insurgency in El Salvador from 1980 to 1992 was to expand the Salvadoran Army, creating a new force of light infantry battalions specially trained for counterinsurgency. Since Congress restricted the U.S. advisor presence in El Salvador to no more than fifty-five personnel, the United States set up a large new training center in nearby Honduras, where Salvadoran units could be sent for training (there was no statutory limit on U.S. advisor and instructor personnel in Honduras). Rebuilding an army takes time, and the Salvadoran army was a badly trained, badly equipped, poorly led force when the insurgency began. The process of dramatically expanding the Salvadoran armed forces, developing competent junior leadership, and deploying the new battalions back to El Salvador went more slowly than anyone in the Pentagon had expected. Only by late 1984, after three years of steady training and large amounts of U.S. aid and military equipment, did the Salvadoran army show a notable turnaround in their combat effectiveness. At that point the tide turned, and the insurgents were put on the defensive. After a long fight, the rebels were essentially defeated and soon began negotiations to end the war on the government's terms.

One critical problem in rebuilding the Salvadoran army was the overall low level of training and lack of competence of the junior leaders. The Salvadoran military, like most third world forces, had no professional NCO corps to provide small-group leadership or handle such technical specialties as maintenance, supply, or communications. The third world military culture typically ignores the need for a professional NCO corps. Even if the value of NCOs is understood, the governments of developing countries are unwilling or unable to provide adequate salaries and benefits to keep skilled NCOs and technical specialists in the force. The Salvadoran military followed this pattern. It takes years to develop good NCOs and technicians. By the time a Salvadoran NCO finished his training and became competent, his enlistment would be up. At this point he would leave the military with his new skills to get a higher-paying civilian job. The excessive personnel turnover within the junior leader ranks slowed the expansion of the Salvadoran army's new counterinsurgency battalions, because elite light forces are extremely reliant upon good junior leaders. The constant shortage of trained technicians and specialist personnel in El Salvador also meant a low standard of maintenance and equipment availability. Usually only 50 percent of the Salvadoran aircraft were operable. Such problems are also the norm in other third world militaries, and in the armed forces of the former Soviet Bloc states. Getting militaries to build an effective corps of NCOs and specialist technicians requires considerable outside assistance, as well as a conscious plan to change a dysfunctional military culture. It can be done, but it takes time.

That most small-nation military and security forces suffer from poor officer leadership is not due to a lack of available talent. Usually the officer corps, drawn from the middle and upper classes, is fairly well educated. Most of the officers have the potential to be capable leaders—if professionally trained. The problem of officer leadership lies entrenched in the nature of the national politics and the long-established military culture.

One of the core problems in supporting the government of El Salvador against a major insurgency in the 1980s was the dysfunctional nature of El Salvador's military leadership. In many respects, El Salvador's situation typifies the problems of military and security forces in developing countries. El Salvador had endured a series of sometimes ruthless military dictatorships from 1932 to 1980. Politically, the military was the primary power in national politics, although civilian politicians often fronted for the military juntas and factions. The officer corps was tightly bound up with the business interests of the leading families of El Salvador. The officers, as in most Latin American countries, were drawn from the small upper and middle class, and trained in an elite four-year military academy. At the academy each class formed lifelong bonds and political alliances that made the officer academy as much a school for conducting coups, as for military operations. Over the four-year course, the classes formed *"tandas,"* closely knit clubs in which officers of a year-group ruthlessly supported each other for position and promotion, engaging in cutthroat rivalries with other class *tandas*. The rivalries within the military were so extreme that during the 1980 to 1992 insurgency a field commander desperately calling for air support might not receive it if the air commander was a member of a rival *tanda*.[22] It was nearly impossible to remove openly corrupt or incompetent officers if those officers were politically well protected, or were members of one of the stronger *tandas*. Even the popular democratic president of El Salvador, Jose Napoleon Duarte, one of the most honest and decent reformist leaders in the history of Central America, was unable to buck the system to relieve openly corrupt and incompetent officers. This was the military that the United States had to support and reform to defeat a Communist insurgency.

Rebuilding the Salvadoran military—whose culture was as much a cause of the insurgency as the government's inability to combat it—required a long-term approach by the U.S. Southern Command (Southcom) and the U.S. advisors. Essentially, U.S. strategists wisely wrote off most of the senior officers of the Salvadoran military as too incorrigible to reform and retrain. A key aspect of the U.S. program to rebuild the Salvadoran military was to send the younger officers, the ones less influenced by the dysfunctional military culture, to extended training courses in the United States and Panama Canal Zone. There they could, over time, absorb not only basic military knowledge, but be part of a professional military environment where corruption, business deals, and *tanda* relations were not part of daily life.[23] The best of the younger Salvadoran officers were sent to the yearlong U.S. Army Staff College course for Latin Americans at the School of the Americas. Along with a high-quality staff education, the U.S. faculty emphasized the importance of basic democratic values and human rights as part of the ethics of the school.[24] Selected Salvadoran lieutenants and captains were sent to U.S. service schools, such as the infantry and artillery officers' courses, where they received the same advanced officer training as U.S. officers. The U.S. Air Force Interamerican Air Force Academy, then located in Panama, provided basic and advanced courses for the Salvadoran air force officers. The guiding idea was that the U.S.-trained officers would not only learn the right leadership skills for the battlefield, but would also absorb an understanding of how a military ought to operate in a democratic society. As the younger, U.S.-trained officers moved up in rank, they brought a new ethos to the armed forces of El Salvador.

The patient, long-term approach by Southcom worked. Over time, the Salvadoran military developed solid leadership and improved its human rights record as the U.S.-trained officers rose to battalion commands and senior staff positions. By the early 1990s, a democratically elected Salvadoran government was able to remove the last layer of senior officers trained under the old regime and replace them with more professional, democratically oriented officers trained in U.S. military schools. Today, the Salvadoran armed forces have the best-led and most democratic officer corps in Central America.[25]

The concept of rebuilding a dysfunctional army into an effective fighting force by carefully selecting and mentoring senior officers has proven successful in numerous cases since the Philippine Insurrection. To rebuild the Chinese army in Burma, General Joe Stilwell found the most promising younger Chinese officers and, using his leverage as theater commander and his control of U.S. military aid to China, insisted that the officers he named be given command of the regiments and divisions under his command. He reinforced his program of developing the Chinese army leaders by assigning American advisors and liaison teams down to regimental level.

In other times and places, the U.S. Army and Air Force have found other officers with the talent to spot good leadership in foreign armies and the diplomatic skill—coupled with the clout of U.S. aid—to insist that incompetent officers be relieved and good officers be given senior commands. When the United States was confronted with the Communist insurgency in Greece, the first head of the U.S. advisory mission, General Livesey, found it difficult to provide a clear strategic direction to the Greek military leadership. In 1948, he was replaced by Major General James Van Fleet, not known as an intellectual, but rather a no-nonsense fighting commander under General George Patton in World War II. He pressured and virtually bullied the Greek government into reorganizing their army, replacing the high command and many of the senior commanders with men he named. As with Stilwell, he insisted that U.S. advisors be assigned down to division, and even regimental, level. The Greek government's offensive against the insurgents quickly gained momentum, and by late 1949 the insurgency was broken.[26]

Van Fleet demonstrated his talents again during the Korean War. In the first year of the Korean War, the South Korean army performed poorly in combat, to put it mildly. Most of the ROK divisions collapsed, first under the North Korean offensive in the summer of 1950, then under the Red Chinese offensive of winter 1950 to 1951. The South Korean army suffered from many problems, including poor training and a lack of equipment, but the greatest deficiency was the shortage of good officers. As is common with a new army in an undeveloped nation, the South Korean officers were highly politicized, often corrupt, and poorly trained, more interested in tending to their family business than in caring for their troops. In 1951, Van Fleet was brought in as the chief advisor to the South Korean army, with the mission of rebuilding and retraining the force. Besides setting up a series of training schools for the South Korean soldiers and junior officers, he personally selected some of the best and brightest of the Korean officers, sending them to the United States to attend the one-year U.S. Army Staff College course at Fort Leavenworth. These officers came back to Korea, with the war still raging, and were placed in top command and staff positions. While still weak, the combat performance of the South Korean army improved noticeably. In 1953, Van Fleet was promoted to serve as the U.S. commander in Korea and, as the war ran down, convinced President Dwight Eisenhower to make an expensive commitment: to provide a comprehensive, long-term military aid program to reequip and train the South Korean forces so they could take over their own defense and allow most of the U.S. forces to return home.[27]

While Van Fleet was rebuilding the Korean army, another remarkable American military figure emerged as the military advisor to the Philippine government—then under severe threat from the Huk insurgency. Air Force Lieutenant Colonel Edward Lansdale became a legend in counterinsurgency circles for his brilliant performance as an advisor to Philippine Defense Minister Ramon Magsaysay. When the highly competent Magsaysay was appointed as defense secretary in 1950, the Huk insurgency was growing at an alarming rate, and the military campaign to contain it was foundering. The rebellion was led by former guerrillas who had fought the Japanese from 1942 to 1945. After the war, the somewhat Marxist Huks took up the cause of the small peasants and tenant farmers of the Philippines, a group that had long suffered under oppressive conditions and government corruption. The elite groups that dominated the Philippine government tended to ignore their basic concerns. As is so often the story, the army and police were part of the problem. Both forces were often corrupt, preferring to respond to any outbreaks of violence by even more violent measures against the peasants. Every government antiguerrilla campaign seemed to serve as a recruiting drive for the peasants, who became more and more alienated from the government and security forces.

Lansdale and Magsaysay worked remarkably well together as a team. At Lansdale's urging, Magsaysay pushed for the retraining of the armed forces, emphasizing a new program of civic action to be carried out by the military. Specialist units were trained and equipped to go after the Huks in their jungle bases. At the same time, the army carried out a large number of small civic action programs—building roads and schools and providing aid to small farmers. Lansdale worked to see that U.S. aid was adequate to support Magsaysay's reform program. For his part, Magsaysay flew around the country holding surprise inspections. He obtained presidential authority to remove officers on the spot, and even to order courts-martial of corrupt officers. He was courageous enough to stand up to the military establishment when necessary. At one point he even rejected an entire army promotion list because of the lack of combat experience of the officer nominees. He worked tirelessly to identify the best officers and was ruthless in firing corrupt and incompetent officers, replacing them with officers who not only were professionally competent, but who understood the need for a program to win over the allegiance of the peasants. The military reforms, combined with free and honest elections and civil government reforms, "drained the swamp" of peasant discontent. By 1954 the Huks had few supporters left, and all but a few had surrendered to the government. As in many counterinsurgency campaigns, the government eventually won by dealing with discontent at several levels—economic, political, and local, as well as in the military. However, for the military side of the equation, selecting and placing good leaders was a key element of the reform program that won the campaign. [28]

U.S. FAILURES IN SECURITY FORCE TRAINING
The U.S. record in training the South Vietnamese Army was mixed. When the American military training groups arrived in force in 1961, they found a poorly trained Vietnamese Army with a highly politicized officer corps and

generally poor leadership. Officer appointment was through political loyalty and connections, not by merit, and officers typically had little regard for their soldiers. A USAF training group arrived in 1961 to train the South Vietnamese to operate the T-28 trainers, A-1 Skyraiders, transports, and helicopters that the American military aid program provided for the counterinsurgency operations that were the primary mission of the South Vietnamese forces. Frustrated with the slow pace of building a third world air force and wanting to get into action themselves, the U.S. Air Force trainers began to fly the combat missions themselves. In a short time, the U.S. Air Force quickly took over the war effort. It was faster and more efficient that way, but it didn't leave a South Vietnamese air force that could confidently stand on its own feet. The U.S. Air Force focus was on winning the war quickly. The South Vietnamese, incapable of quickly winning the war, were pushed to the side.

When the U.S. Army and Marine combat units arrived in 1965, the same impatience prevailed. The United States quickly took over the main war effort. Training for the Army of the Republic of Vietnam (ARVN) was oriented not toward building an effective counterinsurgency force, but toward creating a smaller, paler copy of an American conventional army. American trainers and advisors with the ARVN worked hard to support their allies but never had the authority, whether implicit or explicit, to call a halt to misconceived operations or see that incompetent ARVN commanders were removed. Serving as an advisor or trainer with the South Vietnamese was not considered prestigious, for Westmoreland and the army staff conveyed the attitude that advisory or training duty with the ARVN did not further a professional career or chance for promotion in the way that service with U.S. units or staffs did. So most U.S. professional officers sought to serve in U.S. combat units simply to protect their careers.

Despite all the drawbacks associated with training and advising, the United States helped train and mentor many competent South Vietnamese officers. During the last 1975 campaign, when the South Vietnamese army was completely on its own, some of the well-led ARVN units fought exceptionally well; however, most did not.[29] The great failing was not in the lack of supplies or equipment, but in the lack of effective battlefield leadership. Despite a decade of intensive training and advising, the U.S. military had never broken the culture of highly politicized and poor leadership prevalent in the South Vietnamese forces from its inception to its end. During a decade of American combat involvement, the American commanders in Vietnam never really made a concerted effort to change the South Vietnamese command culture.

While the U.S. effort to train the South Vietnamese cannot be counted as a total failure, the American and international effort to build a new security force in Haiti certainly fits that description. It serves as a perfect case study of how NOT to go about building a security force in a third world nation. When the United States intervened in Haiti with twenty thousand troops in 1994 to depose the military dictatorship and replace it with previously deposed President Jean-Bertrand Aristide, it was confronted with a culture of abject poverty, corruption, and violence built on the authority of a thoroughly rotten military and police force. U.S. forces had the mission of establishing a basic level of civil order in Haiti and creating a new security force that could effectively serve a democratic civilian government. In contrast to the 1992 U.S./UN intervention in Somalia, a plan was actually developed before the invasion to create a new police and security force. The problem was that the plan was utterly unrealistic in its expectations of the Haitians, and so badly supported by the United States and the UN that it never had the slightest chance to succeed.

One of the first steps in the process was to demobilize the corrupt, brutal seven-thousand-man army that had dominated Haiti for more than six decades. While the army was disbanded, some of the soldiers would be permitted to join the newly created national police force. Disbanding the army might have been a good symbolic step toward establishing a democracy, but neither the United States nor the UN was prepared to provide more than a small fraction of the economic aid necessary for Haiti to establish a minimum level of government stability and economic opportunity. In the meantime, the members of the army faced the loss of their status in the nation and almost certain unemployment and poverty.[30] So a large part of the army kept their guns, stayed with their leaders, went underground or to the hills, and simply waited for the occupying forces to leave.

The plan to build a new national police force in place of the army was very hurried, badly conceived, inadequately funded, and poorly executed. The first problem was an inadequate program to screen the 3,400 soldiers initially selected to form the interim police force. Although all police volunteers were supposed to be screened for criminal and human rights violations—as would be expected in a military known for criminality and abuse—in fact, only the officers were given a brief screening. Even less edifying was the participation of Aristide's new high command in the screening process, since some of them had a less than exemplary record in the criminal activity and human rights departments. After the brief screening process, the former soldiers were given six days of training, then sent out in units under the observation (but not control) of international police monitors. To undermine an already inadequate vetting process, no means was set up to properly investigate civilian complaints made against members of the new force. In short, it was mostly the old force—only slightly modified. From the start, the new police force was mistrusted and disliked by the average Haitians, and it failed to quell a mounting wave of crime.[31]

One Haitian idea, supported by the Americans, was to create local provisional police units from civilians selected by the community as well as "vigilance brigades," local civilians who would conduct anticrime patrols. The provisional police and vigilance brigades, given arms and a minimum of training by U.S. Special Forces, were sent out to support the undermanned interim police. The results were not good. While this solution may have helped in some areas, the militia forces were under little control and, in the absence of any functional legal system, soon became a law unto themselves. On one night in March 1995, the vigilance brigades lynched five suspected criminals in Port au Prince.[32]

U.S. plans included the creation of a new national police academy that would rush the former soldiers of the interim police and the new civilian recruits through a four-month course. The academy began under U.S. and UN supervision in early 1995 and had the mission of training 7,000 Haitian national policemen in one year, for the UN security force was scheduled to withdraw from Haiti in February 1996. Not only was the four-month course too short to create competent policemen, but the academy only had room and resources to teach two classes of 375 police candidates at a time.[33] This meant that when the U.S./UN multinational force withdrew, Haitian security would be fully in the hands of a force in which less than half of the members had even minimal training. As for the police leadership, no provision was made for training or mentoring the senior commanders. They would be appointed by the new Aristide regime. It was a recipe for failure, and fail it did.

For the long term, the Haitian security forces suffered from a serious lack of competent leadership, training, and basic equipment. The only significant outside support was provided by a small UN training and aid group that stayed on, but it had few resources, and little authority to change anything. The security situation in Haiti became as bad as, even worse than, before.[34] The culture of the old police and military forces remained. Corruption and abuse remained the norm. Ex-soldiers formed paramilitary groups that still effectively control much of the country. The national police are powerless against the continuing devolution of Haiti from a land of one dictator to a land of multiple warlords.

The U.S. solution at the start was to invade Haiti with large conventional forces and put a new government into power. After that, the primary concern seems to have been to give Haiti the appearance of a new security force at the lowest possible cost, use the smallest number of personnel, and get U.S. forces out of the country at the earliest possible moment. Even in a highly developed country with impressive resources available, the U.S. plan's assumptions about the ability of a former dictatorship to create an effective security force would have been minimal. As a plan for a third world country with a long tradition of incompetent and corrupt security forces, the U.S. approach guaranteed failure. But the long term wasn't important to the Clinton administration and the Pentagon in 1994. What was important was that we looked good in the short term. Because of this, Haiti remains impoverished and unstable—and is getting worse.

TRAINING THE IRAQIS

The U.S. and Coalition attempts to organize, train, equip, and advise security forces for a new Iraqi government after the fall of Saddam's regime is a story of false starts, dead-end roads, and misguided detours. A great deal of time, money, and effort over more than two years have not produced Iraqi police or military forces capable of either taking on the insurgents or providing a basic level of security to the main population centers. More than two years after the end of the conventional phase of the Iraq War, the insurgency is still going strong, with no sign that the Iraqi military and security forces are getting the upper hand. In many respects, the story of organizing and training the Iraqi forces is a textbook example of a wrong approach, based on wrong assumptions.

Although it would have been a fairly easy matter, in the months before the Iraq War, for a dozen good staff officers to come up with a solid plan to build new Iraqi military and security forces, that effort was not made. The failure of the Pentagon and CENTCOM to create a coherent postwar plan for occupying Iraq also extended to the matter of the post-Saddam security forces. The Pentagon's approach was to let the Iraqi exiles sort out the postwar security arrangements—but the Iraqi exiles were so fractious that no general policy or process could be agreed upon. Nor could the exiles agree on a vetting process for admitting members of the current Iraqi military and police forces into the post-Saddam forces. When the U.S. forces drove into Baghdad, these vital issues were still undecided. Still, the United States went ahead with one program to provide postwar Iraq with Iraqi security forces, an expensive plan to train Iraqi exiles to become the cadre for a new Iraqi military. A U.S. major general was appointed to oversee the program, a training site set up, and eight hundred U.S. personnel assigned to support the program. However, disagreement between rival Iraqi groups—problems that were foreseen by area experts who knew Iraqi politics—essentially killed the effort. Although the Joint Chiefs of Staff issued a planning order to train Iraqi exiles on September 22, 2002, the actual training did not begin for another five months. In the end, a mere seventy Iraqi exiles were trained.[35] Thus, the main strategy to build a cadre for a new Iraqi military collapsed even before the war began.

Another U.S. strategic assumption was the hope that, somehow, the UN, NATO, and other nations would step in after the fall of Saddam's regime and generously help train and organize new Iraqi armed forces and police. As with the hope that the UN and allied nations would provide a large peacekeeping and security force for postwar Iraq, this too proved a chimera.

One of the most vital elements of postwar planning—setting up an effective Iraqi police force—was ignored in the run up to the war. It was well known that Iraq under Saddam had the typical police force of a third world dictatorship. It was politicized, incompetent, ruthless, and thoroughly corrupt. Under the Baathist dictatorship, the poorly trained and poorly paid police forces functioned at the bottom of the regime's feeding chain. They existed primarily to threaten and extort bribes from the citizenry—hardly a group to rely on to keep Baghdad and other large cities orderly after the fall of the dictatorship.[36] That Iraq would need to retrain and rebuild its police force and search out decent leadership from the ranks of the less corrupt officers was obvious, and the lack of prewar planning to deal with this demonstrates the failure of the interagency process at the strategic level. The Justice Department and FBI could have been brought into the process, as expert agencies that know about civilian police organization and training. Before the war, it would have been easy to recruit a group of active and retired senior police officers from America's big cities to assess the requirements for policing a city of five million such as Baghdad. However, to my knowledge, little if any effort was made to tap specialized and expert resources outside the DOD before the invasion.

The Pentagon was taken by surprise by the level of postwar criminality in Iraq and the virulence of the insurgency that began only weeks after the fall of Baghdad. Deputy Defense Secretary Wolfowitz remarked with considerable understatement in 2003, "Some conditions were worse than we anticipated, particularly in the security area."[37] Rather than rush more U.S. troops to Iraq to deal with a deteriorating security situation, the U.S. policy emphasized standing up Iraqi security forces as quickly as possible.[38]

With the need to get a police force going after the U.S. invasion of Iraq, several quick fixes were applied. Jordan was contracted to train thirty thousand of the envisioned ninety-thousand-man Iraqi police force in brief eight-week courses.[39] Police officers and NCOs from the old force were expected to take over the leadership of police detachments after three-week courses in human rights and police procedure. Considering the depth of incompetence and corruption of Saddam's police, the quick-course approach to training the police and leaders was reminiscent of the

Haitian police-training program. Even worse, the Iraqis expected to employ the minimally trained and equipped police as the primary force to fight the insurgents.

In a race to field Iraqi police and military forces, CENTCOM and the Pentagon lurched from one quick fix to another, hoping to end the disorder and suppress the insurgency. Their further hope was that the Iraqis could take over their own security, so that most U.S. troops could come home. When political pressure is applied from all sides, the Pentagon can move pretty quickly. In short order, various programs were implemented to build new Iraqi security forces. Most of these programs were established without prior study or serious reflection and were deeply flawed from their conception. In the rush for quick, cheap solutions, critical thinking went by the wayside.

One major mistake in the attempt to stabilize Iraq was the policy of tolerating the armed militias created by Iraqi factions and sectarian groups. Because the United States had too few soldiers to police the large cities and the Iraqi police force was in a shambles, there was no alternative to combating the widespread disorder than to allow the non-Baathist elements in Iraq to organize forces and police themselves. The policing of Sadr City, a mostly Shiite slum of over two million in Baghdad, was carried out by Muqtada al-Sadr's Mahdi Militia, which soon grew to the size of a small army under the highly militant al-Sadr, one of the most violent and radical Shiite leaders in Iraq. In the absence of effective police forces, the U.S. forces at first tolerated al Sadr's force, and the many other party and sectarian militias that sprang up, as necessary to keep order. But the militia solution proved as bad as the original problem of widespread crime. When a semblance of an official police force was organized, the militias persisted in their police functions, refusing to disband. Since the sector police commander for Sadr City had but three hundred poorly armed men, and al-Sadr's Mahdi Militia had up to ten thousand heavily armed men, the police were compelled to accept al-Sadr's authority.[40] It was a poor beginning to establish the rule of law in Iraq. As al-Sadr made ever more extreme demands for political power, open conflict with the U.S. and Coalition forces was inevitable. By late 2003, U.S. forces were engaged in fairly large battles to suppress al Sadr's militia forces.

Seeing that the militias were adding to the disorder and violence in Iraq, in late 2003 the Coalition forces worked to negotiate a deal among the militias to disarm and be transformed into an interim force to fight the mostly Sunni and Baathist insurgents. The solution was the formation of the Iraqi Civil Defense Battalions (ICDC Battalions), recruited mostly from the party and sectarian militias to serve ostensibly under the control of the Coalition forces and interim Iraqi government. The U.S. military placed great hope in the ICDC battalions as a force to break the insurgency.

The ICDC units first raised in 2004 fared poorly in the battle against the growing insurgency. One problem was their lack of loyalty to the Iraqi provisional government. The ICDC units recruited from the militias gave their primary allegiance to their sect or party and only reluctantly accepted government control. Another problem was the lack of training and discipline. The ICDC battalions, expected to support the Coalition forces in highly complex counterinsurgency operations, were nonetheless given only three weeks of training before being committed to urban warfare. Units lacked basic equipment, competent leaders, and heavy weapons. The ICDC battalions were of little help to the Coalition forces that continued to bear the burden of fighting.

A central principle established by the Iraqis as they formed their own government was that police and military forces of the nation could not be concentrated under any one ministry. This was, perhaps, natural among a group of politicians who rightfully feared dominance by any sect or party and who feared the return of a dictatorship. By late 2004, the Iraqi government had plenty of men under arms, but there was little coordination of the different Iraqi forces in the counterinsurgency campaign. In fact, the diffusion of power means that each ministry has raised its own police or paramilitary force. The Oil Ministry has created a considerable force to protect the pipelines and refineries. The Culture Ministry has a force to protect buildings and national monuments. The police come under the Interior Ministry, and the army under the Defense Ministry. At the same time, the Kurds have maintained their fifty-thousand-strong militia, which has most of the attributes of a regular force.

Also present are approximately twenty-five thousand private security personnel from dozens of nations, who were hired mostly to protect foreign

corporations and contractors, and serve as bodyguards for Iraqis and foreign personnel. Private security contractors (many essentially mercenaries)
now constitute one of the larger armed groups in Iraq, yet they are largely
unregulated and often beyond the control of either the government or
Coalition forces. Employing large numbers of security contractors was one
Pentagon method to put manpower on the ground without increasing the
U.S. Army and Marine Corps ground forces. But there have been many drawbacks to employing contract security personnel in lieu of regular forces.
Most of the trainers for the first Iraqi army units to be trained were contract
civilian personnel, and there were complaints from U.S. military personnel
that the contractors were doing a poor job—and the performance of the first
Iraqi units when they went into battle bears out this judgment. Part of the
problem with contractors is a lack of discipline and reliability. The Iraqi government learned, to its dismay, one of the problems with employing foreign
security contractors. The security for the Baghdad Airport, a major strategic
asset of the Iraqi government, was put in the hands of an international security company, Global Security. On September 10, 2005, Global Security shut
down the Baghdad International Airport, Iraq's major transport link to the
outside world, as part of a pay dispute with the Iraqi government. The U.S.
military was forced to quickly send in some of its hard-pressed regular forces
to keep the airport secure while the security contractors and the government
worked out a deal.[41]

In addition to foreign contractors are a variety of private armies that
claim to support the government and have demanded pay and arms from
the government to fight the insurgents. These private armies, too, add to the
general confusion in Iraq. Several skirmishes have occurred when police
have mistaken security contractors or progovernment militia units for
insurgents. As of mid-2005, no one in the U.S. forces or the Iraqi government knows how many men either the government, or organizations allied
to the government, have under arms on any given day.

Initial attempts to set up regular armed forces have been—like most of
the postwar planning for Iraq—poorly conceived and inadequately supported by the United States. At first, having disbanded the Iraqi army, the
Coalition was not in a rush to reconstitute regular armed forces. However,
within three weeks of the fall of Baghdad, with the insurgency in full swing,

it became apparent that Iraq needed to have regular forces—if not to play the central role against the insurgents, then at least to serve as a backup force for the police. A small staff, the Coalition Military Assistance and Training Team (CMATT), was given the very large task of organizing an Iraqi defense ministry and recruiting and training a new Iraqi army, navy, and air force. With a staff of fewer than fifty personnel in late 2003, CMATT had to stand up Iraqi armed forces with completely inadequate resources. Because of the Coalition personnel shortage, contractors were again relied upon to carry out the main task of training the new Iraqi army. When I was with CMATT in Baghdad in early 2004, there were plenty of complaints about the competence levels and effectiveness of the expensive contract trainers. With minimal personnel, however, it was the only practical course to training an army quickly.

The first hastily recruited and trained battalion of the new Iraqi army collapsed even before it saw action. As soon as training was completed in October, more than three hundred of the 1st Battalion's soldiers deserted over pay problems and fear for the security of their families, making the unit operationally ineffective.[42] CMATT soon had another battalion trained, and believed that the problems that had plagued the 1st Battalion had been corrected. Although few soldiers deserted upon completing the short training course, the whole battalion simply collapsed when it was ordered into battle against the insurgent strongholds in 2004. Whole companies melted away, and others refused orders to go into action. Throughout 2004, the police, ICDC battalions, and regular army units experienced high desertion rates before going into action, and the remainder tended to run away as soon as battle was joined.[43]

The Iraqi security forces had been set up for failure by being committed to urban warfare with inadequate equipment and minimal training. Quite simply, the Iraqi security forces lacked confidence that they could fight and win. While the lack of armor, heavy weapons, and adequate equipment was partly to blame for the poor Iraqi performance, the main problem was the lack of competent leadership. In the rush to stand up police, ICDC, and army units, the focus had been on providing at least minimal training to the rank and file, while officer training had been ignored. It's not that the Iraqis are inherently bad soldiers, but throughout history badly led armies and police forces have consistently failed in battle. The Iraqis behaved no differently.

U.S. advisors on the ground with the Iraqi army identified poor Iraqi leadership as the single greatest obstacle in developing effective security forces. Stories abounded of incompetent Iraqi officers engaging in petty corruption. One account was related of an Iraqi lieutenant colonel who stayed behind in headquarters during every major operation, and of other officers who went on leave every time their units were ordered into action.[44] Without effective training, and without understanding the model of a combat-effective, democratic army, the Iraqi officers of the new army fell back into the old habits of complacency and corruption that they had learned so well under Saddam's regime.

In early 2004 in Baghdad, I outlined a plan to send more than fifty hand-picked Iraqi majors and colonels a year to the full U.S. and Coalition staff colleges and senior service schools, and to continue the program for several years. Once completing the full professional training, the Iraqis would take over senior command and staff positions, serving as the cadre for a system of Iraqi schools that would, in turn, provide a much higher level of training to the Iraqi officers than the short courses the contractors were giving. The program would continue for several years until a solidly educated Iraqi leadership corps was in place. I believed then—and still believe—that this is the only possible means to solve the greatest deficiency of the Iraqi forces: the lack of good leadership.

Although the soldiers working with the Iraqi army liked the concept, such a plan could not go far in a U.S. military that was still committed to finding a quick, cheap solution to defeating the insurgency. Indeed, what I saw in Baghdad in early 2004 was a "Mr. Micawber strategy": the hope that "something would turn up," and the insurgency would collapse on its own accord without the need for the United States to plan or reorganize its effort for a prolonged insurgency. Throughout 2003 and 2004, almost no effort was made to ensure that the new Iraqi armed forces would have competent, professional leadership. In the 2004 to 2005 academic year, only one Iraqi officer was sent to the Army Command and General Staff College course. In December 2004, only two Iraqi officers were enrolled in the twenty-week U.S. Army Infantry Officers' Advanced

Course—considered a core requirement in the U.S. military for training effective midlevel combat officers.

It's not as if the U.S. Army and other services lack the training infrastructure; the U.S. military has the best officer education and training system in the world. The bases and courses already exist, and it would have been quite simple to put a large number of Iraqi officers through the U.S. courses. Indeed, one colonel at the Infantry School told me he wished there had been forty Iraqis going through the course instead of two. While the requirement to have basic fluency in English would be a problem for many third world nations, it is not the case for Iraq. English was a major subject in the Iraqi schools and the educated Iraqis, from whom the officers are recruited, tend to be fairly fluent in English. While the old Iraqi military was crippled by a dysfunctional culture, there are plenty of first-rate human resources upon which to build a sound military and police. The Iraqis have long been one of the best educated of the Arab peoples, and many of the Iraqi officers whom I have met are well-educated, idealistic, and deeply motivated by a desire to see their nation transformed into a democracy. They have courageously taken sides with the new Iraqi government—at great risk to themselves and their families. However, even the best of the majors and colonels have little understanding of strategic planning, large unit operations or the function of military leadership in a democracy. Acquiring this understanding requires a first-class military education, and cannot be picked up "on the job." The Iraqi military leadership desperately needs professional training, and U.S. policy has failed them in that regard.

By early 2005, almost two years into the insurgency, the U.S. and Coalition forces in Iraq are beginning to understand that the hasty strategy to stand up large numbers of minimally trained Iraqi forces has not worked. In January 2005, retired General Gary Luck was sent to Iraq to assess the needs of the Iraqi forces. He recommended that the U.S. Army triple the number of trainers to eight thousand.[45] At the same time, U.S. units in Iraq were ordered to assign a ten-man advisor and support team to every Iraqi army battalion.[46] Even with renewed U.S. efforts to train the Iraqis, the process of standing up combat-effective police and military units has proceeded at a snail's pace. By July 2005, the DOD rated only half of the police units, and two-thirds of the army units, as "partially capable" for counterinsurgency missions, which mean that there are very few Iraqi troops capable of conducting any operations at all without considerable U.S. support.[47]

As of this writing, the counterinsurgency campaign in Iraq is in doubt. On the military side, the critical problem has been the setting up of Iraqi military and police units capable of effective counterinsurgency operations. Early efforts to build new Iraqi security forces were hampered by a lack of prewar planning for the postwar requirements. Through 2003 and 2004, the process was hampered by the shortage of funds, equipment, Coalition staff, and trainers. Most of these problems are very slowly being remedied, but the most serious deficiency remains: the lack of competent officer leadership for the Iraqi forces. Simply put, for many centuries, good leadership and good training have been the most important elements of effective armed forces. Although there is a place for minimally trained home guards in counterinsurgency operations, in general, the only police and military forces that have been effective in counterinsurgency have been highly trained and led by first-rate officers and NCOs. The U.S. and Coalition nations have to work hard to overcome the ugly heritage of Saddam's corrupt, dysfunctional military. Unless the U.S. and Coalition nations address the problem of deficient Iraqi leadership and train a truly professional officer corps, the outcome of the insurgency will remain in doubt.

CHAPTER SEVEN

THE WAY AHEAD FOR AMERICA AND THE WEST

Denmark, 1807. Lieutenant Sharpe, 95th Rifles British Army, to Lord Pumphrey, political advisor to the military commander. Sharpe: "What's a civilian doing as an aide to the general?" Pumphrey: "Offering sound advice, Sharpe, offering sound advice." Sharpe: "That's not unusual, is it, my lord?" Pumphrey: "Sound advice is very unusual indeed."

—Bernard Cornwell, 2001

It's time for blunt talk and equally blunt advice. There are serious problems within the U.S. military, especially regarding the U.S. strategy for the Global War on Terror. These problems need to be addressed, and addressed now. First of all, Americans—the political leaders, the military, and the general public—need to understand the nature of the fighting, not just in Iraq but in Afghanistan, Colombia, the Philippines, and any location where U.S. forces and allies are confronting insurgency and terrorism, most of it motivated by radical Islam. This is war, not a law-enforcement operation—a prolonged war. America and its allies are at war with forces that are primarily nonstate organizations, although support for these insurgents and terrorist groups is coming from several states. Regrettably, many of the leaders in Europe and the United States, and many of the elites, do not seem to understand that we are at war. Furthermore, many in the U.S. military seem not to recognize the various insurgencies as true wars. That these are not conflicts with states and conventional forces does not reduce the consequences of failure.

The 9/11 Commission argued eloquently that the United States in the 1990s did not understand either the nature of the enemy or the threat. The loose organization of international terrorist groups, their lack of clear state sponsorship, and the new model of the network-based insurgency did not seem to be a serious threat before 9/11. Yet ever since 9/11, Americans and the West have been slow to understand the nature of the threat posed by networked and culturally based insurgency. American military leaders have been thrown off track by the lack of one specific identifiable enemy upon which our whole doctrine and way of war is based. Today we are not facing a state, such as Serbia, run by a corrupt dictator who can be easily coerced by American military power. The war we have fought since 9/11 is waged against people who are carefully prepared, and even eager, to die. They have been nurtured in a worldwide network of radical *madrassas* and mosques, and organized within a shifting network of groups. Radical Islamic factions are not just at war with America and the West, but also with Muslim governments deemed "impure," or simply too friendly with the United States. This war will go on for many years, carried out at many levels, from conventional war to law enforcement to trade sanctions.

It would be disastrous for the United States to lose the wars in Afghanistan and Iraq. However unpleasant these conflicts are, America must not give in to the desire to pull out and leave these nations to sort themselves out—and probably return to chaos or, at best, dictatorial control. An American pullout from Iraq or Afghanistan would be a signal to the entire world that the United States can easily be beaten. If we refuse to confront insurgencies, we shall hand our enemies a surefire strategy to beat the Americans. Our allies—and there are many, even in the third world, who still look to America for political leadership—will distance themselves, and few governments will be willing to cooperate with us. Some lukewarm allies, seeing American weakness, may well change sides and ally themselves with anti-American coalitions. The stakes are high. A victory by the United States means hope for moderate regimes in the Islamic world and provides an alternative to the radical Islamic model. Success in Iraq and Afghanistan, and defeat of other insurgencies trying to instill dictatorial systems, would be a step toward a more peaceful, cooperative world. During the Cold War, by building functioning democracies in Malaya, El Salvador, and other nations, we defeated Communist insurgencies. It was bloody and costly work over a prolonged period, but the success of many nations that we supported demonstrates the "better state of peace" that Clausewitz said should be the ultimate object of every nation that goes to war.

Many in the U.S. military adhere strongly to the dogma that America should only fight big, conventional, high-tech wars. They prefer that we continue to pile up high-tech weapons, as we await the day our enemies will fight the kind of war that we are best at. Why should anyone engage the Americans in a conventional war, however, when nonstate insurgent and terrorist groups can easily beat us by unconventional means? Yes, we can expect America's enemies to make some stupid mistakes, and we need to be ready to take advantage of them as they arise—but you can't build a national strategy around the assumption that our enemies, both states and nonstate groups, will be so dumb as to fight us on our own ground, where we have every advantage. Enemies will target American weakness—and our great weakness is our lack of forces, organization, doctrine, and strategy to fight insurgencies.

This book has documented a notable reluctance among American military leaders to change their well-established, conventional war doctrine and adapt American military forces to fight insurgency and terrorism. The rigid adherence to fighting only one kind of war is a primary cause for the incredible inertia the defense establishment has shown by its inability to adapt to new realities and enemies since the end of the Cold War. But insurgencies sponsored and supported by radical Islam are not unstoppable forces; they CAN be defeated. Indeed, many insurgencies have been defeated in the past—but only through the application of adequate resources and manpower, and the employment of the right training and doctrine. Effectively fighting insurgencies will not require the U.S. military to give up its expertise in conventional war, or the forces most suitable for conventional war. It means some adjustments in the allocation of manpower and resources, and some likely cutbacks in the most expensive, high-tech weapons, but also the addition of new forces and resources, specialized to fight insurgents and terrorists, added to the existing structures.

Many political commentators argue that the United States must center its efforts on building a grand, international coalition, and that major efforts cannot be made unless they have the full support of both developed and undeveloped nations. Some argue for opposing radical Islamic insurgencies through the auspices of international organizations such as the UN, NATO, or European Union. Getting others to carry most of the financial and military burden appeals to the American taxpayer, but is fundamentally unrealistic. While America needs foreign support, requiring that we wait for it before acting is a guaranteed recipe for strategic failure. It was not long ago that the United States had to chide most of the European nations for their unwillingness to contribute a fair share of spending and effort to NATO for their own defense against the Soviet Union. Since the end of the Cold War, the Western Europeans have shown an astounding inability to deal with military problems in their own region. During the crises in Yugoslavia in the 1990s, the Western European economies outweighed Serbia by a factor of about a hundred-to-one, and the European military forces outnumbered the Serbians at about a forty-to-one ratio. Even though this was in Europe's backyard and not a matter of distant force projection, the Western Europeans dithered for years, incapable of effective military intervention. Only when the United States intervened in the ongoing conflicts, first in Bosnia in 1995 and then in Kosovo in 1999, were the Serbs coerced into accepting peace settlements. There are some important lessons for the United States here. Even in their own region and in their own interests, Western Europeans cannot be counted on to apply military force in any kind of decisive manner.

Donald Rumsfeld's famous comment about "Old Europe" makes a great deal of sense. The "Old Europe," as exemplified by France and Germany, is essentially isolationist and politically weak. While large and wealthy nations with the desire to be major players on the world scene, both nations suffer from stagnant economies, persistent unemployment rates of over 10 percent, and the burden of maintaining ever-more-costly welfare states. The great mass of European voters are now focused on their seemingly insoluble internal problems and, while they loudly expressed sympathy for America in the wake of 9/11—a sympathy that didn't last very long—many of the major democracies are politically incapable of providing significant military or other support. The record of the major democracies concerning support for the new democratic government in Iraq, and support for the rebuilding of Afghanistan, has been long on talk and idealism but short on action. In autumn 2003 in Madrid, the developed nations pledged over $13 billion in aid and grants to Iraq, but by June 2005 less than one-third of this amount had actually appeared. NATO has also proven to be a weak reed. Only in June 2005 did NATO set up its first police training program in Iraq.[1] The international support for the Global War on Terror has also been short of concrete actions. In 2003, a UN monitoring committee complained that 108 nations failed to file required reports on their actions in the war against terrorism—actions such as freezing assets and reporting names of suspected terrorists— although these actions had been required under Security Council resolutions since 2001.[2] But this is not a new story. The ineffectiveness of the UN in conducting any form of military intervention has long been evident, from Somalia to Haiti to Yugoslavia.

In fact, one of the success stories of the Bush administration has been its relative effectiveness in garnering international support for U.S.-led operations in Afghanistan and Iraq outside the major international forums such as the UN and NATO. Doing a political end run around the UN, the United States put together a coalition of thirty nations to actively support the invasion and occupation of Iraq. The "Coalition of the Willing" included old, reliable allies such as Britain and Australia, plus troop contingents from the "new European" states of Poland, Hungary, and Latvia. Italy provided a significant force to Iraq as well as South Korea. El Salvador and Honduras sent troops. In a major change in international policy, and for the first time since the end of World War II, Japan contributed military forces to combat operations when it deployed a force to Iraq. The level of active foreign support for the Iraq War and postwar operations exceeds the level of foreign troop support for the U.S.-led operation in the Korean War, when seventeen foreign countries sent troops to fight alongside America and South Korea. Two divisions of non-U.S. troops ended up in postwar Iraq, one British division and one multinational division—not enough to handle the situation themselves, but a very significant degree of support.

Creating an effective strategy to oppose radical Islamic insurgency and international terrorism requires accepting the unpleasant reality that the

United States will have to do the heavy lifting, providing the majority of forces, resources, and funding for military and civil operations around the globe. Winning the peace after major conventional operations is a long, expensive, and very necessary requirement of policy. While coalition building is politically important and needs to be energetically pursued, we cannot build a military strategy around the hope that the United States will carry out the major conventional military operations and then turn missions such as nation-building over to coalitions and international organizations.

FIRST STEPS

The most important thing is to apply the right strategy and organization to the problem of radical Islamic insurgency facing the world. A national strategy cannot be oriented toward the short term or view the problem as a mostly military one. In successful counterinsurgency campaigns, victory invariably was the product of a long-term strategy that included major political and economic, as well as military, elements. A successful strategy implies an effective interagency process, in which the nonmilitary and military branches of the government communicate effectively, cooperate smoothly, and carry out a strategy that allocates the necessary tasks to the organizations with the right expertise.

Unfortunately, the record of interagency cooperation within the U.S. government is not impressive. In the 1980s, a fair degree of interagency cooperation was achieved to create an effective strategy in El Salvador—but it came only after a long period of confusion and bickering between the agencies. Interagency cooperation was no better during U.S. interventions in Haiti, Bosnia, or Kosovo in the 1990s. Surprisingly, as one moves down the chain of command, interagency cooperation often improves. Out in the field, the military and other government agencies such as the United States Agency for International Development (USAID), the foreign aid specialists of the State Department, all see that there's a job to do and get to work. The problems of interagency competition are centered in Washington, D.C., and in the culture at the higher ranks of the government—the people most removed in space and time from the people at the front, and most concerned about getting ahead by building bureaucratic empires and supporting the special interests of their agency. Since 9/11, there is broad consensus that major organizational, procedural, and cultural changes are needed in the military, the State Department, the intelligence agencies, and other branches of government to deal with a worldwide threat. Yet reform and change have proceeded at a glacial pace—almost as if 9/11 and the wars in Iraq and Afghanistan were minor events that would blow over quickly, without requiring any fundamental change in the way that Washington does business.

The most sensible solution to making the various agencies of the government work together in a coordinated strategy is not to create yet another new coordinating organization—which would simply add yet another layer of bureaucracy to an already too-complex government/strategic structure—but to pass legislation that will force the government agencies to coordinate on military and security matters. There is already a good model for this. Throughout the 1970s and 1980s, there were major problems in getting the different branches of the armed forces to work efficiently together. The problems were highlighted in the Grenada invasion of 1983 when the army found that its communications system and the navy's were incompatible and army units could not contact supporting naval units in the middle of a battle. The problems of joint service coordination were largely solved by the Goldwater-Nichols Act of 1986 in which the different services were simply required to plan together, develop compatible equipment, and train together. Without adding any vast new bureaucracy, the services became far more efficient in warfighting, and joint operations have now become part of an ingrained service culture. The U.S. government today needs a law similar to the Goldwater-Nichols Act that would set the requirements for all the government agencies that would deal with countering security threats and insurgencies to work and train together. In practice, this would mean that the State, Justice, Treasury, and probably other departments would be required to have expert teams available to work in coordination with the DOD in planning and coordinating security training and international counterinsurgency efforts. In conducting strategic planning, the DOD would be required to give other agencies a seat at the table as full partners. Depending on the level and nature of the threat, there will be instances in which the State Department or Justice Department might play the primary role with the military acting in support. There will, of course, be strong resistance within the government agencies to change their cultures. However, an effective strategy to meet the threat posed by international insurgency requires that several government agencies become much more involved than they are today.

The Pentagon culture has proven to be especially resistant to fundamental reform. A few changes have been made since 9/11, but nothing near the degree of change necessary to meet the current and foreseeable threats to the United States. Enacting major changes in organization, doctrine, and force structure requires first-rate military leadership, and leadership has been a weak point of the top rank of the uniformed military. From 2001 to 2005, U.S. Air Force General Richard Myers served as Chairman of the Joint Chiefs of Staff, and as such, was by law the senior officer in the U.S. military, and senior military advisor to the president. As a leader, Myers put in one of the poorest performances as a senior general in the history of American warfare. Under Myers, it would have been hard to discern that the U.S. military has been at war with a tough, capable, and unconventional enemy for four years. Throughout his tenure, Myers consistently fought to preserve the 1990s force strengths and force structure, with no significant changes, and continued to place the budgetary and organizational emphasis on high-tech conventional war weapons and programs—even as insufficient American ground forces battled guerrillas and insurgents with no end in sight. Myers made little effort to make even the most obvious reforms in the military force structure, for example, reorganizing the National Guard to be a major element for homeland security operations. There is broad consensus within the military, even among National Guard officers, that the current National Guard structure based on the Cold War requirements needs to be changed to meet both current and future threats. Only minor, incremental changes were made under Myers' tenure, less change than other reform-minded chairmen of the joint chiefs have accomplished in peacetime. General Myers took a hands-off approach to reforming the force structure, while devoting considerable energy to getting approval for space and other high-tech programs, indicating his possible inability to move past his air force roots and think in terms of the comprehensive requirements of the U.S. military.

In assessing Myers' leadership, one can look at other issues as well, including reforming the military's intelligence system and the army and Marine Corps force structure. In four years under Myers, only minor changes have occurred to meet the requirements of the post 9/11 world. To view Myers' performance as senior general in context, contrast his performance with the forceful and decisive leadership displayed by Colin Powell as Chairman of the Joint Chiefs of Staff during the Gulf War. Indeed, America has a long and impressive tradition of senior military leadership to serve as leadership models for our current conflicts. For an example of how to reform an army in wartime, we can again look at General George Marshall, head of the army and air force from 1939 to 1945. When the 1940 German victories in Europe shocked the world, Marshall embarked on an ambitious program of restructuring and reforming the U.S. Army and Air Force's organization, training, and doctrine to meet the threat of the Axis nations. As one might expect, Marshall's program of fundamental reforms met with enormous resistance, both inside and outside the military. Bureaucratic inertia was prevalent in Washington in 1940 to 1941, as it is today. But Marshall, through superb leadership, overcame the obstacles and pushed his reform program through. Thanks to Marshall, the U.S. Army and Army Air Forces were ready with the right plans, doctrine, organization, and training when the United States entered World War II. Without the fundamental changes that Marshall initiated, the United States might have lost World War II.

We have the greatest industrial and financial resources in the world, along with enormous technological capabilities—but we still need old-fashioned leadership for all that capability to bring victory. Victory in the current Global War on Terror will require imaginative, forceful leadership in several key branches of the government, as well as the will to change long-standing institutional cultures. Nowhere is the need for decisive leadership and long-term strategic vision more important than in the U.S. military.

CHANGING OUR STRATEGY

In the following pages, the primary changes needed in our military doctrine and force structure will be outlined. An effective strategy is required as well to defeat the insurgents and terrorist groups that currently, and for the next several decades, will remain the primary threat to American security.

1. APPROPRIATE DOCTRINE, ORGANIZATION, AND RESOURCES

The U.S. military requires a broad program of organizational and doctrinal reform to meet the challenges of the future. The new American way of war has proven useful in fighting large, conventional wars against conventional states, but has proven highly deficient as a means of fighting insurgents, terrorists, and guerrillas. Despite some common assumptions in the Pentagon that technology has changed the fundamental nature of warfare, the basics of warfare and insurgency have NOT fundamentally changed. In terms of fighting nonstate enemies, the basic counterinsurgency doctrines worked out in the 1950s and 1960s are fundamentally sound. Counterinsurgency is about humans interacting with humans. It's less about conventional firepower and battles and more about intelligence, civic action, psychological operations, and police work. In order to adapt effectively to fight the current and coming insurgencies, the military force structure will require considerably more military police units, more human intelligence specialists, and more civil affairs and psychological operations units. Although there have been some small increases in these forces since 9/11, the recent efforts do not even come close to what will be required for a long-term strategy.

One basic strategic question is how to allocate the nation's manpower and financial and technical resources for warfare. Even before 9/11 and the U.S. engagement in Iraq and Afghanistan, the belief that the nature of warfare had fundamentally changed, and that sizable ground armies would no longer be required, was wearing thin.[3] By the late 1990s, some top Western military theorists were already skeptical of the enthusiastic Pentagon claims, arguing that airpower and high-tech capabilities did not rule out the need for large ground forces in future conflicts. The events of 9/11 and the conflicts in the aftermath have reinforced the arguments of the critics of the new American way of war.

After 9/11, the Pentagon was warned by top analysts and senior retired generals that U.S. Army manpower levels were far too low to carry on the commitments of Afghanistan and Iraq, and that reliance on too small a force in prolonged military commitments would wear the force out.[4] As the conflicts in Afghanistan and Iraq began, recruitment and retention for the U.S. Army remained high for a time, so such concerns were ignored by the Pentagon. Currently, soldiers have routinely had their tours of duty extended and are facing further tours of duty in Iraq and Afghanistan after only relatively short breaks from combat. The predictions that conducting too many operations with too few troops would "break the force" appear to be coming true. One indication of the high stress and low morale of the all-volunteer armed forces is the military divorce rate. The war in Iraq, fought with insufficient forces and requiring repeated unit deployments with no end in sight, has brought divorce rates in the U.S. Army to record levels. For army officers, the divorce rate in 2005 is three and a half times higher than in 2001. Between 2003 and 2005, with most of the Army in Iraq or preparing to go again, the divorce rate rose an astounding 78 percent. On the enlisted side, divorces in early 2005 were up 53 percent from 2000.[5] A further indication of trouble for the ground forces is the inability of the U.S. Army and Marines to recruit enough soldiers. As of June 2005, the army had missed its recruiting quotas for the third straight month, the quota in April being missed by an impressive 42 percent. By June 2005, the U.S. Marine Corps had missed its recruiting goal for the fourth straight month.[6] By September 2005, the regular army recruiting level was more than six thousand below the yearly goal. The situation for the U.S. National Guard and Reserves was even worse, with the Guard meeting only 80 percent of its 2005 recruiting objectives and the Army Reserve only 84 percent.[7]

One of the most puzzling aspects of the U.S. military establishment in the Global War on Terror is its reluctance to change the force structures and concepts of warfare established before 9 September 2001. It is as if the scaled-down force structure of the Clinton era (1993–2001), an era of relatively small conflicts and interventions, was somehow sacrosanct and could not be changed even in wartime. Under Clinton, the manpower of the armed forces was cut by 40 percent, and defense spending scaled back to 3 percent of gross national product (GNP)—the lowest military force and spending levels since 1940. The emphasis at the Pentagon was to cut manpower drastically, in particular cutting traditional ground forces in favor of a small number of high-tech weapons that could be employed quickly, and with precise effects. For the army before 9/11, the primary mission (albeit unstated) was to cut the budget and "do more with less." This was a peacetime strategy suited to making the president, administration, and Congress happy by providing a whopping "peace dividend" of funds from the armed forces to use for other government programs. The belief in the peace dividend passed on into the next administration. Douglas Feith, responsible for planning changes in the Pentagon's global force structure under President Bush, even commented that recent wars have taught us "we are able to bring about very large military effects with smaller forces than anybody thought were capable of those effects in past eras."[8]

But the events of real war have called into question the pre 9/11 assumptions and policies. The prevailing peacetime strategy of "do more with less" can lead to strategic defeat. Since 9/11, U.S. military spending has risen only slightly to approximately 4 percent of the GNP. Despite manpower shortages on every front, the army still has the 480,000-man regular force that it had before 9/11. A Congressional Budget Office report of September 2004 on long-term defense spending noted that U.S. expenditures on ground forces are "about half what they were at the height of the Reagan defense buildup in the mid-1980s." Many senior officers, academics, and knowledgeable political leaders have gone on record to warn that a shortage of manpower for the American ground forces could actually break the force, and America could soon end up with a worn-out army with low morale, low efficiency, and declining standards of competence.

Despite the DOD's reluctance to consider an increase in the size of the army and Marine Corps, many of America's most experienced combat commanders have called for significant increases in the size of the army and the Marine Corps so that the ground forces can carry out their missions. General Barry McCaffrey (Ret.), commander of the 24th Infantry Division during the Gulf War, has called for an increase in army strength of nine brigades—the equivalent of three divisions.[9] In 2004, Major General Robert Scales (Ret.), a brigade commander in the Gulf War, former commandant of the Army War College, and noted military historian, proposed a ground force hike of 150,000 over the next four years, increasing the number of army brigades to fifty from the current thirty-three and adding two USMC expeditionary brigades.[10] Army Chief of Staff General Shinseki, in his retirement speech in 2004, warned against taking the "wrong conclusions" from Operation Iraqi Freedom. He argued for "a force sized correctly to meet the strategy set forth in the documents that guide us, our national security and national military strategy. Beware the twelve-division strategy for a ten-division army. Our soldiers and families bear the risk and hardship of carrying a mission load that exceeds the force capabilities we can sustain."[11]

Adding their voices to experienced generals calling for more ground force manpower, many congressmen—including, significantly, almost all the members of the House Armed Services Committee, the congressmen with the greatest expertise in military affairs—proposed major increases in army manpower in the wake of 9/11.[12] In 2003, Congresswoman Heather Wilson of New Mexico called for increasing the armed forces by 90,000 to 150,000, and she was joined by over 120 other congressmen. Even in the immediate aftermath of the conventional victory in Iraq, there was concern over the strain on active and reserve forces faced with back-to-back deployments.[13]

Many top defense analysts also hold that an immediate increase in army manpower is essential to maintaining an effective national defense.[14] Frederick Kagan noted that the high state of training in the U.S. Army has been largely due to the high quality of its specialist training units, such as the elite 11th Armored Cavalry Regiment, which plays the opposing force at the National Training Center. Then, in 2005, the 11th Armored Cavalry Regiment was deployed to Iraq. The army's training command has been continually stripped of individuals and units to provide manpower for the wars in Iraq and Afghanistan. As Kagan pointed out, the troops replacing the 11th Armored Cavalry won't be able to match their skill level and expertise. Thus, the standard of army training, one of the U.S. military's greatest advantages in warfare, will decline.[15] The policy of robbing the training establishment of manpower and resources is nothing new; the Clinton administration repeatedly used the army's training personnel and resources to man and fund the ongoing interventions and military operations in Bosnia and Kosovo. In the 1990s, the Clinton administration mortgaged the army's future health to meet short-term demands, in the belief that the U.S. interventions in Bosnia and Kosovo would be of short duration. Yet ten years after the Dayton Accords, American troops are still in Bosnia, and U.S. troops are still in Kosovo six years after the conflict there. By pulling experienced trainers out of the United States and sending them to Iraq, the U.S. military is continuing the same manpower policies of the Clinton administration in the hope that the commitments in places like Afghanistan and Iraq will go away quickly—over the long term, an exceptionally risky military strategy.

Officers who have served in the Pentagon have told me that the army remains reluctant to ask for more manpower, because it is afraid to add force structure that Congress will be unwilling to finance—which would mean that any improvements in equipment would have to be shelved, and the army turned into a "hollow force" much like the 1970s. So the army remains wedded to the concept of somehow making do with a force that was considered by most to be far too small even for the relative peacetime requirements of the 1990s. However, the first and most essential duty of a government is to protect its citizens. If it fails in that task, even if it accomplishes many useful social endeavors, the government will have failed the nation. Thus, at a time when the United States faces numerous ongoing conflicts, increasing the defense budget to 5 percent of the GNP (less than in the 1980s, which was a period of major economic growth) and assuring the armed forces of long-term, adequate financial support makes sense. Increasing the percentage of GNP devoted to defense would allow the ground forces to increase manpower, train the force effectively, provide for military families, and continuously improve its equipment so that the United States can maintain a comfortable lead in technology versus the most probable competitors. There is no reason why the United States cannot have armed forces adequate for heavy conventional wars AND other divisions configured for rapid intervention and counterinsurgency operations. The constant short-term, ad hoc solutions, such as employing contractors to fulfill basic military functions, prevents America from building up solid, long-term assets and makes long-term strategic planning difficult.

Even after the experience of Afghanistan and Iraq, in which old-fashioned ground forces have played the lead role in combating guerrilla insurgents, the U.S. military remains committed to the pre-9/11 theories of the high-tech, minimal-manpower, conventional war. The strongly held preference in the Pentagon is to continue allocating resources to high-tech weaponry rather than to the ground forces. As of this writing in 2005, there is strong support in the Pentagon for a new, massive, multi-billion-dollar program to abrogate the long-term ban on weapons in space. The program would include a space vehicle that would carry hypervelocity rods, projectiles made of two-hundred-pound tungsten rods that could be fired from orbiting space vehicles and hit targets on earth at 7,200 miles per hour with the force of a small nuclear weapon. The advantages of being able to hit any place on earth immediately, and with pinpoint accuracy, are admittedly useful. One can imagine a terrorist leader and his staff vaporized in such an attack. However, such capability comes with a huge price tag: the cost of taking out just one target would be approximately $100 million. The per-target cost for the envisioned space attack system would be fifty to one hundred times the cost of a modern ballistic missile that can do the same thing—albeit with less panache. Yet General Lance Lord, the head of Space Command, has argued for massive investment in new space weapons, testifying before Congress: "We must establish and maintain space superiority ... Simply put, it's the American way of fighting."[16]

There is little doubt that the United States can finance such projects—but at the cost of $100 million for the Air Force Space Command to destroy one target, the United States will have to give up a good many other military capabilities due to lack of funds. Yet there are many other more practical alternatives to employing "space power" against America's enemies. In fighting terrorists we might consider putting the $100 million used to destroy one target from space to other uses. With $100 million the United States could raise, train, equip, and deploy two light infantry battalions—one thousand soldiers—for service in Iraq or Afghanistan. Two battalions could destroy and defeat a great many targets, providing security for a sizeable region, and one thousand trained men would be a long-term asset for future conflicts. In another scenario, $100 million could finance a small corps of highly trained, James Bond–type agents able to operate behind enemy lines. Instead of killing Osama bin Laden with a $100 million, space-launched projectile, an American agent could shoot him with a 25-cent bullet fired from a $2,000 sniper rifle. The sniper rifle could then be used again to shoot a few more of Osama's lieutenants. And at the end of the day, those agents, and their sniper rifles and special equipment, would be available for the next mission. If we have intelligence that's good enough to locate a target with exactness, then, as a taxpayer, I wonder why many in the U.S. military would

247

prefer to employ a $100 million projectile rather than a $25,000 bomb or a 25-cent bullet? Technology is good, and America needs to maintain a technological advantage over its enemies. However, basic military capabilities should not to be sacrificed so that the United States can master one form of waging war while being deficient in all the other forms.

It's partly how one views military manpower. Many in the U.S. military establishment see manpower as too expensive, draining resources away from needed high-tech weapons and equipment. Many view each soldier as a long-term liability. Not only do soldiers cost money to pay and train and equip, but the government also must provide adequately for soldiers' families—quarters, medical care, schools for dependents, etc. Retirement pay for soldiers and reservists is also a burden. If the soldier is killed or wounded in battle, then there is the additional cost of paying for long-term medical care and benefits to the families. I prefer to consider each trained soldier, airman, sailor, or marine as a long-term national asset. War remains a highly human and personal activity, and no amount of social theory or technological development will change that. The human brain is still the most important and potent weapon of warfare. A trained soldier, unlike a one-time contractor, is a resource available for many years—as many reserve soldiers have discovered by being recalled to active duty after having served a full term in the regular forces. Some enormously expensive equipment items tend to be useful in just one kind of warfare, often a pure waste of money if the enemy decides to fight another kind of war. On the other hand, once trained in the basic military skills, soldiers can acquire new skills as conditions change. Human beings are far more flexible and adaptable than the most sophisticated equipment ever made. If the equipment a soldier operates becomes obsolete, he can be retrained to operate other equipment, and the equipment discarded.

The idea that a nation should spend more on equipment and technology than on its soldiers is not new. Before World War II, France spent its military budget on the massive concrete and steel defenses of the Maginot Line along the German border, cutting manpower and training expenditure to the bone. In 1940 the Germans, whose military spent their budget on manpower, training, and multipurpose equipment, refused to fight the war that France wanted. Instead, they outflanked the Maginot Line and easily beat the poorly trained French army. Sometimes our faith in high-tech equipment programs as the first line of defense starts to look a lot like the approach of the interwar French military.

In fact, the Pentagon's preference for equipment over manpower has led to a number of embarrassing DOD scandals that have come to public attention since 9/11. One result of failing to adequately fund manpower systems and infrastructure is the broken pay system for the Army Reserve and National Guard soldiers mobilized in large numbers since 9/11. With no permanent increases in the regular force, the U.S. Army has had to rely heavily on reserve soldiers to fight the war and insurgency in Iraq. By 2004, more than 30 percent of the U.S. Army forces in Iraq were reservists. Tens of thousands more were on active duty, carrying out missions in the United States and around the world. Yet the pay system for army reserve soldiers has been broken for years, unable to efficiently get pay and allowances into the pockets of the soldiers and their families. This means that mobilized reserve soldiers and their families suffer financial problems for months while an ancient pay system muddles with their pay. A congressional study done in 2004 found that 95 percent of all reservists deployed or mobilized for the war in Iraq have experienced pay problems.[17] Personally, I'm not complaining because I am one of the lucky reservists who only had to wait nine months to get full pay for duty in Iraq. Other families, especially those primarily dependent upon one income, are in real trouble. Military pay officials have testified to Congress that the problem centers on very old computer systems that require extensive and complicated workarounds to keep them functioning at all. The good news is that the system is due to be reformed in 2007 to 2008—a full seven years AFTER major reserve call-ups began in the wake of 9/11. This is one of the most telling examples of "business as usual" in the Pentagon in the wake of 9/11. One wonders what General Marshall might have done if, in December 1941, he had been told by senior officers and War Department civilians that 95 percent of the National Guardsmen and Reservists mobilized for war were suffering from pay problems—but that it was not a major problem because sometime around 1947 to 1948 the system would get fixed?

Another major scandal of the war in Iraq has been the inability of the U.S. Army to provide all the soldiers in the combat zone with improved body armor able to stop bullets, not just shrapnel fragments like the Vietnam-era body armor. The approach of the Pentagon to the war in Iraq was very much in keeping with the pre-9/11 mentality of "saving money is the first priority" and "do more with less." So the U.S. Army went to war in Iraq without enough modern body armor to equip every soldier. Not expecting an insurgency or a war without front lines, the Army Materiel Command actually put a halt on buying new armor for the troops as the army supply chiefs figured it was only necessary to provide armor for the front-line troops; the fifty thousand support troops not on the front line could do with the old, Vietnam-era armor. The savings? Basically, Pentagon small change, about $700 per set of armor.

When the insurgency was building up, and it became clear there was no front line or rear area in Iraq, modern body armor was ordered for all troops in Iraq. Although there were companies already manufacturing the improved body armor, under the Pentagon contracting system it took 167 days to start getting armor sets to the soldiers in Iraq. Even then, some troops still lacked modern armor in early 2005. Army General Paul Kern (Ret.), who oversaw the procurement system in the Army's Materiel Command, said that the performance of 167 days to get something as simple as body armor to troops under fire was "historically pretty good."[18] The reality is that many deployed soldiers bought their own sets of body armor privately, at $1,400 a set, rather than trust the army to keep its promises.[19] What is especially interesting is that when our allied forces in Iraq realized they needed more bulletproof vests, they bypassed the Pentagon and ordered directly from a manufacturer in Michigan. They began getting armor in twelve days. Former Army Secretary Thomas E. White remarked, "We've never been good at equipping people in a simple, straightforward fashion."[20] Again, I wonder what George Marshall would have done when confronted with a DOD supply system unable to provide basic, inexpensive equipment that could save the lives of the soldiers?

In short, there is an overwhelming case for significantly increasing the size of the U.S. Army and Marines, the forces that seize and occupy ground and deal with populations. There is an equally strong case for giving personnel a higher funding priority than equipment. Taking an average of the many recommendations already made by top soldiers and analysts, it would be reasonable to increase the army by three divisions, and the Marine Corps by two to three expeditionary brigades. This would enable U.S. ground forces to meet basic force requirements for counterinsurgency, nation-building, and occupation, while maintaining adequate units in case of a conventional war.

Recruiting additional men and women for the armed forces, as well as retaining highly trained specialist personnel such as intelligence experts, linguists, and SOF specialists—all necessary to fight unconventional enemies—will be difficult. Fixing the recruiting and retention problems of the services will require a significant turnaround in the equipment-oriented Pentagon culture. For example, the services will have to devote considerably more effort to making military posts and bases as attractive as possible, with better housing and base facilities. Today's military, which contains a much higher percentage of married soldiers than the Vietnam-era force, will have to be far more family-friendly in its assignment policies and provision of medical care. Pay, especially for specialist personnel, will also have to be increased. It makes little sense to pay pilots large bonuses, considering them essential personnel for operating high-tech equipment, but then pay linguists, arguably just as essential to winning a war, small bonuses.[21] Spending moderate amounts to keep well-trained soldiers who can serve a tour of active duty and, afterward, go to the reserves and be available for future emergencies is likely to be a lot cheaper, in the long term, than paying huge sums to contractors—who may not be up to the job, and who cannot be counted on as long-term assets.

If it becomes too difficult to recruit more soldiers without lowering standards—which is to be avoided at all costs—we should consider what other world powers have done in the past, and continue to do today: recruit units of foreigners to fight in the ranks. For 175 years, the French have maintained the Foreign Legion, an all-foreigner force, to fight in their overseas campaigns. The Foreign Legion can only recruit foreigners into its enlisted ranks, and after a term of successful service, the soldiers are offered French citizenship and other benefits. Another nation that employs foreign troops in its regular army is Britain. For almost two hundred years, the British army has maintained a force of thousands of Nepalese soldiers in its Ghurkha regiments. Both the French Foreign Legion and the British Army

Ghurkhas are considered to be elite corps, possibly the best light infantry forces in the world. I don't know any experienced American soldiers who would feel nervous about having the Ghurkhas or Foreign Legion protecting their flank in a tough battle.

Why shouldn't the United States consider creating a foreign legion of one or two divisions on the French model? By offering American citizenship and further military advancement as a reward for good service, we could easily recruit a superb force of highly intelligent, fit young men overseas to serve in an American foreign legion in peacekeeping operations and foreign deployments. We could set up an elite, Marine Corps–style training program, creating light infantry forces of such quality that American officers would compete for the privilege of leading such troops. Both Britain and France have managed to remain strong democracies and maintain strong armed forces by recruiting large units of foreign soldiers. If we need to expand the military ground forces, a foreign legion force makes sense.

2. REFORM OF U.S. MILITARY TRAINING AND EDUCATION

The current U.S. military education and training system, created in the 1940s, was adequate for the requirements for the Cold War. However, it is largely out of date for training officers and NCOs for the types of war that we face today and are likely to face in the future. For the threat America faces today, a major reform program is needed for all the armed services. The military should immediately correct its practice of ignoring the subjects of counterinsurgency and nonstate conflicts in the staff colleges and officer education programs—a practice since the end of the Vietnam War. Although a few courses have recently been added to officer education programs, this is not nearly enough to make up for decades of neglecting nonstate warfare. A new, all-services counterinsurgency school of at least six months' duration is urgently needed. Such a school should teach counterinsurgency and counterterrorism, providing officers from the ranks of captain to colonel with an understanding of the theories, doctrines, and tactics of fighting non-state entities, as well as providing a solid grounding in the principles of civil affairs, human intelligence, and psychological operations. The Counterinsurgency School would be staffed with a world-class international faculty of regional experts and specialists in counterinsurgency and counterterrorism. For starters, the military should look to sending five hundred to one thousand officers a year through the school before they go on to staff positions and unit commands. If the military had a corps of officers with this type of education, many of the mistakes made in the postwar planning for Iraq might have been avoided.

For over a century, the army and navy staff colleges have prepared officers to be senior staff officers and commanders. The courses and school traditions served the country well in preparing officers to fight the big conventional wars, such as World War II and Korea, as well as the Gulf War. What was needed then were officers capable of doing the planning and staff work for mass armies conducting conventional operations. The higher military schools traditionally took a rote-learning approach to teaching the fundamentals of major operations. Yet even in the middle of the Cold War, the staff college education was criticized as insufficient to prepare officers for a highly complex world, where interventions in failed states are more likely than all-out conventional war. For the last two decades, a number of experts, inside and outside of the military, have criticized the current U.S. staff college and senior officer education system for academic weakness, and for discouraging imaginative officers while rewarding the safe, "careerist" approach.[22] Respected military writers such as Edward Luttwak, Martin van Creveld, and Colonel Douglas MacGregor have all argued that current, complex world conditions require a very different approach to the officer education system and have made some sensible recommendations to strengthen the system.[23] I will summarize and comment on a few of the best recommendations.

First of all, education for staff and command should take place much earlier in an officer's career. Instead of sending senior majors in their mid to late thirties to the staff college, the best and brightest senior captains should be identified and sent to the staff college in their late twenties. Instead of the one-year, mass-education model we have now, the general staff and command course should be geared to a smaller number of carefully selected officers, who would be required to compete in a written examination that emphasizes strategic understanding and tactical competence. The officer students should be put through an academically tough, eighteen to twenty-four month program crafted to educate an elite general staff corps, capable of thinking strategically and planning higher operations. In *Transformation Under Fire* (2003), a superb critical analysis of our current military culture, combat veteran Colonel MacGregor argued that the general staff course graduates should be given accelerated promotion, and that most of the army's battalion command positions, the path to higher command, should be reserved for graduates of the general staff college. This would ensure that the best and brightest in the officer corps compete to attend the school.[24] While MacGregor wrote about the army's educational needs, the same model is equally valid for the air force, navy and marines.

Senior officer education at the lieutenant colonel or colonel level also needs considerable reform. Currently, many of the officer students sent to the senior service schools are in their forties, close to the end of their career. Indeed, many retire within two years of completing the one-year war college course. For an armed forces concerned with education costs, this approach is extremely wasteful. If staff college education were provided to captains in their late twenties, then the war college course could be geared to majors or junior lieutenant colonels in their late thirties. In this manner, the military would get a decade of service from the course graduates before their retirement. As with the staff college, the senior officer schools should be academically tough, focused on national strategy, and organized to educate a small number of elite officers, carefully selected for higher command and staff positions.

The U.S. military will need many more trained staff officers to man the basic brigade, division, and wing staff positions than such an elite education system can provide. The solution to filling military staff requirements can be met by sending most midlevel officers to a six-month staff course in the fundamental skills of operational and tactical staff work and planning. Making the changes to the midlevel and senior officer education programs would require neither major additional funding nor even a major reorganization of the current schools. For example, the U.S. Army already teaches the fundamentals of staff operations in the first six months of its ten-month general staff course. [25]

Creation of an elite general staff is a concept that is long overdue in our armed forces. Long ago, Clausewitz noted that war is basically about politics. If anything, this is even truer today. The current wars against nonstate forces are far more politically complex than the wars of Clausewitz's era, and modern conflicts require officers to have a deeper understanding of history, politics, and regional studies than in earlier periods. The changes to the military education system recommended here would provide America with military leaders better able to deal with the problems of insurgency and terrorism.

3. REFORMING THE INTELLIGENCE SYSTEM

The problem with the U.S. intelligence system is rooted in the decades-long, American neglect of human intelligence. The solution is not necessarily to spend more money on intelligence, but rather to redirect a small portion of the current spending on high-tech intelligence systems into developing human intelligence personnel and resources. As Major General Robert Scales noted, the United States "spends billions on weapons but a pittance on training officers and soldiers—especially in the languages and cultures of places like Afghanistan."[26] The issue is not resources or funds but time. It takes years to train a fully competent linguist, so there is no quick fix to providing the U.S. intelligence and military forces with the necessary language capabilities. Unfortunately, because of the slow rate of growth in the language training programs since 9/11, the military, the CIA, and other intelligence agencies are way behind in building the human intelligence force necessary to fight insurgents and terrorists. If we move quickly to test and recruit a large number of suitable linguist candidates for government and military service, contract with universities for language instruction, and also expand the military and government language school program, we could start to meet the most urgent needs of the military and intelligence community in two to three years.

Improving our linguist, analyst, and interrogator capabilities will require another cultural change in the military. This means that the military will need to provide better incentives for soldiers to learn languages and paid time and opportunities for soldiers to learn and keep up their skills. ROTC cadets should be given scholarships and extra pay for learning a language, such as Arabic, Farsi, or Uzbecki, deemed vital by the DOD. Reservists should be given paid time every month to maintain their language proficiency, as well as full funding to attend university language courses. The current bonus system should be overhauled, and major increases made for speakers of vital languages. One simple reform to produce quick results would be to streamline the military language program so that any soldier passing a language aptitude test could quickly embark on a paid course of language study at a local school or university. As soon as the soldier passed a basic proficiency test in the assigned language, he would start getting additional pay. With each additional level of language proficiency, the soldier would get a higher bonus pay. Today, some of the biggest barriers to developing linguists for the military are the arcane and bewilderingly complex regulations concerning who can take language courses, who can get bonuses, and who can be assigned to a language position. Army linguists have told me the system was such a hassle, they didn't bother going through the massive amount of paperwork required to receive the $50-per-month language bonus. As usual, the armed forces, and especially the army, have created their own problems through excessive bureaucracy, and trying to do training on the cheap. As with anything else, in the armed forces you get what you pay for, and for decades we have paid out too little for human intelligence.

As noted in Chapter 4, interrogation and collection of human intelligence must be carried out in accordance with military and international law. Strong-arm interrogation techniques or any treatment that borders on torture should be ruled out—period. However, this should not be interpreted as being "soft" on terrorists. Terrorists and insurgents, captured in civilian clothes and bearing arms, not members of the fighting forces of a state, do not have to be considered prisoners of war. The Geneva Convention is clear on the point. Under international and civil law, insurgents and terrorists are criminals and should be treated as such. We need an effective system of special military courts, in which captured terrorists and insurgents can be quickly tried as criminals and given swift punishment per the rule of law. Penalties should be severe, and insurgents who kill civilians should be executed for murder. Because of the need to use classified information in court, some or all of the military or civil tribunals could be held in closed session. If we and our allies are provided an effective legal means of trial and punishment, we can use the same methods on captured insurgents that American prosecutors use on Mafia and drug-gang small fry: if they cooperate and provide good information, they'll get a light sentence or even their freedom.

If they refuse to cooperate, they'll get a very long prison sentence or the death penalty. Such an approach would be far more likely to elicit intelligence to break insurgent networks than the Abu Graibh methods—and be far more acceptable in world opinion.

Bill Gertz, author of *Breakdown*, the story of the intelligence failure that led to 9/11, has proposed a series of organizational reforms for improving the performance of intelligence at the national level that should be taken seriously. Rather than having the Defense Intelligence Agency (DIA) and CIA duplicating their efforts, he argues that the DIA be abolished, and suggests that many of the intelligence personnel working for the DIA should be moved to support the intelligence units of the major military commands, while others should be moved to the CIA to bolster the military expertise in that agency. He also proposes that the CIA specialize in intelligence analysis, and that the CIA Directorate of Operations be organized into a new service to handle clandestine and special operations.[27] Gertz's proposals would very sensibly elevate the organizational status of clandestine operations, a very important part of the Global War on Terror that was cut back over decades, in a series of misguided reforms that damaged America's ability to conduct espionage and special operations.

4. Aiding America's Allies Against Terrorists and Insurgents

A key element in defeating insurgents and terrorists is helping America's allies to fight their own wars. Many small nations have quite valiantly chosen to side with America to fight insurgents and terrorists in Afghanistan and Iraq. Other small nations are sitting on the fence and will demand aid and assistance from the United States before they provide even minimal cooperation—just like in the Cold War. The point is, many small nations aligned with the West are currently facing internal terrorist and insurgent threats like the Philippines, or such threats on their borders, like Georgia. Many of America's allies might have the will, but lack the financial, technological, and military resources to handle the threat posed by insurgents or terrorists. So that America's allies can effectively fight their own battles, and also be able to fight alongside us, many countries will require considerable support in the form of military training and equipment. Furthermore, considering that economic and social problems help create the conditions for insurgency, many nations will also require foreign aid in the form of economic development and infrastructure improvement.

In the early years of the Cold War, the United States countered the Soviet threat to Europe through the Marshall Plan, whose main component was financial aid to get the devastated European economies back on their feet, suppressing the poverty and instability that bred support for the Communist ideology. The post–World War strategy to defend the West also included a large component of military assistance—a program that began when communist rebels threatened Greece in 1947. The strategy to contain and defeat Communism initiated by President Harry Truman was no "quick fix," and it was criticized by many Americans as too expensive and requiring a very untraditional, long-term commitment. Yet it worked and, looking at a free and prosperous Europe today, there's no doubt it was worth the money and effort.

At the grand strategy level today, we need to think in the broad terms of the Marshall Plan that played such a central role in defeating the aims of the Soviet Union. Few of the small nations that have supported the United States in the Global War on Terror can confront such threats by relying only on their own resources. Defeating terrorists and insurgents will require a long-term strategy of military and economic assistance, both to fight insurgents and terrorists, and to address the problems of poverty and unemployment that make a more congenial atmosphere for terrorist and insurgent recruiting. A workable strategy to defeat terrorists and insurgents will require the full involvement not only of the DOD, but also of the State Department, Commerce Department, Justice Department, and other agencies. We can hope that the wealthier European nations will fully support such a strategy and we should build a broad coalition whenever possible, for defeating insurgency—especially radical Islamic insurgency—is clearly in the broad interests of the Western democratic nations. Realistically, our strategy cannot depend on the full support of the developed democracies as a condition of success. As in the Cold War, I suspect America will have to bear the primary burden of military and economic aid. It will be expensive, but it will be worth the price.

After the end of the Cold War, U.S. security assistance to small nations threatened by crime, terrorism, and insurgency slipped to very low levels. The policy to cash in the peace dividend by cutting security assistance was short-sighted, ultimately working against America's interests. For example, the Central American countries that became major transit points for drugs into the United States, and whose fragile democracies have been under-mined by narcotics gangs, saw their security and police assistance cut to only a few million dollars a year in the 1990s—a minuscule sum considering the problems they faced. Haiti is again a failing state, largely because the United States and the West were unwilling to adequately fund a new police force for that nation. Yet, even after 9/11, we have seen only marginal increases in the security assistance program for small nations. Nepal, facing a significant insurgency, was slated to receive only $10 million in military aid in fiscal year 2004. Georgia, a struggling new democracy in a volatile region, facing incursions of Chechen Islamic insurgents on its borders, received only $10 million in aid in 2004. The Philippines, a large nation fac-ing a major Islamic insurgency and a longstanding ally of the United States, was allocated only $17 million in military aid in 2004.[28] The U.S. Defense and State Departments continue to think in terms of small pro-grams to help allies fight terrorists and insurgents. For example, the U.S. military is currently concerned about an al Qaeda recruiting and organiz-ing drive in the North African Muslim states, and has asked Congress for $125 million over five years to help train African security forces, especially in Mali, Mauritania, Niger, Chad, and Senegal. This works out to less than $5 million per country per year—in a region that is becoming a major field for al Qaeda activities.[29] Simply put, this level of aid will not enable the poorly trained and poorly equipped security forces of those nations to take on al Qaeda in a serious fashion. At our current level of effort, al Qaeda is likely to outspend the United States in a program to undermine the North African states.

Providing significantly more military and security assistance to small allies in the Global War on Terror will not necessarily require any large, addi-tional expenditure, as money can be diverted from existing programs. One of the most notable examples of the glacial pace of the American strategic response to 9/11 is the foreign military assistance budget. For every year since the 1970s, Israel and Egypt have received the overwhelming majority of U.S. security assistance funds. In the fiscal year 2002 budget, drawn up before 9/11, Israel and Egypt took 82 percent of the military aid budget of $4.052 billion. In the two years after 9/11, the military aid budget for fiscal year 2004 was only modestly increased to $4.414 billion, and Israel and Egypt—despite being massively armed and facing no urgent threats to their security—still receive most of the military assistance funds, with their share only dropping to 78 percent.[30]

While I have no personal axe to grind per the U.S. policy toward Egypt and Israel, I would also note that both nations have gotten a pretty good deal from the United States in terms of military aid for the last thirty years. Would it cause a crisis if we were to tell Israel and Egypt that the world situation and threat to the United States have changed rather dramatically over the last four years, that we have urgent new priorities for our military assistance programs, and that we need to reallocate $2 billion or so of the $3 billion a year in military assistance that now goes to those nations? Reallocating a major portion of our military assistance budget to small nations that are directly threatened by terrorism and insurgency, and who have far fewer resources than Egypt and Israel, is an obvious move. I suspect Egypt and Israel would complain, but accept this reasoning.

Helping small nations to reform, train, and equip their security forces to effectively fight terrorists and insurgents will require training and assistance programs far larger in scope than those we have today. Many of the third world police and armed forces require years of extensive training and advice before they are capable of defeating the current threats—so we have no time to lose. As we did in El Salvador in the 1980s, we should use U.S. aid as a lever to push recipient nations toward necessary reforms and to improve their human rights compliance. Many third world countries have well-trained officers but lack a professional NCO corps, and indeed have no idea how to train such a force. Even basic tasks such as this will require considerable assistance from the United States.

Although America has ample resources, the U.S. military, and especially the army, is not properly organized to undertake the large-scale training

programs needed by allied nations. Under current doctrine and organization, the special operations forces have the primary responsibility for sending advisors and training missions to countries requesting military aid. The
SOF sends out small teams of superbly trained and experienced personnel,
who train a few selected host country personnel in the expectation that that
group will become the expert trainers for their nation's forces. Programs like
this take a long time to show results and, simply put, such a process is much
too slow to meet current needs. The major problem with using SOF as lead
trainers is the relatively small size of the U.S. Special Operations Command:
there are simply too few SOF soldiers to support the training missions and
to carry out the direct-action combat missions. The SOF, which only accepts
soldiers with years of experience, cannot be quickly expanded.

The simplest solution would be to take most of the training missions
away from the special forces and assign them to a command that focuses
on training as its primary purpose—such as a joint, all-services version of
the U.S. Army Training and Doctrine Command (TRADOC). TRADOC,
formed in the 1970s in the aftermath of Vietnam to serve as the primary
agency for army training, education, and doctrinal development, proved
its worth in the 1970s and 1980s, taking a demoralized force and making
it the most effective of the NATO armies. TRADOC is exceptionally good
at training troops, so creating a large new branch of TRADOC and making it responsible for training foreign forces fits its culture and organization. But even before 9/11, during the massive defense cuts of the 1990s,
TRADOC was seriously short of funds and personnel.[31] After 9/11, the
problems of limited budgets and staffing have become still more acute,
for TRADOC has been virtually the only major army command that has
no direct combat role—and combat forces receive the top priority for
funds, equipment, and personnel. However, in a war against insurgents
and terrorists, training foreign forces is of equal importance as the direct-
combat operations of U.S. troops. By giving a multiservice TRADOC the
mission to train foreign military personnel and to conduct training missions overseas, we would be making the training organization what it
should be—a primary arm in the battle against terrorists and insurgents.
By assigning a combat role to a new joint TRADOC organization, we
could ensure it would receive adequate, long-term funding from the

Pentagon, which has shortchanged the training establishment for too long in the mistaken impression that training troops was somehow not a "combat" mission.

Due to their combat orientation and elite status, special operations forces can best be employed as combat advisor teams to serve with allied nations. SOF should not be completely cut from the training mission, as they are the best suited for training the elite security units of allied forces. However, the greater part of the training for third world forces can be done by U.S. personnel without the specialist language and regional background training that the SOF requires. Typically, the greatest weakness of the armed forces of small nations is in the training levels of the support personnel—mechanics, logisticians, administrators, communicators, equipment operators, and medical personnel. For training personnel in those skills, the most important requirement is instructor expertise. The U.S. reserve forces contain a large pool of NCOs and officers with experience as trainers and certified in the specialist skills that a training command needs. Reserve personnel could support a new training command by teaching short specialist courses for foreign troops during their yearly service. Such an arrangement would take some of the burden from an overstretched regular force, while putting the reserves to good use.

A modest increase in the current budget for the military training and education commands will enable the U.S. military to absorb a much larger number of foreign officers in our staff colleges and specialist courses. The forces of our small allies urgently need assistance to improve the professional standard of their officer corps. The United States, with the best and most comprehensive system of military training and education in the world, can adapt to increased numbers of foreign officers without much trouble. Many American military leaders have focused so long on the high-tech side of warfare, they have lost sight of one of America's key advantages in the Global War on Terror: our military training infrastructure.

While training foreign armed forces is important, we should not forget that the police are often the most important force in waging an effective counterinsurgency campaign. Like the military, police need thorough training and highly professional leadership to defeat insurgents and terrorists. One of the key elements of success in the Malayan counterinsurgency campaign was Sir Arthur Young's program to select the police recruits and NCOs with the best potential and send them to the full, one-year police college courses in Britain. There they were fully trained in all aspects of criminal investigation and police operations. Once properly trained, they came back to Malaya to fill key leadership posts in the police and intelligence services. The Justice Department could make a major contribution in our own campaign by setting up a program of intensive, six- to twelve-month courses for foreign police officers. The Justice Department could establish a new branch of the FBI, responsible for training foreign police and intelligence forces. Plenty of highly qualified trainers who have special expertise relevant to counterinsurgency could be recruited from America's law-enforcement agencies. The Justice Department and FBI have long experience in breaking up organized crime families, a task very similar to that of breaking up insurgent organizations. Retired American big-city police officers could be hired to teach foreign police officers how to keep order in large cities. The superb U.S. law-enforcement training system can play an important role in the grand strategy to defeat insurgency. Police work in countries facing insurgency or terrorist threats is exceptionally complex, and the current policy of short courses won't provide the kind of expert police leadership that is needed. Good police leadership has been proven to be a vital element in successful counterinsurgency campaigns. For a relatively small expenditure in creating professional programs for foreign police in the United States, we can get a tremendous payoff. All that is needed is a new attitude toward interagency cooperation between the DOD and other branches of government.

5. Supporting a Media Campaign

Although the United States has begun an effort to increase its media campaign in the Islamic world, we need a much larger, and much better, media campaign as part of our strategy against terrorism and insurgents.[32] An essential element in the Global War on Terror must be a long-term media program to counter the power of the radical *madrassas* that serve as the recruiting pool and intellectual base for radical Islamic terrorists and insurgents.[33]

In many respects, the radical Islamic ideologues have more media savvy than we do. Al Qaeda and other radical Islamic groups understand this is a war for the hearts and minds of the people, and thus they put media considerations at the center of their strategy. Targets, such as the Khobar Towers in Saudi Arabia or the USS *Cole*, are often carefully chosen to gain the maximum advantage in the Islamic world. Radical Islamic factions also have an advantage in an international media culture that tends to be anti-American, often expressing a romanticized, 1960s view of revolutionaries. For example, even after the suicide bombings of the London transit system in July 2005 that left over fifty Britons dead and hundreds wounded, the BBC refrained from describing the mass murderers as "terrorists."[34] In much of the politically correct media culture of Western Europe and the United States, the preferred media term for people who mass murder civilians is "militant." Al Qaeda also understands how to exploit the international media for sympathy. An al Qaeda handbook seized in 2005 instructs its fighters to make false charges of torture if they are captured and to remember their duty to "spread rumors and write statements that instigate the people against the enemy."[35]

In contrast, the American understanding of the role of media in counterinsurgency is distressingly thin. Although the military has a small corps of psychological operations specialists, they are usually considered minor staff functionaries and their role in a campaign given the lowest possible priority. When they have been called upon for planning input, their role has traditionally been to develop media campaigns geared to undermining the morale of the enemy's conventional armed forces, not to influence civilians. While the military puts considerable effort into public relations campaigns designed to influence the U.S. people and media, the concept of mounting a major effort to influence foreign civilians is not viewed as a proper mission for soldiers. A clear disconnect exists between published policy and actions. Current U.S. doctrine correctly places the mind of the civilian populace in the center of counterinsurgency operations when it makes the legitimacy of the threatened government one of the strategic centers of gravity. However, the small effort the military devotes to the hearts and minds campaign illustrates that the U.S. military leadership still fails to understand counterinsurgency basics.

As media campaigns are essentially civilian in nature, one might expect the State Department to have a better handle on the situation. But the State Department has not done much better than the military in developing appropriate media campaigns. Mounting an aggressive media campaign goes against the State Department institutional culture, which values quiet diplomacy over open media advocacy. As with the military, the State Department has many other traditional priorities, and overseeing a strategic media campaign is not high on the list.

The most effective organizational means of implementing a strategic media campaign to counter the influence of radical Islamic ideology can be found in the U.S. strategy of the Cold War. In the early days of the Cold War, the United States set up the U.S. Information Service (USIS) as an independent agency with the mandate of promoting democracy and a positive view of America overseas. The USIS was created specifically to counter the influence of Communist propaganda by creating and supporting educational institutions; sponsoring public events; and supporting radio, television, and film programming. The USIS played an important role in the Cold War. By the 1990s, however, it was seen as an anachronism so the agency was disbanded and its functions taken over by the State Department.

Given the pervasive role of the media today, meeting the current threat requires a specialist agency with a similar mission to that of the USIS during the Cold War. Indeed, an agency responsible for America's strategic media campaign should have more prominence than the old USIS. The agency director should have a seat on the National Security Council, and a senior agency representative should be on the staff of each military theater commander, with a status equal to the other top staff officers. We should never again intervene in a country, or mount military operations, without a coherent plan to influence the civilian population that we are going to have to deal with. We should also plan to employ ample resources before, during, and after any military operations, to support the efforts of democratic and moderate elements in unstable regions to establish a free and democratic media.

FINAL COMMENTS

I have recently come across some influential staff officers in the U.S. military who believe that the Coalition forces and Iraqi government cannot defeat the insurgency in Iraq. I strongly disagree. The United States and its allies CAN defeat insurgencies. We can win in Iraq and help the Iraqis establish a just peace and functioning democracy, although it will be a very long and arduous process.

Of course, those in the U.S. military who say that we cannot win in Iraq are also assuming that we are somehow permanently stuck with the strategy, doctrine, intelligence system, force structure, and military culture that we have now. If that is the case—that the doctrine and structures created in the 1990s are sacrosanct and cannot be changed—then perhaps those staff officers are right.

If we are to defeat insurgents and terrorists, then our current strategy, doctrine, and force structure are woefully inadequate to the task. As a long-time soldier, I want to see the United States win in Iraq and Afghanistan. I want to see the radical Islamic insurgencies threatening other developing nations defeated. I do not want to see my son inherit a world where American power and influence are in obvious decline—and being replaced by the violent forces of a radical ideology. However, the United States cannot prevail against insurgency and terrorism without a coherent strategy and fundamental changes in our intelligence system and military force structure. Most of all, the U.S. military needs to change the way it thinks about warfare. Military doctrine, training, and especially the military culture have to be reoriented away from the false prophets of technological determinism and back to some basic concepts. We need to bury the Vietnam Syndrome that has convinced many military and civilian leaders each insurgency is another Vietnam, and that all counterinsurgency campaigns are doomed to failure—just like in Vietnam.

The central theme of this book is that there is nothing fundamentally new in conducting an effective counterinsurgency campaign. Insurgencies cannot be defeated via the rapid, decisive campaigns favored by American doctrine—but they can be, and often have been, defeated by forces employing a superior strategy over the long term. The basic principles of effective counterinsurgency are well known to those who have studied the subject. While history rarely provides a perfect analogy or perfect model to follow, it can offer an excellent starting point to analyze current problems. History also offers important insights into the best means of adapting current resources, doctrine, and policies to meet the threat posed by nonstate enemies. The strategies that I have espoused in this book are firmly grounded in experience and historical evidence. Furthermore, these strategies have already proven highly successful under a variety of conditions.

Epigraph
Rudyard Kipling, "The Lesson," *The Five Nations* (1903; repr., Amsterdam: Fredonia Books, 2001).

CHAPTER 1
Epigraphs
Carl von Clausewitz, *On War*, edited and translated by Michael Howard and Peter Paret (Princeton: Princeton University Press, 1976). In my opinion, the best edition of Clausewitz in English.
Major C. E. Callwell, *Small Wars: Their Principles and Practice* (1899; repr., London: Harrison and Sons, 1903).

1. Clausewitz's main discussion of guerrilla war is found in Book 6, chapter 26 of *On War*. He touches on aspects of insurgency in Book 3, chapter 5; Book 5 chapter 17 and Book 8, chapter 3.
2. Major C. E. Callwell, *Small Wars*, 1.
3. Ibid., 3.
4. Ibid., 14–24.
5. Philip Towle, *Pilots and Rebels* (London: Brassey's, 1989), 40–43. Field Marshal Milne, Chief of the Imperial General Staff, criticized the RAF for its air control techniques in Aden, arguing that constantly bombing the tribesmen would not create the conditions for a peaceful administration.
6. For an example of interwar British small wars doctrine see Major General Sir Charles W. Gwynn, *Imperial Policing*, rev. ed. (London: MacMillan and Company, 1934).

7. For a good overview of the careful use of force applied by the USMC in Nicaragua, see Wray Johnson, "Airpower and Restraint in Small Wars: Marine Corps Aviation in the Second Nicaraguan Campaign, 1927–1933," *Aerospace Power Journal* (Fall 2001).

8. The most useful overview of Mao's works on revolutionary warfare theory in English is found in the *Selected Military Writings of Mao Tse-tung* (Peking, 1963).

9. James Corum and Wray Johnson, *Airpower and Small Wars* (Lawrence: University Press of Kansas, 2003), 230–233. For a thorough study of the Vietnamese approach to revolutionary war doctrine see Wray Johnson, *Vietnam and the American Doctrine for Small Wars* (Bangkok: White Lotus Press, 2001).

10. For an overview of the Greek civil war see Edgar O'Ballance, *The Greek Civil War 1944–1949* (New York: Praeger, 1966), 52–110.

11. See Howard Jones, *"A New Kind of War": America's Global Strategy and the Truman Doctrine in Greece* (New York: Oxford University Press, 1989), 184–187, 197. In fiscal year 1949 the Truman administration provided $200 million in military aid to Greece, a vast sum at the time and equal to several billion dollars today.

12. For an overview of the successful counterinsurgency strategies of the Huk campaign, see Douglas Blaufarb, *The Counterinsurgency Era: U.S. Doctrine and Performance* (New York: The Free Press, 1977), 24–40.

13. Some of the best works on counterinsurgency operations include Sir Robert Thompson, *Defeating Communist Insurgency* (London: Chatto & Windus, 1966). Also important is Thompson's *No Exit From Vietnam* (London: Chatto and Windus, 1969). An outline of basic counterinsurgency theory and practice is Frank Kitson, *Low Intensity Operations* (London: Faber and Faber, 1971). An important American work was John J. McCuen, *The Art of Counter-Revolutionary War* (London: Faber and Faber, 1966). See also the memoir of one of America's leading counterinsurgency practitioners, Edward Lansdale, *In the Midst of Wars: An American's Mission to Southeast Asia.* (1972; repr., New York: Fordham University Press, 1991).

14. Roger Trinquier, *Modern Warfare: A French View of Counterinsurgency* (London: Pall Mall Press, 1964). The French version was published as *La*

Guerre Moderne (Paris: Editions de la Table Ronde, 1961). An important work outlining the French approach to counterinsurgency in Algeria is General Paul Aussaresses, *Services Speciaux: Algerie, 1955–1957.* (Paris: Perrin, 2001). English translation: *The Battle of the Casbah; Terrorism and Counter-Terrorism in Algeria 1955–1957* (London: Enigma Books, 2003).

15. See Frank Kitson, *Low Intensity Operations* (London: Faber and Faber, 1971). Also see Sir Robert Thompson, *No Exit From Vietnam* (London: Chatto and Windus, 1969), 163–167.

16. On the U.S. experience in Vietnam and the failure to employ a coherent counterinsurgency campaign, see W. Scott Thompson, and Donaldson D. Frizzell, eds., *The Lessons of Vietnam* (New York: Russak and Co., 1977). In it are articles by Major General Edward Lansdale on counterinsurgency and an article on the small but successful U.S. program to train local self-defense forces by Colonel Robert Rheault, "The special forces and the CIDG Program," 246–255. See also Thomas Thayer, "Territorial Forces," 256–262, in the same volume.

17. Thompson's sharp critique of American strategy in Vietnam is found in *No Exit From Vietnam* (London: Chatto and Windus, 1969), 122–144. However, Thompson also pointed out that some potentially effective counterinsurgency programs were weak because the effort was too thin and spread out and that programs to build the economic and social infrastructure lacked coherence. See pp. 152–155.

18. Sir Robert Thompson, *No Exit From Vietnam* (London: Chatto and Windus, 1969), 122–139.

19. Ibid., 197–198.

20. See Mark W. Woodruff, *Unheralded Victory* (London: HarperCollins, 1999), 29–60, 246.

21. See Richard Locke-Pullan, "An Inward-Looking Time": The United States Army, 1973–1976," *Journal of Military History*, Vol. 67, No. 2 (April 2003): 483–512.

22. On the thinking on counterinsurgency in the post-Vietnam U.S. Air Force, see Dennis Drew, "U.S. Airpower Theory and the Insurgent Challenge: A Short Journey to Confusion," *Journal of Military History*, Vol. 62, No 4 (October 1998): 809–832.

23. For the background of the war and the U.S. policies in El Salvador, see

James Corum, "The Air War in El Salvador, *Airpower Journal* (Summer 1998).

24. Ambassador Edwin Corr and Courtney Prisk, "El Salvador: Transforming Society to Win the Peace," from Edwin Corr and Stephen Sloan, *Low Intensity Conflict: Old Threats in a New World* (Boulder: Westview, 1992) 223-254.

25. Max Manwaring, "The Threat of the Contemporary Peace Environment: the Challenge to Change Perspective," *Low Intensity Conflict: Old Threats in a New World* (Boulder: Westview, 1992), 46-59, see esp. 52-53.

26. Ibid., 54.

27. See Max Manwaring and John Fishel, "Insurgency and Counter-Insurgency: Toward a New Analytical Approach," *Small Wars and Insurgencies* (Winter 1992): 272-305. The authors provide a matrix of requirements needed to oppose insurgency successfully.

28. Ambassador Edwin Corr and Ambassador David Miller, "United States Government Organization and Capability to Deal with Low-Intensity Conflict," *Low Intensity Conflict*, 17-45.

29. Ibid., 42.

30. Max Manwaring, "The Threat in the Contemporary Peace Environment: The Challenge to Change Perspectives," *Low Intensity Conflict*, 54.

31. Anthony Burton, *Urban Terrorism: Theory, Practice and Response* (London: Leo Cooper, 1975), 75-79. On the Foco theory, see also John Shy and Thomas Collier, "Revolutionary War," *Makers of Modern Strategy*, ed. Peter Paret (Oxford: Clarendon Press, 1986), 815-862, see esp. 850-851.

32. Burton, *Urban Terrorism*, 80-87.

33. A useful overview of terrorism in a strategic and tactical sense is found in Philip Jenkins, *Images of Terror* (New York: Aldine de Gruyter, 2003).

34. Christopher Harmon, "Five Strategies in Terrorism," *Small Wars and Insurgencies* 12, no. 3 (Autumn 2001): 39-66.

35. There are several useful books on the religious motivations for supporting al Qaeda's war against the West, including: Peter Berger, *The Holy War, Inc.: Inside the Secret World of Osama bin Laden* (New York: Phoenix, 2004); Stephen Schwartz, *The Two Faces of Islam: The House of Sa'ud from Tradition to Terror* (New York: Doubleday, 2003); and Jane Corbin, *The Base: Al-Qaeda and the Changing Face of Global Terror* (New York: Pocket

Books, 2003).

36. Bin Laden's *fatwa*, "Jihad Against Jews and Crusaders," World Islamic Front Statement, Feb 23, 1998. See pp. 251-254 in James Carafano and Paul Rosenzweig, *Winning the Long War* (Washington, D.C.: Heritage, 2005).

37. Ibid., 253.

38. See Lieutenant Colonel Thomas X. Hammes, USMC, "*The Evolution of War: A Fourth Generation*," Thesis of the National Defence College, Kingston, Ontario, June 1994, 25-27.

39. Colonel Thomas X. Hammes, USMC, *The Sling and the Stone: On War in the 21st Century* (St. Paul: Zenith Press, 2004), 100-101.

40. On Hezbollah and the Israeli campaign against them, see James Corum and Wray Johnson, *Airpower and Small Wars* (Lawrence: University Press of Kansas, 2003), 409-415.

41. On the Palestinians and the media, see Hammes, *The Sling and the Stone*, 104-105.

42. On the Israeli campaign against the PLO and Hezbollah and the use of the international media by both insurgencies, see Corum and Johnson, *Airpower and Small Wars*, 398-425.

43. On the Soviet war in Afghanistan, see Corum and Johnson, *Airpower and Small Wars*, 387-397.

44. Jonathan Schanzer, "Ansar al-Islam: Back in Iraq," *Middle East Quarterly* (Winter 2004).

45. Scheherezade Faramarzi, "Death Toll in Iraq Attacks Rises to 109," *Washington Times*, February 4, 2004.

CHAPTER 2

Epigraphs

General Merrill McPeak, USAF, "Leave the Flying to Us," Washington Post, June 5, 2003. Air Force Chief of Staff (1990-1994).

Hans von Seeckt, Essay on "Schlagworte (Buzzwords)," *Gedanken eines Soldaten* (Leipzig: K. F. Koehler, 1935), 7-18. Commander of the German Army (1920-1926) and one of the most influential military thinkers of the twentieth century.

1. Cited in Thomas Keaney and Eliot Cohen, *Revolution in Warfare?* (Annapolis: Naval Institute Press, 1995), 188.

2. An army officer present at the conference circa 1994 provided me with an account of Shinseki's statement.

3. For some examples of the statements common in the 1990s, see Barry Watts, *Clausewitzian Friction and Future War* (Collingdale, PA: Diane Publishing Co., 1996).

4. Colonel John Warden, "Employing Airpower in the 21st Century," *The Future of Air Power in the Aftermath of the Gulf War,* eds. Richard Schultz and Robert Pfaltzgraff Jr. (Maxwell AFB, AL: Air University Press, 1992), 81. Colonel Warden is the author of numerous articles and some short books that argue that airpower and strategic bombing are now the dominant and decisive form of waging war.

5. Lieutenant Colonel John F. Jones, USAF, "Giulio Douhet Vindicated: Desert Storm 1991," *Naval War College Review* (Autumn 1992): 97–101.

6. Colonel Jeffrey Barnett, USAF, "Defeating Insurgents with Technology," *Airpower Journal* (Summer 1996): 69–75.

7. General Ron Fogleman, USAF, "Global Engagement: A Vision for the 21st Century Air Force," United States Air Force, November 1996.

8. General John Shalikashvili, Chairman of the Joint Chiefs, *Joint Vision 2010,* 1996. See pp. 17, 19, 25.

9. See John Mueller, *Policy and Opinion in the Gulf War* (Chicago: University of Chicago Press, 1994).

10. For an overview of the force size debates after the Gulf War, see William W. Kaufmann, *Assessing the Base Force: How Much is Too Much?* (Washington, D.C.: Brooking Institution, 1992).

11. Ibid., 83.

12. Thomas Keaney and Eliot Cohen, *Revolution in Warfare?* (Originally published as the *Gulf War Air Power Survey Summary Report*) (Annapolis: Naval Institute Press, 1995), 199, 209–210.

13. Ibid., 211.

14. Jeffrey Record, *Hollow Victory* (Washington: Brassey's, 1993), see especially 136–157.

15. Lieutenant Colonel John Orndorff, "Aspects of Leading and Following: The Human Factors of Deliberate Force," *Deliberate Force: A Case Study in*

Effective Air Campaigning. Final Report of the Air University Balkans Air Campaign Study, ed. Colonel Robert Owen (Maxwell AFB: Air University Press, 2000), 351–379.

16. Colonel Robert Owen, "Summary," *Deliberate Force: A Case Study in Effective Air Campaigning. Final Report of the Air University Balkans Air Campaign Study*, ed. Colonel Robert Owen (Maxwell AFB: Air University Press, 2000), 486.

17. Norman Cigar, "How Wars End: War Termination and Serbian Decisionmaking in the Case of Bosnia," *South East European Monitor* (January 1996): 3–48.

18. *International Herald Tribune*, May 11, 2000.

19. Allied Force Munitions Assessment Team, *Kosovo Strike Assessment Final Report*, October 14, 1999.

20. "The overall quality and level of intelligence surveillance, and reconnaissance (ISR) support provided during Operation Allied Force was far superior to that provided in the Gulf War." DOD, Report to Congress, *Kosovo/Operation Allied Force After-Action Report*, January 31, 2000, 131.

21. "U.S. Missiles Pound Targets in Afghanistan, Sudan," CNN, August 1998. http://www.cnn.com/US/9898/20/us.strikes.02/.

22. Yossef Bodansky, *Bin Laden: The Man Who Declared War on America* (New York: Forum, 2001), 283–284.

23. United States Navy, Fact File, http://www.chinfo.navy.mil/navpalib/factfile/missiles/wep-toma.html.

24. Amir Shah, "Taliban Leader, U.S. Won't Attack," *Associated Press News*, Sunday, September 30, 2001.

25. *Army Times* "Cohen Dashes Services' Hopes for More Troops," August 2, 1999.

26. The author was in an Army Reserve training division from 1994 to 2002 with the mission of managing large-unit training exercises for regular army, National Guard, and Army Reserve units. The author has direct experience of many exercises canceled, shortened, and cut back during this period. Budgets were reduced so that units could bring only half their staffs to training. Commanders complained that the ability of their units to perform to a high standard was suffering because key personnel were not getting the

necessary training.

27. One of the primary causes of the Abu Graibh prison scandal in Iraq noted by the army investigators is that the army military police units (National Guard and Army Reserve in this case) had been very poorly trained and prepared to carry out their wartime mission.

28. Robert Burns, "Ex-General Says War Games Were Rigged," *Associated Press* and *Army Times*, August 16, 2002.

29. Greg Jaffe, "Pentagon's Draft Spending Plan Calls for a 42% Increase in Arms Budget," *Wall Street Journal*, May 1, 2001.

30. Colonel Douglas McMaster wrote in an early 2003 Army War College paper that the army's modernization program was built on "an unrealistic vision of future war... that overlooked wars' human and psychological dimensions." Cited in Greg Jaffe, "Defining Victory as Chaos Mounts" *Wall Street Journal*, page A-1, December 8, 2004.

31. "Army Officials Fear More Cuts," *Washington Times*, June 4, 2002.

32. Max Boot, "The New American Way of War," *Foreign Affairs* Vol. 82, No. 4 (July/August 2003): 42.

33. On the "new model of warfare," see Stephen Biddle, *Afghanistan and the Future of Warfare: Implications for Army and Defense Policy* (U.S. Army War College, Carlisle, PA: Strategic Studies Institute, November 2002), 1–4.

34. Ibid.

35. Several excellent articles and studies have been written about the planning and command problems of the Anaconda operation. See Elaine Grossman, "Anaconda: Object Lesson in Poor Planning or Triumph of Improvisation?" *InsideDefense.Com*, August 12, 2004; Major Mark Davis, SAASS Thesis, May 2004, Maxwell AFB AL; Also cited in *Inside the Pentagon*, "Army Analyst Blames Afghan Battle Failings on Bad Command Set-Up," July 29, 2004. Davis is the most important source for this analysis: he conducted extensive interviews with the senior commanders and staff officers involved in the March 2002 operation.

36. Biddle, *Afghanistan and the Future of Warfare*, 29.

37. During several major rebellions against British rule in Iraq (1918–1932), Iraqis were, at first, greatly demoralized by British air attacks that easily found the rebels and inflicted heavy casualties. Then the rebels learned to cope with the air attacks by camouflage, dispersal, and simple, but

effective, air raid warnings. British air operations had less and less effect. See James Corum and Wray Johnson, *Airpower and Small Wars* (Lawrence: University Press of Kansas, 2003), 51–86.

38. Grossman, "Anaconda: Object Lesson in Poor Planning."

39. Sean Naylor, "Army Complains About Air Support in Afghanistan," *Army Times*, September 30, 2002.

40. Biddle, *Afghanistan and the Future of Warfare*, 38–43.

41. Ibid., 38–43.

42. The material from this section comes from some draft, unclassified briefings by U.S. Army personnel that were based on primary documents and 176 interviews with U.S. Army, Marine, and Air Force personnel as well as British personnel who participated in the campaign. The army has not yet released a final version of the analysis of the Iraq War.

CHAPTER 3
Epigraphs
Lieutenant General Thomas Gage, Commander of His Majesty's Forces in North America, to the War Minister, November 1774.
General Anthony Zinni, USMC, former Commander of U.S. Central Command. March 6, 2003.

1. The best historical work on the subject is Bill Linn, *The Philippine War* (Lawrence: University Press of Kansas, 2002).

2. See James Corum, "Operational Problems in UN Peacekeeping" in *Peacekeeping in Africa*, Vol. 2, ed. Jakkie Cilliers (Centre for Strategic Studies: Pretoria, 1995). The chapter details the poor multinational planning, the ineffective command and control, and the poor performance of the UN in large, multination peace enforcement operations.

3. An excellent history of the Malayan Insurgency is Anthony Short, *The Communist Insurrection in Malaya, 1948–1960* (London: Frederick Muller, 1975).

4. James T. Quinlivan, "Force Requirements in Stability Operations," *Parameters* (Winter 1995): 59–69.

5. Ibid., 65.

6. See James T. Quinlivan, "Burden of Victory: The Painful Arithmetic of Stability Operations," *Rand Review* (Summer 2003).

7. Rowan Scarborough, "Post-Saddam resistance unforeseen, U.S. officials say," *Washington Times*, September 1–7, 2003, 17.

8. Ibid.

9. Ibid.

10. Frederick W. Kagan, "War and Aftermath," *Policy Review Online*, August/September 2003, 2–3.

11. Bob Woodward, *Plan of Attack* (New York: Simon and Schuster, 2004).

12. There were various efforts for prewar planning that included a group at the Army War College and the National Defense University. These groups coordinated their efforts in conferences in November and December 2002. ORHA was officially formed on January 20, 2003, with some of the personnel from the planning groups becoming part of the initial cadre.

13. Conrad C. Crane and W. Andrew Terrill, *Reconstructing Iraq: Insights, Challenges, and Missions for Military Forces in a Post-Conflict Scenario* (U.S. Army War College: Strategic Studies Institute, February 2003).

14. Ibid., 40–41.

15. Ibid., 18–20, 34–39.

16. Ibid., 31.

17. Ibid., 42-73.

18. U.S. Army Colonel Douglas MacGregor was a key player in pushing the Pentagon's new theories of high-tech warfare. The Secretary of Defense sent MacGregor to the CENTCOM staff before the war so that he could show them how a 50,000-man corps could take Baghdad. Information from Colonel Paul Hughes, U.S. Army (Ret.).

19. Cited in James Fallows, "Blind into Baghdad," *Atlantic Monthly*, January/February 2004.

20. Rowan Scarborough, "Wolfowitz criticizes 'suspect' estimate of occupation force," *Washington Times*, February 28, 2003.

21. Cited in Greg Jaffe, "Defining Victory as Chaos Mounts," *Wall Street Journal*, December 8, 2004, p. A-1.

22. There were more units available for the Iraq War of 2003. The Army was preparing the 1st Cavalry Division for deployment in early 2003, but this was turned off at the order of the Pentagon on the grounds that it wasn't needed.

23. General Anthony Zinni, USMC (Ret.). Edited copy of speech to directors of the Center for Defense Information, May 30, 2004.

24. General Franks, interview, *Parade Magazine*, New York, July 30, 2004.

25. "U.S. 'Never' had enough Troops in Iraq: Bremer," *Agence France Presse*, October 5, 2004.

26. Ibid.

27. Letter to author by Lieutenant Colonel Lazslo Pazstor, USAR (Ret.), November 2004. Pazstor served with the Civil Affairs command in Iraq and made many of these trips to Baghdad himself.

28. Letter to the author by Colonel Paul Hughes, U.S. Army (Ret.), November 2004. Hughes was involved with the prewar planning for the Iraq occupation and served as an army strategist with ORHA during the 2003 invasion of Iraq.

29. Major Vicki Rast, USAF, *Interagency Fratricide: Policy Failures in the Persian Gulf and Bosnia* (Maxwell AFB: Air University Press, 2004), 171.

30. Ibid., 170.

31. Ibid., 171. One NSC member commented on the interagency breakdown. "When the system has to push the president, it does not work—the president must lead the NSC."

32. For a good analysis of the cultural and bureaucratic barriers that prevented effective State Department and DOD planning for the occupation of Iraq, see Donald R. Drechsler, "Reconstructing the Interagency Process After Iraq," *Journal of Strategic Studies* (February 2005): 3–30.

33. Mark Mazzetti and Solomon Moore, "Insurgents flourish in Iraq's wild west," *Los Angeles Times*, May 24, 2005.

34. Tom Lasseter, "Officers Say Army Lacks Troops To Protect Gains," *Miami Herald*, June 1, 2005, p. 1.

35. Ibid.

36. Kenneth McCreedy, "Planning the Peace: Operation Eclipse and the Occupation of Germany," *Journal of Military History*, Vol. 65, No. 3 (July 2001): 713–740. See also 716–717.

37. Ibid., 716–717.

38. Ibid., 717–721.

39. Ibid. See 721–739, 715–717. Eisenhower's papers also show that even in May 1944, when the battle for Normandy was about to begin,

Eisenhower was corresponding with Washington about the postwar occupation of Germany. See: *The Papers of Dwight D. Eisenhower, The War Years Vol. III*, ed. Alfred Chandler (Baltimore: Johns Hopkins University Press), 1872–1876. Memo to Walter Bedell Smith, May 20, 1944. See also 2122–2123, Cable to Combined Chiefs September 5, 1944; also 2269–2271, Letter to John J. McCloy, November 1, 1944.

40. McCreedy, "Planning the Peace," 714, 735–739.
41. Lieutenant Colonel Antulio Echevarria, *On the American Way of War*, U.S. Army War College Strategic Studies Institute Paper (Army War College SSI: Carlisle Barracks, PA, May 2004).

CHAPTER 4
Epigraph
Unnamed British officer, Malaya, 1954. Cited in *Army Quarterly*, April 1954.

1. Cited in David Talbot "How Technology Failed in Iraq," *Technology Review* (November 2004).
2. As of October 2004, Former Honduran Army Military Intelligence Chief, Colonel Juan Lopez Grijalba, is facing trial in the United States for torture, extrajudicial killings, and disappearances in Honduras in the 1980s. Grijalba was chief of the DNI (Special Intelligence Service) and commanded the army's special intelligence battalion, Battalion 316, which had a well-earned reputation for death-squad activities. Both organizations were so outside the law they were feared by ordinary Hondurans and even members of the military.
3. Chris Mackey with Greg Miller, *The Interrogator's War: Inside the Secret War Against Al Qaeda* (London: John Murray, 2004), xxi.
4. Ibid.
5. Thomas Ricks, "Intelligence problems in Iraq are detailed" *Washington Post*, October 25, 2003, p. A1.
6. Ibid. See also document. "JRTC Observations from Operation Iraqi Freedom and Enduring Freedom (May 31, 2003–June 13, 2003)" *U.S. Army CALL Newsletter* 03-27, Chapter 2.
7. "3rd Infantry Division (Mechanized) After Action Report. Operation Iraqi Freedom. July 2003," 67.
8. Ibid.

9. Interview with General Tommy Franks, USMC (Ret.), *Parade Magazine*, July 30, 2004.

10. Douglas Jehl and Eric Schmitt, "Prison interrogations seen as yielding little data on rebels," *New York Times*, May 27, 2004.

11. Ibid.

12. A good look at the tactical-level intelligence operations in Vietnam is seen in Eric Smith, *Not by the Book: A Combat Intelligence Officer in Vietnam* (New York: Ivy Books, 1993). On the problem of intelligence feedback, see pp. 172–173.

13. Some of the policy documents that stress the importance of language skills in the military include the *National Security Strategy, Joint Vision 2020, DOD Guidance on Transformation and Joint Doctrine*. See Science Applications International Corporation, *SAIC Defense Language Transformation Report*, Washington D.C., 2004, 6-8.

14. In September 2002, Air Force Chief of Staff General John Jumper said, "our expeditionary force requires airmen with international insight, foreign language proficiency and cultural understanding... These international skills are true force multipliers and essential to our ability to operate globally." "Chief of Staff's Sight Picture," September 2002. Wonderful sentiments—but as of 2004 (two years after this statement) the Air Force Reserve had 212 validated foreign language requirements, of which only 137 were funded. See *SAIC Defense Language Transformation Report*, 27, 38.

15. Interviews with senior officers in CENTCOM in 2003–2004 were unanimous on the issue that the inadequate numbers and quality of linguists was a major issue. *SAIC Defense Language Transformation Report*, 32.

16. *SAIC Defense Language Transformation Report*, 16, 21.

17. Jack Kelly, "Military Talent Drain: Army Losing Valuable Linguists," *The Washington Times*, commentary, May 17, 2003.

18. *SAIC Defense Language Transformation Report*, Executive Summary, iv-v, Washington, D.C., 2004.

19. *SAIC Defense Language Transformation Report*, 48–49.

20. Stephen Losey, "482,000 Wait for Clearance," *Federal Times*, August 16, 2004, 1.

21. John Newsinger, *British Counterinsurgency: From Palestine to Northern*

Ireland (New York: Palgrave, 2002), 48.

22. *The Taguba Report*, documenting the abuses at Abu Graibh through 2003, was released in April 2004 and can be found online at http://news.findlaw.com/cnn/docs/tagubarpt.html.

23. *The Taguba Report*. See also Rowan Scarborough, "Interrogators pressured to make inmates talk," *Washington Times*, May 5, 2005.

24. Neil King, "Army hired Cuba interrogators via same disputed system in Iraq," *Wall Street Journal*, July 15, 2004, p. 4.

25. Sherwood Moran, USMC Major, "Suggestions for Japanese Interpreters Based on Work in the Field, Division Intelligence Section," 1st Marine division, July 17, 1943. Report in the Center for Marine Corps History, Quantico, VA.

26. On Scharff see Raymond F. Toliver, *The Interrogator: The Story of Hans Joachim Scharff* (Pennsylvania: Schiffer, 1997).

27. A good account of interrogating captured al Qaeda fighters in Afghanistan is found in Chris Mackey, *The Interrogator's War: Inside the Secret War Against Al Qaeda* (London: John Murray, 2004). Mackey is an Army Reserve Arabic-speaking intelligence specialist who was called to active duty and served in Afghanistan in 2002-2003.

28. Mackey, *The Interrogator's War*, 178-181.

29. James Corum and Wray Johnson, *Airpower and Small Wars* (Lawrence: University Press of Kansas, 2003), 297.

30. Ibid., 345.

31. There is a large number of excellent works on the insurgency in Malaya. As a general work, I recommend a fine critical study by Anthony Short, *The Communist Insurrection in Malaya 1948-1960* (London: Frederick Muller, 1975).

32. Short, *The Communist Insurrection*, 154-155.

33. Ibid., 136-139.

34. See Short, *The Communist Insurrection*, 235-237, for the text of the "Brigg's Plan."

35. A good account of how the committee and intelligence collection system functioned in Malaya is found in Frank Kitson, *Low Intensity Operations* (London: Faber and Faber, 1971), 54-58. On intelligence, see 95-131.

36. Brian M. Linn, *The Philippine War 1899–1902* (Lawrence: University Press of Kansas, 2000), 296.

37. *U.S. Marine Corps Small Wars Manual 1940*, Chapter 2, 24.

38. Anthony Cordesman, "The Current Military Situation in Iraq," Washington, D.C.: Center for Strategic and International Studies Paper, November 14, 2003, 13–14.

39. Anthony Cordesman, "The Lessons of Afghanistan: A First Analysis," Washington, D.C., Center for Strategic and International Studies Paper, 2002, 9–12.

40. For an account of the Marine Japanese language training, see Roger Dingman, "Language at War: U.S. Marine Corps Japanese Language Officers in the Pacific War," *Journal of Military History* (July 2004): 853–884.

41. Edward M. Coffman, "The American 15th Infantry Regiment in China, 1912–1938: A Vignette in Social History," *Journal of Military History* (January 1994): 67–69.

42. Bill Gertz, *Breakdown: How America's Intelligence Failures Led to September 11* (Washington: Regnery Press, 2002).

43. See especially Bill Lind, "Outside View: Still No U.S. Intel Reform," *UPI Outside Commentary*, September 9, 2004.

44. Ibid.

CHAPTER 5

Epigraphs
Major General Robert Scales, U.S. Army (Ret.), cited in Stephen Hedges, "Military Voices say Blame isn't all on Civilians," *Chicago Tribune*, August 15, 2004. Noted military historian and former commandant of the U.S. Army War College.

Colonel T. E. Lawrence, "The Science of Guerrilla Warfare," *Encyclopedia Britannica*, Fourteenth Edition, 1929.

General Sir Gerald Templer, British High Commissioner for Malaya, 1952.

1. America in 1775 had 38 newspapers, two magazines, dozens of almanacs, and numerous printers who printed broadsheets and pamphlets by the thousand. Often newspapers from one colony were read in several surrounding colonies. See Neil R. Stout, *The Perfect Crisis: The Beginnings of the Revolutionary War* (New York: New York University Press,

1976), 5–6.

2. An account of the U.S. public opinion monitoring of the Germans during the occupation is found in Anna Merritt and Richard Merritt, *Public Opinion in Occupied Germany: The OMGUS Surveys 1945–1949* (Urbana: University of Illinois Press, 1970).

3. Anthony Short, *The Communist Insurrection in Malaya 1948–1960* (London: Frederick Muller LTD., 1975), 416.

4. Ibid., 417–419.

5. John A. Nagl, *Counterinsurgency Lessons from Malaya and Vietnam* (Westport: Praeger, 2002). On the use of former insurgents in the propaganda campaign, see 93–94.

6. Short, *The Communist Insurrection*, 418–419.

7. Ibid., 420–421.

8. Ibid., 422–423.

9. A useful overview of the FLN and its politics is Abder-Ramane Derradji, *The Algerian Guerrilla Campaign: Strategy and Tactics* (Lewiston, New York: Edwin Mellen Press, 1997).

10. On the French civic action programs, see Peter Paret, *French Revolutionary Warfare from Indochina to Algeria* (London: Pall Mall Press, 1964), 40–51.

11. Ibid., 40–41.

12. James Corum and Wray Johnson, *Airpower and Small Wars* (Lawrence: University Press of Kansas, 2003), 170–172.

13. Alistair Horne, *A Savage War for Peace: Algeria 1954–1962* (London: Penguin, 1977), 249–250.

14. W. Byford-Jones, *Grivas and the Story of EOKA* (London: Robert Hale, 1959), 54, 58.

15. An excellent overview of the Cyprus insurgency is found in Nancy Crawshaw, *The Cyprus Revolt* (London: George Allen and Unwin, 1978).

16. George Grivas, *Guerrilla Warfare* (Athens: Longmans, 1964), 5–10.

17. Ibid.

18. Ibid.

19. One of the most dramatic instances of the breakdown in discipline occurred when whole British battalions broke discipline after the killing of two British women and looted part of Famagusta, and indiscrimi-

nately beat hundreds of Greek civilians, killing some and putting hundreds in the hospital. See W. Byford-Jones, *Grivas*, 142–150.

20. Charles Foley, *Island in Revolt* (Longmans: London, 1962), 219.
21. Thomas Ehrlich, *International Crises and the Role of Law. Cyprus 1958–1967* (Oxford University Press, 1974), 16–17.
22. Robert Holland, *Britain and the Revolt in Cyprus 1954–1959* (Oxford: Clarendon Press, 1998), 210.
23. Foley, *Island in Revolt*, 228–229.
24. David Anderson, "Policing and Communal Conflict: The Cyprus Emergency, 1954–60," *Policing and Decolonisation. Politics, Nationalism and the Police, 1917–65*, eds. David Anderson and David Killingray (Manchester: Manchester University Press, 1992), 187–217.
25. Foley, *Island*, 140–141.
26. On *dich van* see Mark Woodruff, *Unheralded Victory* (London: Harper Collins, 1999), 197–199.
27. Ibid., 199–207.
28. Ibid., 198–199.
29. James S. Corum, "Airpower and Peace Enforcement," *Airpower Journal* (Winter 1996): 16–17.
30. Donna Leinwand, "Iraqis Can't Believe Everything They Read," *USA Today*, September 18, 2003.
31. Conrad Crane, and W. Andrew Terrill, *Reconstructing Iraq*, U.S. Army War College, SSI Study, February 2003, 65.
32. Ibid.
33. Special Study, James S. Corum, "Lessons on Occupying an Enemy Country," Section 2. Sent to Planning Cell September, 2002. Author's files.
34. "Media Development in Post-War Iraq, International Media Support," Lancaster House, London, April 24, 2003, 1.
35. Ibid., 4. See also Tina-Marie O'Neill, "Commission Seeks to Regulate Iraqi Media Sector," *Sunday Business Post*, July 4, 2004. "Unregulated media allowed scores of local and foreign stations to lay siege to its airwaves."
36. The Governing Council in Iraq only issued a temporary code of media ethics to regulate the media in July 2004.

37. Michael McDonough, "Retired General Discusses Iraqi Occupation," *Washington Times*, November 26, 2003.

38. Tina-Marie O'Neill, "Commission Seeks to Regulate."

39. Cited in Richard Halloran, "U.S. Is Losing the Public Relations War," *Honolulu Advertiser*, August 22, 2004.

40. In April 2004 a group sponsored by the U.S. Marine Corps raised $1.5 million to support six Iraqi-owned and -operated TV stations in Al-Anbar province. See Spirit of America website, http://www.spiritofamerica.net/cgi-bin/soa/project.pl?rm=view-project&request-id=51. March 9, 2005.

41. On January 20, 2005, the Harris Corporation received a $22 million contract from the Iraqi government to train personnel of the Iraqi Media Network.

42. Cited in "U.S. Is Losing the Public Relations War," *Honolulu Advertiser*, August 22, 2004.

43. Cited in James Jay Carafano and Paul Rosenzweig, *Winning the Long War* (Washington, D.C.: Heritage Books, 2005), 183.

44. Carafano and Rosenzweig, *Winning the Long War*, 184.

45. Ibid., 195.

46. Richard McKenna, *The Sand Pebbles* (New York: Harper and Row, 1962), 342–344.

47. In 2005 I polled two dozen of my students (field-grade Army and Marine officers) at the U.S. Army Command and General Staff College who had recently served in Afghanistan and Iraq. Not one rated the U.S. military information operations as effective.

CHAPTER 6

Epigraphs
Order issued by King Frederick William III of Prussia on August 6, 1808, inaugurating a series of fundamental reforms in the Prussian Army. Cited in Hugh Smith, *On Clausewitz: A Study of Military and Political Ideas* (New York: Palgrave, 2005), 40–41.

George Orwell, "No, Not One," *Adelphi*, October 1941. *The Collected Essays, Journalism and Letters of George Orwell* (1968).

1. On the nature of the Salvadoran military before the civil war and the

U.S. process of transforming that force, see James S. Corum, "The Air War in El Salvador," *Airpower Journal* (Summer 1998), 27–44.

2. For the best historical account of the Philippine War see Brian M. Linn, *The Philippine War 1899–1902* (Lawrence: University Press of Kansas, 2000). On details of the early Philippine Constabulary and Philippine Scout operations, see Brian Linn, *Guardians of Empire: The U.S. Army and the Pacific, 1902–1940* (Chapel Hill: University of North Carolina Press, 1997), see esp. 10–47.

3. Julian Paget, *Counter-Insurgency Campaigning* (London: Faber and Faber, 1967), 51–55.

4. One of the greatest needs for the police was for armored cars to patrol the roads and guard vehicle convoys. The insurgents inflicted heavy casualties on the police in particular in setting up road ambushes for police patrols and then also ambushing the unit that came to their relief. The British had fewer than twenty armored cars in Malaya when the insurgency began and, although there were plenty of war surplus armored cars readily available in 1948, the police leadership opposed the idea of acquiring a large number even though the police commanders experienced in insurgency were begging for them.

5. Richard Clutterbuck, *Riot and Revolution in Singapore and Malaya 1945–1963* (London: Faber and Faber, 1973), 72–73. On formation of the Special Branch, see 178–181.

6. The collected papers of Sir Arthur Young are to be found in the library of Rhodes House, a center for imperial and commonwealth history, found at Oxford University. Young's memos and reports to the British cabinet and to Templer all put training the police NCO and officer leadership as the top priority for fighting the insurgency.

7. John A. Nagl, *Counterinsurgency Lessons from Malaya and Vietnam* (Westport: Praeger, 2002), 92–93.

8. Peter Paret, *French Revolutionary Warfare from Indochina to Algeria* (London: Pall Mall Press, 1964). On the SAS, see 40–51.

9. Ibid., 40.

10. Ibid., 50.

11. For a good account of the SAS and *harkis* see Alistair Horne, *A Savage War of Peace: Algeria 1954–1962* (London: Penguin Books, 1977), 109,

220–221, 255–256.

12. Stephen Hoadley, *Soldiers and Politics in Southeast Asia* (Cambridge: Schenkman Publishing, 1975), 72–81. This book provides a useful analysis of the politics of the South Vietnamese officer corps.

13. Anthony James Joes, *Resisting Rebellion: The History and Politics of Counterinsurgency* (Lexington: University Press of Kentucky, 2004), 114–115.

14. Ibid., 115–116.

15. Ibid., 116–118.

16. Ibid., 113–114.

17. Howard Jones, *"A New Kind of War": America's Global Strategy and the Truman Doctrine in Greece* (New York: Oxford University Press, 1989), 97.

18. A good account of the French strategy in Algeria is found in Paret, *French Revolutionary Warfare*, 38–39.

19. See Anthony James Joes, *Resisting Rebellion*, 32, 118–120.

20. The best account of Stilwell and his program to change the Chinese army is found in Barbara Tuchman, *Stilwell and the American Experience in China 1911–1945* (New York: Bantam Books, 1971).

21. Orr Kelly, *From a Dark Sky: The Story of U.S. Air Force Special Operations* (Novato: Presidio Press, 1996), 174–192. The usually outgunned Laotians, supported by USAF combat controllers and CIA pilots, were often able to hold their own in fierce battles with the North Vietnamese.

22. James Corum, "The Air War in El Salvador," *Airpower Journal* (Summer 1998): 39.

23. The basic military strategy for the U.S. support for the Salvadorans was worked out in early 1981 when Brigadier General Fred Woerner and a small staff met for ten days with the Salvadoran general staff and developed a five-year plan to support, retrain, and reorganize the Salvadoran armed forces—then facing likely defeat at the hands of the rebels. General Woerner later became the U.S. commander in chief of Southcom in the late 1980s. Woerner was the right man in the right place at the right time. He spoke fluent Spanish; had spent much of his career in Latin America; had served as a military advisor in Guatemala; and knew the region, its politics, and its armed forces like few other American soldiers. He was under no illusions about the nature of the

Salvadoran regime, the dysfunctional military culture, and what needed to be done to reform the Salvadoran military. Because of his in-depth knowledge of the military issues, the culture, and the politics of the region, he was able to develop a very effective strategy in a short time with a small "pick up" team from Southcom and the Pentagon, who were rushed to El Salvador virtually as an emergency operation. It's a useful lesson: you don't need a huge staff or complex procedures to develop an effective strategic plan to fight an insurgency. You do, however, need some genuine regional expertise.

24. The School of the Americas, now called WHINSEC and moved to Fort Benning, Georgia, has for many years been derided by American leftists as a "school for dictators" and "school for assassins," where U.S. officers supposedly teach Latin American officers how to torture and abuse the populace and manage military dictatorships. Nothing could be further from the truth. Officers from El Salvador did not need to be taught by Americans how to abuse their population or develop contempt for human rights. I have lectured many times at the School of the Americas and have an intimate knowledge of the curriculum, the faculty, and the philosophy of the school. I have always been impressed by the great dedication of the faculty to their mission and the seriousness they have in imbuing the students with professional skills and an appreciation for democracy and human rights.

25. This is the author's judgment, having visited the Salvadoran military and worked with and visited most of the armed forces of Central America—including Mexico, Guatemala, Honduras, Nicaragua, and Panama. The Salvadorans stand clearly at the top in professionalism and a serious commitment to democratic government.

26. A good account of Van Fleet's leadership as head of the U.S. Military Aid Mission to Greece, 1948-1949, is found in Howard Jones, *"A New Kind of War"* (New York: Oxford University Press, 1989), 184-197.

27. Allan Millett, "The South Korean Army's American Godfather," *Military History Quarterly* (Autumn 2004): 26-37.

28. A good account of the Philippine/U.S. counterinsurgency campaign is found in Douglas Blaufarb, *The Counterinsurgency Era: U.S. Doctrine and Performance* (New York: The Free Press, 1977), 24-40.

29. For an account of the South Vietnamese Army and its leadership in the final days, see George Veith and Merle L. Pribbenow II, "Fighting is an Art: The Army of the Republic of Vietnam's Defense of Xuan Loc, 9–21 April 1975," *Journal of Military History* (January 2004): 163–213.

30. The UN financed a six-month job training course for former soldiers, but after that time the soldiers would be on their own. Since there were few jobs of any sort to be had, the unemployed soldiers naturally turned to crime and joined paramilitary groups that established power in rural areas.

31. Human Rights Watch Report. *Haiti. Security Compromised: Recycled Haitian Soldiers on the Police Front Line*, Vol. 7, No. 3, March 1995.

32. Ibid., 15–16.

33. Report, The Washington Office on Latin America, *Policing Haiti*, September 1995.

34. On the failure of the multinational force to create an effective police force in Haiti, see E. Mobekk, "International Involvement in Restructuring and Creating Security Forces: The Case of Haiti," *Small Wars and Insurgencies* (Fall 2001): 97–114.

35. Bob Woodward, *Plan of Attack*, 322.

36. Several major studies published before the war and immediately after the fall of Baghdad assessed the Iraqi police as thoroughly corrupt and inefficient. See The Fund for Peace, *Iraq as a Failed State, report #1* (September 2003): 15. See also U.S. Institute for Peace, *Establishing the Rule of Law in Iraq*, April 2003. http://www.U.S.ip.org/pubs/special reports/sr104.html.

37. Rowan Scarborough, "Post Saddam resistance unforeseen, U.S. officials say," *Washington Times*, Sept. 1–7, 2003, 17.

38. Deputy Secretary Paul Wolfowitz testified to Congress on June 22, 2004, that he had underestimated the strength of the insurgency—expecting that once Saddam had been captured the insurgency would die away. But he continued to argue that the U.S. didn't need more troops and that, "Getting Iraqi forces up and fighting for their country is the answer." See Rowan Scarborough, "Iraq insurgency surprised Pentagon." *Washington Times*, June 28–July 4, 2004, 3.

39. Jack Fairweather, "Jordan to Train Iraqi Police Force," *Daily Telegraph*,

September 30, 2003.

40. Tom Lasseter, "Al-Sadr Militia, Warriors and Traffic Cops," *Detroit Free Press*, July 14, 2004.

41. Richard Oppel, "Security Company Closes Baghdad Airport Over Pay," *New York Times*, September 10, 2005.

42. Christine Spoler, "Iraqi Soldiers Deserting New Army," *Chicago Tribune*, Dec. 9, 2003.

43. Tom Squitieri, "Long Way to Go Before Iraqis Take Over Security," *USA Today*, Dec. 14, 2004. When the police in Mosul came under attack in November 2004, 3/4 of the 4,000-member force ran away. Most of the ICDC battalion in Mosul also ran, but not before looting their base of weapons and equipment.

44. See Mark Bowden, "When Officers Aren't Gentlemen..." *Wall Street Journal*, February 8, 2005, p. A-18.

45. Eric Schmitt, "General Seeking Faster Training of Iraqi Soldiers," *New York Times*, January 23, 2005.

46. Eric Schmitt, "U.S. May Add Advisors to Aid Iraq's Military," *New York Times*, January 4, 2005.

47. Eric Schmitt, "Iraqis Not Ready to Fight Rebels on Their Own, U.S. Says," *New York Times*, July 21, 2005.

CHAPTER 7

Epigraph
Bernard Cornwell, *Sharpe's Prey* (London: HarperCollins Publishers, 2001), 185.

1. Editorial, "Iraq and the World," *New York Times*, June 21, 2005.
2. Betsy Pisik, *The Washington Times,* "108 Nations Decline to Pursue Terrorists," December 2, 2003.
3. See Colonel John English, *Marching Through Chaos: The Descent of Armies in Theory and Practice* (Westport: Praeger, 1998), 194–195 for an analysis of why large ground armies are still required.
4. One of the most eloquent calls for increasing the army's size came from Medal of Honor winner Journalist Joe Galloway, who compared Secretary Rumsfeld with the Vietnam-era Secretary McNamara in his policies and argued that the army leaders were "in denial" about the manpower problem. See Joseph Galloway, "How to Ruin a Great

Army in a Short Time," *Miami Herald*, September 28, 2003. Frederick Kagan of the Hoover Institute pointed out that even if the army committed itself to no further operations, it would still need fourteen divisions (four more than present) to conduct current operations efficiently. See Frederick Kagan, "War and Aftermath," *Policy Review Online*, No. 102, August/September 2003.

5. William Lowther, "Iraq War Failed U.S.," *Daily Mail* (London), June 9, 2005.

6. "Pentagon Delays Release of May Recruiting Data," *Washington Post*, June 1, 2005.

7. "Uncle Sam's Recruiting Problems," *The Washington Times*, October 13, 2005.

8. Cited in "Even with Moves, Military's Ranks Thin," *Atlanta Journal Constitution*, August 19, 2004.

9. General Barry McCaffrey, "We Need More Troops," *Wall Street Journal*, July 29, 2003.

10. "Increasing Our Ground Forces," *Washington Times*, January 26, 2005, 18.

11. Cited in "Even with Moves, Military's Ranks Thin," *Atlanta Journal Constitution*, August 19, 2004.

12. November 2003—bipartisan group of 128 house members—including 54 of the 61 members of the House Armed Services committee asked the Bush administration for funding for 30,000 troops—two more divisions. Lieutenant General Theodore Stroup (Ret.) said the army should be expanded by 40,000–50,000 troops. David Brownfeld, Fox News Online, "Debate Over Size, Shape of Army," August 30, 2004.

13. Miguel Navrot, "Wilson calls for Bigger Military," *Albuquerque Journal*, September 21, 2003. Senators John Kerry and Carl Levin, the ranking Democrats on the Senate Armed Services Committee, called in late 2004 for increasing the army and marines by 40,000. *Washington Times*, "Increasing Our Ground Forces," January 26, 2005, 18.

14. Robert Kagan and William Kristol called for increase in troops to cover Iraq and the Global War on Terror. Robert Kagan and William Kristol, "Too Few Troops," *Weekly Standard*, April 26, 2004, Vol. 9, Issue 31. Edward N. Luttwak, on the lack of troops to police Baghdad, noted that there are 39,000 police officers in New York City alone—and they speak the language and don't have to contend with heavily armed enemies. See Edward

Luttwak, "So Few Soldiers, So Much to Do," *New York Times,* November 4, 2003. Political commentator Tony Blankley argued that the U.S. military was overstretched, "But as we have learned in the Persian Gulf, numbers of boots on the ground count in this kind of fight—even when it comes to training indigenous forces." See Tony Blankely, "The U.S. Needs a Larger Military," *Washington Times,* November 12, 2003, 17. Other studies by defense experts calling for a larger army include Keith Mines, "On Fighting a 16-Division War with a 10-Division Force," March 8, 2005, *Foreign Policy Research Institute.* *"E-Notes,"* from Foreign Policy Research Institute, 1528 Walnut St., Philadelphia, PA. Mines retired from the Army Reserves and served seven months in Al Anbar Province. Eliot Cohen, one of America's top professors of strategic studies, criticized the British policy of cutting manpower in favor of high-tech weapons that would leave the UK unable to meet its defense requirements. See Eliot Cohen, "Thin Red Line Getting Thinner," *Washington Post,* August 13, 2004, 25.

15. Ibid., Kagan and Kristol, "Too Few Troops," Vol. 9, Issue 31.

16. Rupert Cromwell, "The Real Star Wars," *The Independent,* May 30, 2005, 20–21. See also Frances Fitzgerald, "Immaculate Destruction," *New York Times,* June 3, 2005.

17. Vince Crawley "Financial Friendly Fire," *Army Times,* August 2, 2004, 20. See also Sean Naylor, "GAO: Pay Problems are a Threat to Reserve Retention," *Army Times,* September 6, 2004.

18. Michael Moss, "Many Actions Tied to Delay in Armor for Troops in Iraq," *New York Times,* March 7, 2005, 1. The author was in Iraq in January 2005 when the Pentagon publicly announced that all the troops deployed to Iraq now had the new body armor. This was not correct. Not all the members of my army team deployed to Iraq at that time had it.

19. "Despite U.S. promise, soldiers in Iraq still buying their own body armor," *Jefferson City News Tribune,* April 4, 2004. Senator Susan Collins of Maine of the Senate Armed Service Committee stated, "We lagged far behind in making sure that our soldiers who are performing very difficult and dangerous missions had protective equipment."

20. Michael Moss, "Many Actions Tied to Delay in Armor for Troops in Iraq," *New York Times,* March 7, 2005, 1.

21. For some excellent insights into the army culture and the need for the

senior leadership to adapt the army culture to retain a younger genera-
tion of officers, see Dr. Leonard Wong, *Generations Apart: Xers and
Boomers in the Officer Corps* (Carlisle, PA: Army War College Strategic
Studies Institute Monograph), October 2000.

22. See James Fallows, *National Defense* (New York: Vintage Books, 1981),
116–117. Fallows argued about too much careerism in officer corps and
the "zero defects approach" to the profession that was endangering the
effectiveness of the military. See also Edward Luttwak, *The Pentagon and
the Art of War* (New York: Simon and Schuster, 1984), 43, 185–192,
188–192. Luttwak argued that the U.S. system produced too many
"careerist" officers and that the U.S. needed a true general staff with a
proper general staff education.

23. On reforming the staff colleges, see Martin van Creveld, *The Training of
Officers* (New York: The Free Press, 1990), 108–110. Van Creveld argues
for lowering the age of staff college entry to the late twenties and the
war college to the late thirties. The war college course should be a two-
year course, much like a Ph.D. course with a thesis. Standards should be
set very high and not everyone should graduate. See also James
Carafano and Paul Rosenzweig, *Winning the Long War* (Washington, D.C.:
Heritage Foundation, 2005), 42. The authors, one of whom is a retired
army lieutenant colonel, argue for reforming military education with
earlier staff college entry and point out that the staff colleges should
include postconflict operations in their curriculum.

24. Colonel Douglas A. Macgregor, *Transformation Under Fire: Revolutionizing
How America Fights* (Westport: Praeger, 2003), 31, 212–215.

25. The author is a graduate of three U.S. intermediate and senior officer
schools (Army Command and General Staff College, the Air Command
and Staff College and the Army War College) and served for two years
on the faculty of the Army War College and fourteen years on the faculty of the U.S. Air Force School of Advanced Air and Space Studies (a
one-year program for majors and lieutenant colonels). I have visited and
lectured at the staff colleges of Britain, Germany, Paraguay, South
Africa, Zimbabwe, New Zealand, Norway, and Canada. I believe I have
enough experience in the officer education system to make some sound
assessments as to what can and should be done to improve it.

26. Major General Robert Scales (Ret.). Cited in Stephen Hedges, "Military Voices Say Blame isn't all on Civilians," *Chicago Tribune*, August 15, 2004.

27. Bill Gertz, *Breakdown* (Washington, D.C.: Regnery, 2002), 166–169.

28. U.S. Dept. of State figures *2004—Military Assistance, International Military Education and Training, Foreign Military Financing, Peacekeeping Operations*. Some aid figures for countries facing insurgency: Afghanistan—$150 million in fiscal year 2004; Nepal, $10 million; Philippines, $17 million; Georgia, $10 million.

29. Craig Smith, "U.S. Training African Forces to Uproot Terrorists," *New York Times*, May 11, 2004.

30. U.S. Dept. of State figures *2004—Military Assistance, International Military Education and Training, Foreign Military Financing, Peacekeeping Operations*.

31. *Report of the Defense Science Board Task Force on Training Superiority and Training Surprise*, Office of the Secretary of Defense for Acquisition, Technology and Logistics, January 2001. The shortfall of training resources at the end of the Clinton administration is thoroughly documented and the 2001 DOD task force feared that the quality of U.S. training would severely erode. See especially 2, 9, 12, 24.

32. Since 9/11, the United States has increased its Voice of America broadcast programming to Iran and has established a twenty-four-hour Arabic news channel. VOA spending is $652 million for fiscal year 2006. Donald Lambro, "VOA Funding Rise Aimed at Muslims," *Washington Times*, February 17, 2005.

33. See James Carafano and Paul Rosenzweig, *Winning the Long War* (Washington, D.C.: Heritage Foundation, 2005), 173–197.

34. Tom Leonard, "BBC Edits Out the Word Terrorist," *London Daily Telegraph*, July 12, 2005.

35. Rowan Scarborough, "Captives Told to Claim Torture," *Washington Times*, May 31, 2005.

INDEX